LAW AND ELECTION POLITICS

Law and Election Politics

The Rules of the Game

EDITED BY
Matthew J. Streb

LYNNE
RIENNER
PUBLISHERS

BOULDER
LONDON

Published in the United States of America in 2005 by
Lynne Rienner Publishers, Inc.
1800 30th Street, Boulder, Colorado 80301
www.rienner.com

and in the United Kingdom by
Lynne Rienner Publishers, Inc.
3 Henrietta Street, Covent Garden, London WC2E 8LU

Library of Congress Cataloging-in-Publication Data
Law and election politics : the rules of the game / edited by Matthew J.
Streb ; contributors Antonio Brown ... [et al.].
   p.   cm.
  Includes bibliographical references.
  ISBN 1-58826-304-5 (hardcover : alk. paper) — ISBN 1-58826-329-0 (pbk. :
alk. paper)
    1. Election law—United States. 2. Elections—United States.
3. Electioneering—United States. I. Streb, Matthew J. (Matthew Justin), 1974–
  KF4886.L39   2004
  342.73'07—dc22

                       2004007058

British Cataloguing in Publication Data
A Cataloguing in Publication record for this book
is available from the British Library.

Printed and bound in the United States of America

5 4 3 2 1

For Logan

Contents

Preface

As is true for many books, the idea for *Law and Election Politics* emerged during lunchtime conversations with colleagues. On the face of it, elections and constitutional law seem like two separate topics, although certainly anyone who teaches either subject is aware of a relationship between the two. Just how much overlap exists, though, became apparent from my discussions with one colleague in particular: Evan Gertsmann. I teach political behavior and elections; Evan teaches constitutional law. Over sandwiches, we would pick each other's brain to get a different perspective on our current research or the topics we were covering that week in our classes. A discussion of the role of money in elections would lead me to ask Evan to explain more clearly the Supreme Court's rationale in *Buckley v. Valeo* (1976), one of the most important election-related court cases in U.S. history. A discussion of a recent court ruling regarding a redistricting plan would lead Evan to quiz me on the politics behind the redistricting process and the kind of representation that emerged as a result. I quickly realized that one cannot truly understand elections without being aware of election law, nor can one fully grasp the importance of election-related court rulings without understanding the politics of elections.

My students have also challenged me to think about how election law and electoral politics are connected. Because many political science majors are blossoming lawyers, they often hunger to learn more about the law as it relates to elections—and are disappointed to discover that their assigned books rarely expend more than a sentence or two addressing significant court rulings. As a result, questions in class invariably revolve around the rules of the electoral game and why those rules are constitutional or not.

I became convinced that a clear assessment of election law as it relates to the political aspects of elections would be indispensable for me, my students, and my colleagues. Certainly there are many books on election law, but they are designed primarily for advanced law students and are usually devoid of any discussion of election politics. Nor are they easily digestible for most people. And there are myriad books on elections, but, as noted, these rarely include analysis from a legal standpoint. The goal of *Law and Election Politics,* then, is to bridge the legal and the political, to help readers realize and appreciate their interconnectedness in a way that is both engaging and understandable.

The chapters in this book cover a wide range of subjects, all of which are essential to understanding elections in the United States. It is my hope that students of elections—whether those taking their first course on elections or those teaching elections for the hundredth time—will be captivated by the issues in the book and will come away with a greater understanding of how politics and laws shape the kind of democracy we have and the government under which we live.

*   *   *

There are several people to whom I owe a great deal of gratitude. First and foremost, the contributors to this book all shared their expertise and passion for the topics at hand. I have heard horror stories about contributors not meeting deadlines or refusing suggestions; my experience editing this book was exactly the opposite. I couldn't have worked with a better group of people, and I'm honored to have them associated with the book.

I owe tremendous thanks to Evan Gerstmann, Brian Schaffner, Lee Goodman, Chris Shortell, Seth Thompson, and Michael Genovese, all of whom were willing sounding boards. It is a much better book because of their suggestions and insight. Katie Jones and Danny Cup Choy, my research assistants, kept me organized through the process and were an immense help in tracking sources and developing the bibliography. It has been a great pleasure working with Leanne Anderson and the people at Lynne Rienner Publishers. I have enjoyed working with few people as much as Leanne; she always had answers to my questions, and her enthusiasm for the project was contagious. Finally, my wife, Page, and my son, Logan, constantly remind me what is really important.

—Matthew J. Streb

LAW AND ELECTION POLITICS

1

Linking Election Law and Electoral Politics

Matthew J. Streb

After thirty-five days of madness, confusion, legal wrangling, and political posturing, the Supreme Court finally brought the spectacle of the 2000 presidential election to an end with its decision in *Bush v. Gore*. In a highly controversial 5–4 ruling, the Court voted to end all recounts, arguing that the various standards used by Florida counties for recounting punch-card ballots violated the equal protection clause of the Fourteenth Amendment. Headlines across the country, such as the *Boston Globe*'s "Supreme Court Compromises Its Legitimacy,"[1] the *New York Daily News*' "High Court's Integrity at Risk,"[2] and the *San Francisco Chronicle*'s "Turbulent Election Taints Top Court's Reputation for Neutrality,"[3] condemned the Court's ruling and raised questions about its involvement in the electoral process. In his national column, journalist E. J. Dionne simply asked, "Supremely Partisan, Will the High Court Besmirch Itself?"[4] Even Supreme Court justice John Paul Stevens recognized the danger of the Court's ruling. "Although we may never know with complete certainty the identity of the winner in this year's presidential election, the identity of the loser is perfectly clear," wrote Stevens in his dissenting opinion. "It is the nation's confidence in the judge as an impartial guardian of the rule of law."[5]

Although the country was surprised by—and often extremely critical of—the Court's role in the election outcome, federal courts have always played a pivotal part in interpreting the laws governing elections. Certainly, no decision was more covered or scrutinized than the *Bush v. Gore* ruling, but it would be wrong to conclude that the courts rarely involve themselves in matters concerning the conduct of federal—and in many cases state and local—elections. Indeed, for decades the courts have played a major role in deciphering such contentious issues as campaign finance, voting rights, redistricting, party primaries, and campaign advertising.

The importance of the rules of the game and the courts' interpretations of those rules was again thrust into the spotlight with the recall of California governor Gray Davis in 2003. Amid the media's obsession with the circuslike atmosphere of the campaigning were serious questions about California's election laws regarding the recall of a governor. California law states that, in order for the recall to occur, recall supporters must obtain the signatures of registered voters equal to 12 percent of the previous gubernatorial election turnout (in this case, close to 900,000 signatures). But once the recall makes the ballot, potential candidates have an extremely low threshold to meet in order to be placed on the ballot. The low threshold led an unprecedented 135 people to throw their hats into the ring.

Many were upset with the limited requirements to run for office in a recall election. California law was surprisingly ambiguous regarding the rules of a gubernatorial recall, and the state was forced to rely on the interpretation of the law by Secretary of State Kevin Shelley. Shelley followed a standard used in two recall elections for offices other than governor. Critics of Shelley's interpretation argued that the rules were unconstitutional. The California Supreme Court refused to hear the case, arguing that the law had ambiguities and required Shelley to use his discretion. According to the court, Shelley's interpretations did not violate state law.

The argument against the low threshold for candidates to be put on the ballot was certainly not the only case challenging the recall. In all, there were close to two dozen lawsuits filed. Perhaps the most controversial law regarding the recall kept Davis from being a candidate to replace himself if he were recalled. It was possible (and most scholars studying the election thought most likely) that Davis would be recalled but would still receive around 45 percent of the vote. Because of the large number of candidates on the second question, many thought it would be difficult for one candidate to win a large percentage of the vote. In other words, Davis could be recalled by only receiving 45 percent of the vote (he needed a majority to vote against the recall to remain in office) but still win more votes than the person who would replace him.[6] The court unanimously agreed not to hear the case.

The election also forced the courts to revisit the controversial *Bush v. Gore* ruling. Six counties in California, including Los Angeles and San Diego, were still using the antiquated punch-card machines that were responsible for many of the problems in Florida during the 2000 presidential election. If the recall were to take place in March of the following year—a time that most analysts believed would benefit Davis because the recall would be held in conjunction with the Democratic presidential primaries—instead of October, the six counties would have new voting systems in place. The American Civil Liberties Union (ACLU) filed suit arguing that, if the election were held in October, voters in those six counties (many of which had large minority populations) would be more likely to be disenfranchised, thus violating the equal protection provision enunciated by the Supreme Court in *Bush v. Gore*. Initially, the Ninth Circuit Court of Appeals delayed the recall, citing *Bush v. Gore* in their ruling. The Ninth Circuit then heard the case *en banc* and unanimously (11–0) ruled that the recall should proceed as scheduled. "Interference with impending elections is extraordinary, and interference with an election after voting has begun is unprecedented," the court ruled.[7] "Investments of time, money, and the exercise of citizenship rights cannot be returned."[8] Again, the courts were at the center of a controversy regarding an election.[9]

The cases of *Bush v. Gore* and the California recall clearly illustrate the important role that courts (and electoral law in general) play in elections. Though the courts have been extremely active in interpreting the rules of the electoral game, this role is misunderstood and understudied—as, in many cases, are the rules themselves. *Law and Election Politics* analyzes what the rules of the game are and some of the most important—and most controversial—decisions the courts have made on a variety of election-related subjects, including campaign finance, political parties, issue advocacy electioneering, voting, campaigning, redistricting, and judicial elections. The book is much more than a typical law book, however. Instead, it examines how election laws and electoral politics are intertwined; you cannot understand one without understanding the other. The contributors look at how the law and judicial interpretation of the law shape politics.

Politics is often murky; the rules are sometimes unclear, and the winners are often surprising. Law should not be; the rules should be explicit, and these rules should—in theory anyway—allow us to easily predict the winners. Because of the differences, too often we ignore how election law and electoral politics interact. *Law and Election Politics* addresses this vital subject head-on.

The subjects covered in this book are incredibly important because they all shape the U.S. government and the strength of its democracy. One cannot truly analyze how well our "great democratic experiment" is working without thinking about topics such as the ones addressed in this book. What is the quality of candidates we get to choose from when voting? Are there drawbacks to the two-party system? What role do money and campaign advertising play in terms of which types of candidates win? How do the media cover campaigns, and how does that influence the amount and quality of the information we bring into the voting booth? How is the Internet changing the way candidates campaign, and what kind of voice does it give to the people? Do current laws adequately protect voters? How does the drawing of congressional and state district boundaries affect the kind of representation we get? Are judicial elections giving us strong candidates from which to choose, or are the elections being sold to the highest bidder? Each of these questions has a profound impact on the quality of U.S. democracy and the answers to these questions are provided here.

The Format of the Book

The book addresses several major, contemporary issues—although certainly not all issues—dealing with elections. We begin with a discussion of political parties. In Chapter 2, Kristin Kanthak and Jeffrey Williams examine party primaries, specifically the different types of primaries and how the type of primary can influence the election outcome. They then focus on the relevant case law dealing with primaries and explore how the courts have balanced the parties' rights to freedom of association with the states' rights to regulate elections. In Chapter 3, Marjorie Randon Hershey chronicles the obstacles that third parties have faced in getting on the ballot and winning elections. As Hershey notes, the rules of the game—rules usually made by the two major parties—are stacked against third parties, and the courts have been reluctant to come to their rescue.

In Chapters 4 and 5, the focus turns to the important role that money plays in elections. In Chapter 4, Victoria Farrar-Myers examines the issues of representation and the First Amendment as it relates to the current campaign finance debate. She provides a historical overview of the Federal Election Campaign Act and the *Buckley v. Valeo* ruling. She then discusses the recent campaign finance legislation passed by Congress and signed by George W. Bush, the Bipartisan Campaign Reform Act (BCRA), as well as the Supreme Court's 2003 ruling in *McConnell v. Federal Election Commission* on the legislation. In Chapter 5, Allan Cigler focuses on the increasingly prominent role that organized interest money has played in recent elections, specifically through the use of issue advocacy ads. He analyzes how BCRA and the Court's recent ruling in *McConnell* will affect organized interests' abilities to run issue advocacy ads in the future.

In Chapter 6, we turn to the role of the media in elections. Brian Schaffner looks at the changing nature of the local media resulting from recent legislation, changes in Federal Communication Commission (FCC) regulations, and court rulings that allow companies to own stations reaching a greater share of the population. Schaffner argues that the consolidation of media outlets has the potential to seriously change how (or whether) the media cover local campaigns. These changes may have important consequences for the amount of information citizens have available to them when casting their ballots in local elections.

Chapter 7 looks at elections from a campaign's perspective. Lee Goodman writes about the newest campaign tool that candidates, interest groups, and citizens have at their disposal: the Internet. Goodman argues that the Internet has the potential to revolutionize campaigning and opens the door for the voices of many people to be heard in the democratic arena. As Goodman notes, however, Internet technologies stress old campaign finance laws designed for more expensive media, and election law regarding the use of the Internet is still in its infancy stages and is often unclear.

In Chapters 8 and 9 we move away from the candidate and campaign aspects of elections, instead focusing on voters. In Chapter 8, Evan Gerstmann chronicles the infamous 2000 presidential election that culminated with the controversial Supreme Court decision in *Bush v. Gore*. Gerstmann dissects the Court's ruling and discusses the effect the ruling could have on elections in the future, arguing that the decision sets a dangerous precedent. In Chapter 9, Antonio Brown continues the discussion of voters' rights under the law with an examination of the Voting Rights Act and the effect it has had on protecting minority voters. He focuses, specifically, on possible violations of the Voting Rights Act in the 2000 presidential and the 2003 California recall elections. He concludes by arguing that new voting technology has the potential to further disfranchise some voters.

In Chapter 10, the focus is one of the most controversial and complex aspects of election law: redistricting. Charles Bullock looks at the politics behind the redistricting process. Few issues are dominated by politics as much as redistricting because of the incredible effects the drawing of district lines has on who controls the city councils, state legislatures, and the House of Representatives as well as on the types of representatives we elect. Likewise, few aspects of elections have seen more legal challenges than the redistricting process. Bullock clearly explains how the Voting Rights Act (and its extensions) have guided the redistricting process and brings the reader up to date on the courts' most recent decisions regarding the extremely important process of drawing district lines.

Finally, in Chapter 11, I examine judicial elections, an often less-studied but increasingly controversial topic. Judicial elections are fascinating because they are unlike most elections in this country. The laws regarding campaigning and fund-raising are different than the rules for other offices, and judicial elections are often subjected to certain norms not found in other elections. These laws and norms have recently come under attack, and, as I note, because of recent court rulings the landscape of judicial elections may change immensely.

Notes

1. Balkin, "Supreme Court Compromises Its Legitimacy."
2. "High Court's Integrity At Risk."
3. Sandalow, "Turbulent Election."
4. Dionne, "Supremely Partisan."
5. Quoted in Walsh, "Ruling Marked by the Words of a Dissenter," p. A32.
6. In reality, Republican Arnold Schwarzenegger won more votes on the second question than Davis received on the first.

7. Several thousand people had already cast their votes via absentee ballots at the time the court issued its ruling.

8. Quoted in Weinstein, "Courts See Delay as Too Disruptive," p. A22.

9. In its ruling, the Ninth Circuit did not actually make a decision on whether the use of punch-card machines in the six counties violated the Fourteenth Amendment. Instead, it focused on the much narrower, and less controversial, question of whether a U.S. District Court judge clearly misinterpreted the law in his earlier ruling dismissing the ACLU's lawsuit.

2

Parties and Primaries:
The First Electoral Round

Kristin Kanthak and Jeffrey Williams

Incumbents rarely face tough reelection fights until the general election. Potential candidates of the incumbent's party generally sit out the primary election in the hope that presenting a united front in the general election will help the party keep the seat. Yet this was not the case in 2002, when Cynthia McKinney ran for a sixth term as the congresswoman from Georgia's Fourth Congressional District. Instead, she faced a tough primary challenge from Denise Majette, a former state judge. After the results were tallied and Majette was declared the winner, many McKinney supporters cried foul. They did not argue that Majette ran a dirty campaign but instead pointed the blame at Georgia's system of open primary elections. In open primary states, voters who are not members of the party may vote in a party's election. McKinney's supporters filed a lawsuit, claiming that it was too easy for non-Democrats to vote in the Democratic primary and that enough of them did so to throw the election to Majette.

Clearly, McKinney's supporters felt that the rules governing the primary election affected the outcome of the race. This issue concerns not only Georgia elections; nearly half of the other states have similar rules. Running in one's party's primary election is the first step toward winning elective office in forty-nine of fifty states in the United States. Evidence from scholars who have studied the issue supports the Georgia voters' claims that primaries *do* affect the outcomes of elections, and they often do so in very dramatic ways. Primary electoral rules can help determine the winners and losers of elections. We should not be surprised, then, that disputes over primary laws often, as was the case in Georgia, end up in courts of law. In this chapter, we detail how primaries work, describe the most common types of primaries in the United States, and discuss how the type of primary used affects electoral outcomes. We then explain relevant case law regarding primaries, focusing on how courts must answer the question "What is a party?" to resolve cases involving primary election law.

What Is a Primary?

Simply put, a primary is the means by which parties select candidates for the general election. According to Article 1, Section 4 of the U.S. Constitution, states are responsible for passing laws governing the "times, places, and manner" of holding all elections for federal offices. This rule also applies to primary elections, which states first held in the early part of the twentieth century as part of a tide of Progressive reforms.[1] States can determine when primary elections will be held, whose name can go on a primary ballot (most states have signature requirements or filing fees or both), and who is allowed to vote in a primary. As may be expected, states vary a good deal on the rules they have implemented to govern how primary elections will work. But, as will become clear, primaries matter a great deal to party members, and parties will often sue to attempt to change state primary election laws if they think the laws violate their rights.

All states (save for Louisiana) use primaries to determine which candidates will run in the general election. In all states, a primary win guarantees a spot on the general election ballot, although many states have different rules allowing independent candidates to have their names listed on the general election ballot (see Chapter 3). Nonetheless, winning a primary is necessary for being placed on the ballot as a party's nominee in the general election.

Variation in Primary Type

It is up to the state legislature to determine which primary system a state will use. Primaries vary on how *open* or *closed* they are to voter participation. There are five primary types: open, closed, semiclosed, blanket, and nonpartisan. Table 2.1 lists primary types by state.

In an *open* primary, like that of McKinney's Georgia, voters do not have to declare their party affiliation until Election Day. There are two types of open primaries. In a *pure open* primary, voters privately select the ballot for one party. Although no one else knows which party the voter has selected, the voter casts ballots only in the primaries of that party. In a *semiopen* primary, voters must declare their party affiliation at the time they vote. Of course, they may select any party they wish and are not limited to picking the party they chose in the last election.

One somewhat controversial variation on an open primary is the *blanket* primary. In such a primary, previously used in Washington, Alaska, and once in California, voters receive a ballot with all of the candidates' names on it, regardless of the candidate's party. Voters can select among the entire list for each office. But votes for each party are counted separately, with the top candidate for each party facing each other in the general election. For example, suppose there were five candidates, two parties, and vote totals after the blan-

Table 2.1   Primary Types by State

State	Primary Type	State	Primary Type
AL	Open	MT	Open
AK	Blanket	NE	Closed
AZ	Closed	NV	Closed
AR	Open	NH	Closed
CA	Closed	NJ	Semiclosed
CO	Closed	NM	Closed
CT	Closed	NY	Closed
DE	Closed	NC	Closed
FL	Closed	ND	Open
GA	Open	OH	Open
HI	Open	OK	Semiclosed
ID	Open	OR	Semiclosed
IL	Open	PA	Closed
IN	Open	RI	Semiclosed
IA	Open	SC	Open
KS	Closed	SD	Closed
KY	Closed	TN	Open
LA	Nonpartisan	TX	Open
ME	Semiclosed	UT	Open
MD	Semiclosed	VT	Open
MA	Semiclosed	VA	Open
MI	Open	WA	Blanket
MN	Open	WV	Closed
MS	Open	WI	Open
MO	Open	WY	Open

Source: Kanthak and Morton, "Turnout and Primaries."

ket primary that looked like those depicted in Table 2.2. In this case, Candidate Number 1 wins the Party A primary, and Candidate Number 2 wins the Party B primary. This is the case even though Candidate Number 3 received more total votes than Candidate Number 2, because Candidate Number 3 was not the candidate with the most votes *in Party A*. Therefore, Candidate Number 1 is Party A's nominee and Candidate Number 2 is Party B's nominee, and

Table 2.2   A Hypothetical Blanket Primary Outcome

Candidate	Party	Number of Votes
1	A	552
2	B	435
3	A	512
4	B	152
5	B	326

they face each other in the general election. As will be discussed, because of constitutional challenges, no state currently uses a blanket primary format.

A blanket primary should not be confused with a *nonpartisan* primary, however, which occurs only in Louisiana and is not really a primary at all. As in a blanket primary, voters receive a ballot that lists all of the candidates' names. As the name implies, candidates in a nonpartisan primary do not run based on party affiliation. Therefore, the top two vote-getters, *regardless of party*, face each other in the general election. In other words, if the vote count in a nonpartisan primary were like that of Table 2.2, Candidate Number 1 and Candidate Number 3 would face each other in the general election, known in this type of system as a runoff election. So in a nonpartisan primary, it is possible for two candidates of the same party to move on to the next election, an impossibility in a blanket primary election. Further, if any candidate wins a majority of the votes in the "primary," there is no general election, a fact that distinguishes Louisiana from all other states.

Not all states have open primaries, however. In several states, primaries are *closed*, meaning that only members of the party can participate. In a closed primary state, a registered Democrat could not decide to vote in the Republican primary. Instead, voters must change their party affiliation long before the day on which they wish to cast their ballots. States vary on how long before an election voters can make such a change. In New York, for example, voters must register their party affiliation more than six months before the election is to take place. In all closed primary states, a voter who is registered as an independent (registered without any party affiliation) cannot vote in either party's primary. Independent voters must instead wait until the general election to cast a ballot. Likely because of this rule, in closed primary states, fewer voters register as independents.[2]

Other states have *semiclosed* primary systems, in which some, but not all, voters can vote in a primary on Election Day. In those states, people who are registered as members of one party may not vote in the primary of any other party. Depending on the state, voters who are independents may participate in any one primary, or voters who are unregistered may register and vote in any one primary. After voting, in many states, unregistered voters are officially registered as members of that party, and independents have their registration automatically changed to reflect their new party membership.

With all these variations in types of primaries, researchers have examined how these differences might affect electoral outcomes. If different types of primaries all yield similar candidates and have similar effects on voters, then which type of primary a state uses is an unimportant question. All primaries would have the same effect. It turns out, however, that this is not the case; the type of primary a state holds has very real effects on both candidates and voters. We review some of those effects in the next section.

The Effect of Primary Type

Research has shown that primary type can affect the kinds of candidates who win primaries and, therefore, the types of candidates who win general elections.[3] And, although much of the research on this issue focuses on the House of Representatives, the conclusions likely apply to the Senate as well.[4] Further, intraparty competition through primary competition may be key to parties that are responsive to voters.[5]

Some research has found that members of Congress vote differently based on what kind of primary they had to win in order to gain a seat in the U.S. House of Representatives.[6] Those legislators whose states hold closed primaries, holding all else equal, have more ideologically extreme voting records than legislators whose states have semiclosed or open primaries because candidates in semiclosed or open primaries are trying to garner votes from independent voters or voters from the other parties. In closed primary states, however, only those voters who are registered as members of the same party as the candidate may vote. This means that there is no reason for candidates in closed primaries to try to appeal to voters outside of their own parties, thus making the candidates more ideologically extreme.

There is some evidence, however, that these results might not tell the whole story. For example, King disagreed with the results described above, finding that open primary systems actually yielded more extreme candidates.[7] Kanthak and Morton found that separating out pure open primaries from semiopen primaries changed the effect.[8] They showed that semiclosed and semiopen primaries tended to lead to more ideologically moderate candidates than did closed primaries, but that pure open primaries actually led to even more ideologically extreme candidates than did closed primaries. This may be because the secrecy involved in pure open primaries might make it easier for voters from the other party to attempt to "spoil" a party's primary by supporting a candidate so extreme as to be unelectable in the general election, thus throwing the election to the voter's preferred party.

Two other studies found that the type of primary affects whether candidates run for office as major party candidates, minor party candidates, or independent candidates.[9] In addition, as Marjorie Hershey shows in Chapter 3, states differ on the requirements for getting on the ballot for party nominees and independent candidates. These requirements to get on the ballot influence candidates' decisions on whether to run. Taking into account all these differences, potential candidates who are running for a particular office for the first time are more likely to enter as minor party candidates when the primary system is closed. This is because, again, closed primary systems limit primary participation to only those voters who are registered as members of the party. Yet these new candidates are likely to need to rely on new or independent voters to attract enough support to win. Following this logic, research has also found that new candidates in semiclosed or open primary states are more likely to run as independents or major party candidates. In the major party primary, these more open primary systems allow the opportunity for these new candidates to attract new, independent, or crossover voters (those voters who generally vote in the primary of one party, but "cross over" to vote in another party's primary).

Primary type, then, affects decisions that candidates and potential candidates make, but primaries can also affect decisions that voters and potential voters make. Kanthak and Morton found that open primary states tended to see higher voter turnout than did other states.[10] This fact should not be surprising since there are fewer barriers to voting in an open primary system. Further, the authors found that having a contested primary increased voter turnout in the general election, particularly for the party holding the contested primary. This result is contrary to the findings of some of the previous literature.[11] Kanthak and Morton's conclusion is especially significant given the result reported earlier that primary type can affect the chances of holding a contested primary; primary type can, therefore, indirectly influence turnout in general elections. In other words, states can affect general election turnout by selecting primary systems that encourage greater participation at the primary stage.

Primary Type and the Law

It is no wonder, then, that primary type would be of much interest to those who participate in the electoral process, both candidates and voters. This interest often translates into disagreements about how primary elections should be conducted. Further, those disagreements often end up in court.

Why You Don't Have a Constitutional Right to Vote

Many Americans would claim that the right to vote is guaranteed in the Fourteenth Amendment to the Constitution. That amendment, passed after the Civil War in an effort to guarantee civil rights to former slaves, required states (once the Supreme Court applied the amendment to states in 1925 in *Gitlow v. New York*) to provide "equal protection of the laws" to all citizens. Further, any state that prevented otherwise eligible voters from casting ballots would have its representation in Congress reduced by the proportion of people the state illegally prevented from voting. The language of the amendment seems straightforward to us now: everyone has the right to vote.

It is no wonder, then, that sixty-year-old homemaker Annabelle Barkman was surprised to be denied a ballot when she showed up at her Monroe Township, Bedford County, Pennsylvania, polling place in April 1997. Barkman was refused a ballot because, as a registered independent, she was not eligible to vote in primary elections in Pennsylvania, a closed primary state. Barkman was unaware of the law, because she had recently moved from Illinois, where independents like her could vote in whichever primary they choose. "If you are an American citizen and you move between states, what civil liberties go with you? You'd better know that you can't count on them," Barkman said.[12]

As a result of being denied what she thought was a fundamental right, Barkman sued for the right to vote. Barkman first took her case to the Court of Common Pleas of Bedford County, Pennsylvania. She argued that the local election board should be required to provide her with any available ballot, despite being registered as an independent. The County Court disagreed and denied her petition. She then appealed to the Commonwealth Court of Pennsylvania, which also denied her petition. She has not continued with the case.

In fact, the case was not even a particularly difficult one to decide for either court. The case law, specifically the Supreme Court case *Nader v. Schaffer* (1976), is clear. In that case, Nathra Nader and Albert C. Snyder Jr., residents of Connecticut, were, like Barkman, refused ballots in a primary election because they were not registered as members of a party. The plaintiffs argued that the closed primary laws in Connecticut violated their constitutional rights in three ways: denial of equal protection, freedom of association, and the right to vote. First, Nader and Snyder Jr. believed they were denied equal protection under the law because party members were allowed to vote and they, as independents, were not. Second, they felt that requiring them to associate themselves with a political party in order to vote deprived them of their right to free association, guaranteed in the First Amendment of the Constitution. And third, they argued that their right to vote was abridged, because they were not allowed to participate in the primary election, which they deemed to be an "integral part" of the electoral process.

The Supreme Court rejected these arguments. The plaintiffs pointed to several previous cases in which the Court had determined that states and parties could not prevent people from voting in primaries (the so-called White Primary Cases, which we will return to in a moment). Yet the Court said the issues in the *Nader* case were different. In its decision, the Court concurred with the lower court (the U.S. District Court for the District of Connecticut) that the requirements were not sufficiently onerous to preclude Nader and Snyder from registering as members of a major party and thereby being allowed to participate in the party's primary. The plaintiffs could, the Court said, register with a party but still make campaign donations or sign petitions for candidates outside the party for which they were registered.

It is important to note that the courts did not accept Nader's and Snyder's arguments about free association but made reference in the decision about the *party members'* rights to free association. In the decision, the lower court said that party members have associational rights, which allows them not to have to associate with nonparty members in their primaries if they choose not to do so. In other words, parties can prevent nonparty members from participating in their primaries if they so choose.[13]

A party's right to choose who associates with them was the key to another case, *Van Allen v. Democratic State Committee of New York* (2003).[14] In this recent case, the Supreme Court of New York, Albany County, a lower state appellate court, determined that the plaintiffs, H. William Van Allen and Christopher Earl Strunk, did not have the right to vote in a party primary because they were registered independents in a closed primary state.

The Independence Party of New York had a provision in its rules allowing open primaries. In other words, they invited people of other parties to participate in their primaries. This rule made them different, the court ruled in *Van Allen*, and the plaintiffs could participate in the Independence Party primary election if they so chose. This ruling created an important distinction: Only the party that allowed open primaries could be subjected to them, according to the decision. The other parties, who preferred to keep their primaries closed, were off-limits to voters who were not registered as members of the party.

Limits on the Associational Rights of Parties

The parties' right to determine who participates in their elections is not without limit. In a series of cases beginning in 1927, the Supreme Court stated that discrimination on the basis of race was not allowed in primary elections. Taken together, these cases are known as the White Primary Cases.[15] In the wake of the Civil War, many southern states passed laws attempting to make it difficult for African Americans to vote. One means of discrimination was the so-called white primary. These laws precluded African Americans from voting in primary elections, on the basis that white party members had rights of free association and that these rights implied a right *not* to associate with African American voters in primary elections. The white primary laws therefore provided states with a means to disenfranchise African American voters.

The Supreme Court saw these white primaries for what they were: an attempt to circumvent the Fourteenth Amendment. As stated, white voters tried to argue that forcing them to allow African American voters to participate in their primaries violated their right to free association. Indeed, discrimination on the basis of race is perfectly legal for private organizations. But parties are different from other private organizations, the Court ruled, because they play an integral role in deciding who represents the people of an area. Further, the Court said, primaries are a "state action." In this sense, parties do not have all the rights to free association of other groups. The Court declared white primaries unconstitutional, largely because discrimination in this manner would require the state to have discriminatory laws on the books (see Chapter 9 for more discussion of the white primary).

It was this issue that turned the case in favor of African American voters. Since states are required by the Fourteenth Amendment and *Gitlow* to provide equal protection under the law, an all-white primary by definition fails to provide equal protection. As a result, the white primaries were declared unconstitutional. It is important to remember, however, that white primaries were unconstitutional not because the parties refused to allow African American voters but because the *states* put into practice laws that were discriminatory. The decision therefore implied that parties have much more say over primaries than states do.

Powers of the State and Federal Governments

Although parties have considerable control over the ways primaries are conducted, that say is not unqualified. In fact, the states also have broad powers to regulate elections of federal officeholders under Article 1, Section 4 of the U.S. Constitution, which asserts that states can regulate the "times, places, and manner" of holding elections. Therefore, states can regulate elections in ways that assure that the election is fair and honest. For example, in a Hawaii case (*Burdick v. Takushi* 1992), the Supreme Court ruled that states could ban write-in candidates. The Court's reasoning was that the right to vote is not absolute but is meaningful only as far as the electoral system maintains its integrity. Since the integrity of the system is based largely on the rules the states create, the states' ability to make those rules must be protected.

A state's right to regulate elections reaches to the role of parties, too. In 1994, the New Party, a small Minnesota political party, selected a candidate to represent the party on the ballot for the office of state legislator. The problem, however, was that a major party had also selected the same candidate as *its* nominee. In most states, this would not be a problem. Minnesota, on the other hand, is one of the few states that has a law banning *fusion* candidates, or candidates who run for an office as the nominee from more than one party. In this case, neither the major party nor the candidate objected to the New Party's nomination. As a result of the antifusion law, though, local election officials refused to accept the New Party's nomination petition, since the major party had already filed one on behalf of the candidate. The candidate's name therefore appeared on the ballot only as a major party nominee.

In response, the New Party sued, claiming that the state's antifusion law violated the party members' rights to free association, and the case ended up in the Supreme Court. There, in *Timmons v. Twin Cities Area New Party* (1997), the justices ruled in favor of the state. The Court argued, as they did in the *Burdick* case, that the state has the right to regulate elections. They further found that the prohibition against fusion candidates did not overly burden the New Party membership, because their preferred candidate's name still appeared on the ballot, albeit only as a major party nominee.

Even though the state has power in administering elections, the power is not absolute and, in fact, can be subservient to that of the federal government. The state (under Article 1, Section 4 of the Constitution) and federal (under Article 1, Section 4 and the Fourteenth Amendment to the Constitution) governments' claims to regulate elections clashed in Louisiana, as a result of Louisiana's unusual nonpartisan primary system. Indeed, the so-called open primary system (different from the open primary discussed earlier) is not a primary at all. Instituted in 1975, the law called for one election in which all candidates appeared on the same ballot. This "primary" occurred before the first Tuesday in November of even-numbered years, which is the mandatory uniform federal election date in the United States.[16] According to Louisiana's law, if no candidate received more than 50 percent of the vote, the top two vote getters would then run against each other in a runoff election that would occur on the mandatory federal election date.

In most cases, one candidate would receive the required 50 percent of the vote and thus be declared the winner. In these circumstances, there was no election held for that office on the federally mandated, uniform election day. Several voters in Louisiana sued, saying that the Louisiana law violated the federal law mandating a uniform federal election day. In *Foster v. Love* (1997), the Supreme Court sided with the voters, stating that elections held before the federal uniform election day were void. Their decision was based on the fact that the federal government had passed laws stating that there should be one uniform election day for all federal offices. Further, the federal government's ability to do so is justified by Article 1, Section 4 of the Constitution. Although that section, as described above, gives states the power to regulate elections, it also says that "Congress may at any time by law make or alter" the states' election regulations.

The decision in the *Foster* case did not preclude Louisiana from keeping its unusual nonpartisan primary system, nor did Louisiana opt to change it. The case was based on the fact that the 1975 Louisiana law provided for a means for federal offices to be filled prior to the uniform federal election day, a violation of the federal law. But the nonpartisan system itself was not in question. Further, the federal laws requiring the November election allow runoff elections to be held *after* the uniform election day. In other words, the federal law prevented Louisiana from filling its offices early but specifically allowed the state to fill them *late*, as did many other states that require runoff elections. So Louisiana simply changed its primary date to the November uniform election day. Now, the primary is held in November, and if no candidate receives more than 50 percent of the vote, a runoff between the two is held at a later date. Indeed, that was the case in 2002, when the sitting U.S. Senator from Louisiana, Mary Landrieu, failed to garner a majority of the votes. She held on to her seat, but not before facing Republican elections commissioner Suzanne Terrell in a runoff several weeks after the uniform election date.

Powers of the Party

Clearly, the states and the federal government have a great deal of power in determining how primary elections will be held. But parties are not simply at the mercy of the government. On the contrary, the courts have been clear that parties' associational rights give them a great deal of influence over how primary elections are held in the United States.

Perhaps the archetypal case on the parties' associational rights is *Democratic Party of the United States v. Wisconsin ex. Rel. La Follette* (1981). In the *La Follette* case, the national Democratic Party objected to being required to seat a group of delegates from Wisconsin at their national convention. This convention, held every four years, determines who will be the party's nominee for the president of the United States and sets out the party's agenda. A key issue of the case is the nature of presidential primary voting in the United States. Voters go to their polling places every four years and select a name from a list of potential presidential nominees from their party. In reality, however, they are engaging in a presidential preference primary. Voters are not in fact selecting candidates but instead are selecting delegates to go to the national convention, with the promise that those delegates will vote for their preferred presidential candidate. Further, the party's national convention exists not just to select a presidential nominee but also as a means for party members to make and hear political speeches and to vote on the party's political platform for the next four years.

The state of Wisconsin argued that its interests in the election allowed it to require an open primary. Wisconsin's claims were based on its interest in protecting the integrity of the electoral process, an important issue in the *Burdick* case. Further, the state argued that open primaries increase voter participation, allow voters to cast truly secret ballots, and protect voters from harassment stemming from their having to declare a party affiliation, as is required in a more closed system. The state argued that its interests outweighed the party's claims that open primaries violated the associational rights of the party.

Yet the Supreme Court sided with the party, saying that the party cannot be required to seat delegates at its convention if the delegates were not elected in accordance with the party's rules. The Court's basic argument was that the party members' First Amendment rights to free association could not be infringed by the state, due to the Fourteenth Amendment's inclusion of the states in the prohibition on government intervention into these rights. Parties, therefore, had a right to free association, at least with regard to seating delegates at its own convention. Wisconsin could not force the party to associate with people not meeting the party members' definition of "Democrat."

Further, the party's right to free association works both ways. The *La Follette* case is clear: States cannot force parties to associate with those with whom they choose not to associate. At the same time, states cannot preclude parties from associating with people, when both the party and the people in question desire the association. At issue here is not states requiring open primaries but states requiring closed primaries.

The Republican Party of Connecticut voted, in 1983, to allow independents to vote in Republican primaries for state legislative positions. At the time, Connecticut was a closed primary state. Therefore, the state prevented independent voters from voting in Republican primaries despite the facts that Republicans chose to allow their participation and that the independents chose to participate. The state argued that their laws did not preclude such voters from participating in the Republican primary, since they could do so by changing their party registration at least one business day before the primary election.

In *Tashjian v. Republican Party of Connecticut* (1986), however, the Supreme Court again sided with the party. In its decision, the Court made similar arguments to those in the *La Follette* case. Specifically, states did not have the power to violate First Amendment rights to free association. If the party itself chose to associate with nonparty members, the state is precluded by the Constitution of the United States from preventing that association.

Not surprisingly, then, the Court has also ruled that states cannot make laws that dictate how a party organization may operate (*Eu v. San Francisco County Democratic Central Committee*, 1989). In this case, a California law stated that parties were not allowed to endorse candidates in primary elections.[17] Further, the law set out a required form for parties' governing structure. The Court's decision pointed out that these requirements were a violation of the party members' First Amendment rights to free speech and association.

The End of the Blanket Primary
Up until 2000, the Supreme Court had never stated unequivocally that a particular primary system was unconstitutional. Even in the *Foster* case in Louisiana, it was the time of the primary, not its structure, that was at issue. This changed, however, when residents of the state of California voted to switch to a primary system that the states of Alaska and Washington had been quietly using for years: the blanket primary.

After the 1992 senatorial election in California, Tom Campbell was angry. Democratic nominee Barbara Boxer had beaten Republican nominee Bruce Herschensohn. Campbell, a moderate Republican, was sure he could have beaten Boxer in the general election, but he lost the Republican primary to the far more conservative Herschensohn. At the time, California used a closed primary, and Campbell argued that had independents or even Democrats been able to vote in the Republican election, he would have won. As a result, Campbell decided to attempt to reform the primary system of California. California has a long history of direct democracy, putting issues on the ballot in the form of propositions that voters either support or reject. Campbell took advantage of this process by getting Proposition 198 on the ballot in 1996. That proposition called for a blanket primary like that used in Washington and Alaska. Remember that a blanket primary includes all of the candidates' names in all of the races on one ballot. Using this mechanism, voters can vote in different parties' primaries for different offices. Campbell and his supporters reasoned that such a primary would increase the likelihood that an ideological moderate would represent the party in the general election.

Indeed, the proposition garnered the necessary support, and in 2000 California used the blanket primary system. The California Democratic Party joined with the California Republican Party, the Libertarian Party of California, and the Peace and Freedom Party, however, in suing California's secretary of state, Bill Jones. The political parties argued that each of them had rules that prohibited the participation of a voter who is not a registered member of their party. The parties claimed that California's blanket primary violated their First Amendment right to free association, or more specifically the freedom not to associate.

The state argued that it was within its constitutional rights to administer elections to allow a blanket primary if the voters of California so chose. The state said that it had an interest in administering elections that produced more representative elected officials, expanding the debate beyond the traditional confines of the party system, preventing the disenfranchisement of voters who had not registered by party, providing voters with more choices, increasing participation, and protecting the voters' rights to keep their party affiliations secret. The Supreme Court, however, once again came down on the side of the parties and agreed with the argument that parties have a right to choose with whom they associate.

In *California Democratic Party v. Jones* (2000), Justice Antonin Scalia, writing for the majority, said that the party members' rights to free association (here, the right not to associate) trumped the state's interest in keeping the blanket primary system. Indeed, Scalia's decision declared that the state's reasons for wanting the blanket primary were not compelling and, even if they were compelling, that the blanket primary was not the "most narrowly tailored" way to achieve the state's end. Therefore, the state's blanket primary was deemed unconstitutional, and the state resumed the closed primary system that had been in operation before Proposition 198.

But the Jones case had implications beyond the borders of California. Washington State had been quietly holding blanket primaries since 1935. Shortly after the Jones decision, three political parties in Washington (Democratic, Republican, and Libertarian) entered a lawsuit against Washington secretary of state Sam Reed. As in California, the parties sought to have the blanket primary system declared unconstitutional. On September 15, 2003, the parties got their wish. The Ninth Circuit Court of Appeals, using the precedent set in the *Jones* case, declared the Washington State blanket primary unconstitutional (*Democratic Party v. Reed*, 2003). As for Alaska, the state legislature there voted to create a closed primary system in 2001, thus avoiding a legal standoff.

What Is the Future of the Open Primary?

Given the affirmation of the party's associational rights in the *Jones* case, one could wonder about the future of the open primary. It could be argued, after all, that the open primary, like the blanket primary, requires party members to associate with voters who do not meet their definition of "member" of their party. In his decision on the *Jones* case, Scalia clearly stated that the ruling in *Jones* did not require the Court to take a stand on the open primary.[18] But some scholars have argued that the decision in the *Jones* case would apply to any primary system in which voters do not have to be party affiliates to vote in the party's primary.[19]

Clearly, the issue of the open primary will also have to be decided in the nation's courts. We began this chapter by discussing one such case: Congresswoman McKinney's loss to challenger Majette. Democratic voters in the district claimed that "malicious crossover voting" by Republicans in the Democratic primary caused McKinney to lose the election.[20] Further, they stated that the open primary system in Georgia discriminated against African American voters.

In this case the state of Georgia won. In *Osburn v. Cox* (2003), U.S. District Court Judge for the Northern District of Georgia, Charles A. Pannell, ruled that the plaintiffs (individual voters within the district) did not have standing to determine which voters were actual Democrats. The decision went on to say that the only body that had the right to make such associational claims was the Democratic Party, which was actually a defendant in the case.

Pannell's decision brings up an important question: What if a *party*, rather than a group of voters, had initiated the lawsuit? Would they, then, have the right to stop open primaries? We shall have to wait until a political party chooses to make those claims in court for an answer.

Notes

The authors would like to thank Laura Langer and Barbara Norrander for their comments on previous versions of this chapter.

1. Key, *American State Politics*.
2. Norrander, "Explaining Cross-State Variation."
3. Rice, "Gubernatorial and Senatorial Primary Elections"; Schantz, "Contested and Uncontested Primaries."
4. Kenney, "Explaining Primary Turnout."
5. Geer and Shere, "Party Competition and the Prisoner's Dilemma."
6. Gerber and Morton, "Primary Election Systems and Representation."

7. King, "Congress, Polarization, and Fidelity."

8. Kanthak and Morton, "The Effects of Electoral Rules on Congressional Primaries."

9. Gerber and Morton, "Electoral Institutions and Party Competition"; Gerber, Kanthak, and Morton, "Selection Bias in a Model of Candidate Entry Decisions."

10. Kanthak and Morton, "Turnout and Primaries."

11. Kenney and Rice, "The Effect of Primary Divisiveness"; Kenney and Rice, "The Relationship Between Divisive Primaries and General Election Outcomes"; Kenney, "Sorting Out the Effects."

12. "Independent Voter Sues," *Pennsylvania Law Weekly*, p. 2.

13. We will revisit the lower court's statements on these issues in a moment, when we discuss *California Democratic Party v. Jones*.

14. It is important here to note that court cases are often referred to using the name of only one of the plaintiffs or defendants. So, for example, in this case, Van Allen and Strunk are both plaintiffs, yet only Van Allen's name is used to reference the case. This practice simply saves time, confusion, and ink. In a more dramatic example, the full list of defendants in the *Van Allen* case is "Democratic State Committee of the State of New York, New York Republican State Committee, The New York State Committee of the Independence Party, State Committee of the Conservative Party of New York State, State Committee of Liberal Party of New York State, State Committee of the Right to Life Party of the State of New York, State Committee of the Green Party of New York State, State Committee of the Working Families Party of New York State; The New York State Board of Elections with: Carol Berman, individually and as Chairman; Neil W. Kelleher, individually and as Vice-Chairman; Helena Moses Donohue, individually and as Commissioner, and Evelyn J. Aquila, individually and as Commissioner," clearly quite a mouthful. But pointing out the practice here is important, because the court decided to treat some of the defendants differently.

15. The White Primary Cases are *Nixon v. Herndon* (1927), *Nixon v. Condon* (1932), *Smith v. Allright* (1944), and *Terry v. Adams* (1953).

16. Congress passed the law in 1872.

17. For more information about the effects of party endorsements, see Jewell and Morehouse, "What Are Party Endorsements Worth?"; McNitt, "The Effect of Preprimary Endorsement Competition"; and Morehouse, "Money Versus Party Effort."

18. Interestingly, Scalia also said in the *Jones* decision that a nonpartisan primary, like that of Louisiana, would avoid the constitutional issues of association altogether.

19. Persily, "Toward a Functional Defense."

20. See Wekkin, "Why Crossover Voters Are Not Mischievous Voters," on the effects of crossover voting.

3

Third Parties:
The Power of Electoral
Laws and Institutions

Marjorie Randon Hershey

Brad Warren's race for the U.S. Senate was an exercise in frustration. His party, the Libertarian Party, had done the hard work of meeting the Indiana state requirements for getting on the ballot—only to see the state legislature increase those requirements substantially for the next election. He was treated fairly by reporters, he felt, until the Democratic and Republican primary elections took place. After that, his media coverage dried up; the primaries seemed to anoint the major party winners as the "real" candidates in the race, and reporters didn't want to waste their efforts on a third-party candidate with no realistic chance to win. It was very difficult to attract campaign contributions without media coverage. Without campaign contributions, he couldn't purchase much advertising, so most voters never heard that he was running. It was no surprise when he lost the election in November.

The two major parties, Warren says, have a "death grip" on American politics.

> If I need a new pair of socks, I can go to dozens of stores and pick from several different brands and dozens of colors—for something as insignificant as socks. But when it comes to politics, which has a monopoly on the lawful use of force in our society, we have only two choices. . . . If you get angry with the incumbents, you can throw them out, only to reelect the nasty incumbents you had thrown out in the previous election. Four years from now, you'll be throwing out the incumbents you elected today. There's no choice.[1]

Warren concluded from the experience of his Senate campaign that the role of a third party is "like that of a bee: You rise up, you sting, and then you die."[2]

The Impact of Third Parties

Even in spite of the many disadvantages they face, third parties have made a difference at several key points in the political history of the United States.[3] Consider the case of the 2000 presidential race. The election was nearly a tie; no winner could be determined until disputes about Florida's vote count were resolved. When the dust (and the chads) cleared, election officials announced that Republican George W. Bush had beaten Democrat Al Gore by only 537 votes in Florida. With that tiny margin, Bush won all of Florida's electoral votes; that gave him a majority in the Electoral College and, thus, the presidency. Ralph Nader came in third in Florida; running as the candidate of the Green Party, Nader received 97,488 votes in the state. In postelection polls, almost half of Nader's supporters said that if their candidate had not been on the ballot, they would have voted for Gore. Less than a quarter said they would have supported Bush. It could plausibly be argued, then, that Nader's third-party candidacy gave the presidency to Bush.[4]

In the 2002 midterm elections, although only one independent candidate won a federal office, minor party and independent candidates won 6.3 percent of the popular vote for the highest state office elected—the first time this percentage had topped 5 percent in a midterm election since the mid-1930s (see Table 3.1).[5] Libertarian candidates attracted enough votes to tip the South Dakota U.S. Senate race and the Wisconsin governorship to the Democrats, and eight minor party candidates won state legislative seats. Four states had elected independent or third-party governors during the 1990s,[6] and Ross Perot had won 19 percent of the vote for president as an independent candidate in 1992. At the local level, Libertarians claimed to have run 1,420 candi-

Table 3.1   Percentage of the Vote for Third-Party Candidates in 2002: U.S. Congress and Governors

	House	Senate	Governor
Libertarian	1.6	0.2	1.3
Reform	0.4	0.4	0.2
Green	0.4	0.3	1.3
Constitution	0.2	0.1	0.2
Natural Law	0.1	0.03	0.4
Other parties	0.8	0.1	2.2[a]
Independent candidates	0.5	0.7	0.7

Source: "2002 Vote for U.S. Senate, U.S. House of Representatives, Governors." Ballot Access News 18. January 1, 2003. Http://www.ballot-access.org/2003/0101.html (accessed September 16, 2003).

Note: a. This percentage is skewed heavily because New York gubernatorial candidates from "other parties" received more than one million of the 1,396,408 votes.

dates in 2000; by 2002, about 500 Libertarians held elected or appointed local offices ranging from justice of the peace to school board member.[7]

Minor parties have played notable roles at other critical times as well. Just before the Civil War, for example, when both of the major parties— Democrats and Whigs—shook in the face of the powerful issue of slavery, several minor parties gained strength. One of these, the newly formed Republican Party, needed only six years to field a full slate of candidates and to elect its presidential nominee, Abraham Lincoln, in a four-candidate race.

But Third Parties Rarely Win Power

It is significant, however, that, at that critical time, the Republicans did not remain a third party. They displaced the Whigs and thus became part of the two-party system that has dominated American politics ever since.[8] Similarly, after popular third-party candidates attracted votes at the turn of the 1900s, two-party politics triumphed again, this time by co-opting the supporters and the issues of the new parties. Figure 3.1 shows the peaks in third-party voting for president in the 1890s, 1910s, and 1920s; most of these votes were cast for Populist and Progressive candidates. But the Democratic Party soon absorbed the main ideas of the 1890s Populists and therefore undermined their appeal to voters. The process was repeated in the 1990s, when Republican leaders designed appeals to capture the large number of voters who had supported

Figure 3.1   Percentage of the Vote for Third-Party Presidential and House Candidates, 1876–2002

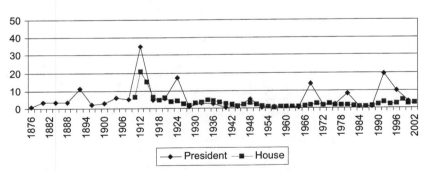

Sources: For presidential votes: *U.S. Election Atlas,* on the Web at www.uselectionatlas.org. For House votes: 1946–2000 calculated from Norman J. Ornstein, Thomas E. Mann, and Michael J. Malbin, *Vital Statistics on Congress, 2001–2003* (Washington, DC: AEI Press, 2002), p. 62. Raw data for House elections prior to 1946 can be found in Michael J. Dubin, *United States Congressional Elections, 1788–1997* (Jefferson, NC: McFarland, 1998), and Edward Franklin Cox, *State and National Voting in Federal Elections, 1910–1970* (Hamden, CN: Archon Books, 1972), p. 257.

Ross Perot as an independent candidate in 1992. The Republican appeals worked, and the Reform Party later faded.[9] Even at their moments of greatest strength, then, we can see the weakness of third-party status in U.S. politics. If a growing third party does not succeed in displacing one of the major parties, as the Republicans of the 1850s were the last to do, it is most likely to see its support lured away by one of the two major parties.[10]

The result is that although third parties may win votes, an occasional major office, and the rare opportunity to tip the balance in an election, they have not been able to maintain power. No such candidate has ever won the presidency; only one party, the Progressives, has won even a single state's electoral votes more than once. There have been more than a thousand state governors elected since 1875, but only about twenty ran solely on a third-party ticket, and just a few have been elected as independents (see Figure 3.2).[11] Although minor parties were represented in the House and Senate in the late 1800s and in the first half of the 1900s, in recent years their number has ranged from zero to two. In 2003 there was only one independent House

Figure 3.2   Number of Third-Party Senators, House Members, and Governors, 1876–2002

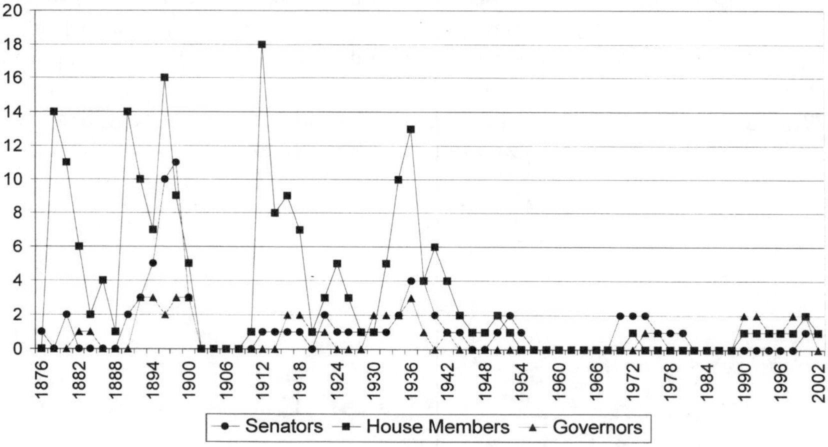

Sources: For Senate and House members: Norman J. Ornstein, Thomas E. Mann, and Michael J. Malbin, *Vital Statistics on Congress, 2001–2003* (Washington, DC: AEI Press, 2002), pp. 56–58; for governors: calculated from *Congressional Quarterly's Guide to U.S. Elections,* 3rd ed. (Washington, DC: CQ Press, 1994), pp. 639–663, and, for 1994–2000, Richard M. Scammon and Alice V. McGillivray, *America Votes* (Washington, DC: CQ Press, 1995, 1997, 1999, 2001).

Note: These are raw numbers of elected officials. The total number of House members increased from 293 in 1876 to 435 today, senators from 76 to 100, and governors from 28 to 50. Fusion candidates are counted as majority-party officeholders. If fusion candidates were classified as third party, there would be twelve more governors shown here: in 1877, 1883, 1892, 1895, 1897 (3), 1899 (2), 1901, 1903, and 1911.

member and one in the Senate; both are from Vermont and both caucus with the Democrats. In fact, a comparative study found that the United States had the smallest number of effective "electoral parties" and the second-smallest number of effective "parliamentary parties" among twenty-seven democratic nations examined.[12]

This situation poses a puzzle. In a nation as diverse as the United States, the constitutional guarantees of free speech and freedom of assembly nurture large numbers of political organizations reflecting differing views on important issues. Why, then, have third parties and independent candidates arisen again and again in American history but failed to achieve real power? Minor parties have a more secure position in most other democracies, so the answers to this question could tell us something important about the American version of democracy. Is it that Americans coalesce so easily into two major groupings—liberal and conservative, business and labor, or traditionalist and modernist—that they are inclined to limit the alternatives to two when they make big decisions? Not likely, as the array of choices at car dealerships and real estate offices suggests. Is it that in a democracy, it is simply natural to have one governing party and one party in opposition? If so, then it would be hard to explain why most other democracies have more than two viable parties.

A much more convincing argument is that U.S. electoral institutions and electoral law (the latter, of course, written by legislators who have won office under the label of the two major parties) discriminate against third parties in a variety of effective ways. These institutions and laws might not be able to protect a two-party system against a massive swell of public discontent. But they have done a remarkable job of sustaining two-party politics to this point.

How Do American Political Institutions Hinder Third Parties?

Several institutional features of the U.S. government make life difficult for ambitious third parties. Four of the most influential are the rules for electing representatives and counting votes, the existence of a single executive office rather than a plural executive, the Electoral College, and primary elections. Each of these institutional choices distinguishes the American version of democracy from that of many—and, in the case of the Electoral College, all—other democracies.

Single-member Districts and Plurality Rules
As political scientist Maurice Duverger argued, single-member districts with plurality elections tend to produce two-party systems.[13] A single-member district is one in which only one candidate is elected to each office—for example, one individual, rather than several, is elected to represent a particular dis-

trict in the U.S. House of Representatives. In plurality elections, the candidate who gets the largest number of votes wins, even if he or she does not win a majority.

In most American elections, candidates are elected to single-member districts using plurality rules. The candidates who fall short of a plurality get nothing. A second candidate who has a viable base of support may well decide to run, on the chance that the front-runner may stumble. But there's little to encourage a third or fourth candidate to contest an election; as the odds of winning a plurality get smaller, it becomes more pointless to invest the resources that would be needed to run even a bare-bones campaign.

The alternative to the single-member district/plurality election system is a multimember district with proportional representation (PR)—a system used by many European nations. In this system, each legislative district will be represented by a group of legislators, not just one. Each political party puts forward a slate of candidates; each voter then chooses a party slate, not an individual candidate. The party's representation is proportional to the vote it receives—at least for parties that win more than a particular minimum percentage of votes. If a party wins 25 percent of the vote in a district, then 25 percent of the legislators from that district will be drawn from that party's slate. So if the district has four representatives in the state legislature, one of the four will be from this party. When a party can put a candidate into office even if the party has won only one in every four votes, it will be encouraged to keep running campaigns.

Most democracies that use this proportional representation system to elect their legislators do have viable minor parties—parties that regularly nominate and elect candidates. In fact, multimember districts were common in the United States prior to the 1950s. Most U.S. House members represented multimember districts in the 1800s—a time when, as Figure 3.2 shows, third-party legislators were more common in the House than they are currently. Even as recently as 1954, 58 percent of state assembly members were still elected from such districts; only nine states chose all their state legislators in single-member districts.[14] But after a wave of reform, based in part on the belief that multimember districts were too amenable to party control and discriminated against minorities, these districts are rare at the state level now and nonexistent at the federal level (see Chapter 10 for further discussion of multimember districts).

Some other democracies whose electoral rules are similar to those of the United States do, however, have more than two major parties. Canada and Britain also have single-member district systems yet regularly support three or more parties, although the impact of plurality rules keeps third parties in Britain from winning as large a proportion of legislative seats as they do of the popular vote. So these rules for representation and voting can't be the only explanation for the weakness of American minor parties.

A Single Executive

In particular, the single-member nature of the American presidency helps to undercut the viability of third parties in the United States. The presidency is the biggest prize for a party, the focus of an enormous amount of coverage by thousands of media outlets. Candidates with a serious chance of winning the presidency are in the news for years before an election. But competing for president is not a feasible choice for most third parties. It is extremely difficult, as we will see, to get on the ballot in all fifty states; the cost of getting on the ballot is beyond the reach of all but a few minor parties. In addition, the possibility of winning a national plurality is remote, so third parties will not get the media coverage and public recognition that come with a presidential campaign.

In contrast, in many other democracies the executive consists of a cabinet of several officials, rather than just one. In such cases, the prize can be divided among two or more parties. A party that finds itself close to the majority needed to control the executive can offer a few positions in the cabinet to smaller parties, in exchange for their votes. These cabinet positions can sustain a minor party; if the Green Party, perhaps winning just 10 percent of the vote, has a chance of putting one of its leaders into the cabinet as environment minister in exchange for its support of a larger party, then the Greens can justifiably argue that a citizen's vote for their candidate is not a wasted vote.

The Electoral College

Another "rule" of the electoral system in the United States, closely related to those discussed above, is the American oddity of the Electoral College.[15] Designed to protect the infant republic from the risks of popular democracy, the Electoral College vote determines which candidate is elected president. Because the candidate who gets the most votes in a state receives all the state's electoral votes (in all but two of the states), a minor party's candidate rarely has a chance to win any electoral votes. Fewer than a dozen minor party candidates have ever succeeded in doing so throughout U.S. history. Nader was not among them, nor was Perot, though he funded his campaign with more than $60 million of his own money.

The only third-party candidates likely to win electoral votes are those whose appeal is geographically concentrated, such as George Wallace's American Independent Party in 1968. Wallace's candidacy had substantial appeal in some southern states because of his anti-integration, pro-military stance. Yet by the same token, its regional character suggests that such a party will not have the broad appeal necessary to win a plurality in a large number of states.

Even among those third-party candidates for president who have registered in the Electoral College, almost all have received a smaller proportion of electoral votes than they did of the popular vote as a whole.[16] Thus, partly because of the "rule" of the Electoral College, as well as the single-member district/plurality election system more generally, voters often feel that it would be futile to cast a ballot for a third-party candidate. In 2000, for example, only one in five respondents in a preelection survey who said they preferred Nader actually voted for him, as did only three in ten of those who ranked him first in a postelection survey.[17] The rules, as always, affect the outcome.

Primary Elections

The existence of the direct primary helps to protect the major parties as well. When a prospective candidate has the opportunity to run for a dominant party's nomination, he or she is less likely to take the rocky path of third-party candidacy. This may be what kept the American South from developing a stable third party during the long period of Democratic dominance, when the Republican Party was simply not a socially acceptable option for ambitious southerners.[18]

Primary elections disadvantage third parties in other ways. Primaries receive a lot of media coverage, which brings increased name recognition and fund-raising opportunities to the candidates of parties that hold primaries— the Democrats and Republicans. By the end of the year before the 2004 presidential election, for instance, the candidates for the two major parties' nominations had received barrels of ink and large amounts of media time. Almost nothing had been reported in the mass media about the potential candidates of the Libertarian, Green, or other third parties, in part because these smaller parties were not preparing for state primaries and caucuses to be held in early 2004. Most minor parties use conventions to nominate their candidates. These events are unlikely to be considered newsworthy unless they contain unusual drama or conflict, as in the 2000 convention of the Reform Party, at which fistfights broke out among delegates. (The resulting media coverage, of course, did not add to the party's credibility among voters.)

These institutional hurdles are very high. They create an atmosphere in which third parties find it difficult to recruit candidates and win votes. In consequence, journalists and voters are led to think of third-party candidates as irrelevant and to doubt their pragmatism and, sometimes, even their sanity. But these are not the only hurdles that third parties face. American elections are governed by a blizzard of state laws. The legislators who pass these laws and the judges who interpret them come almost exclusively from the two major parties. Understandably, the major parties have an interest in protecting the system that advantages their candidates and weakens their minor-party competitors.

Laws and Court Rulings Handicap Third Parties

In the 1800s, elections were run by the political parties, not by the government. People voted either by stating their candidate preference aloud or by placing colored paper ballots, printed and given to them by the political party they favored, into a ballot box. The voting was public; anyone present could see the color and size of each voter's ballot. That made sense for party "machine" bosses; if they had paid for a vote, they wanted to make sure that they got it. But this system didn't please reformers, who in the 1890s promoted the use of the secret ballot. The government printed these ballots, on which parties and their candidates' names were listed. Because the state governments were in essence giving official recognition to the parties whose names were on the ballot, the presumption was that the states had the legal right to regulate the parties.[19]

States have made extensive use of that right, passing an enormous number of laws specifying what a party must do to get on the ballot.[20] New parties or independent candidates typically have to file petitions signed by a certain percentage of voters. Democratic and Republican candidates usually do not. Parties that have won a line on the ballot normally have to receive a certain minimum percentage of the vote for one state office—typically, the governor or the secretary of state—in order to keep that line. The numbers and percentages range widely. These rules are not a problem for the major parties but can be an insurmountable hurdle for many minor parties.

Ballot Access Laws

The laws governing parties' access to the ballot vary greatly from state to state. To get on the Louisiana ballot for the U.S. Senate in 2000, a new party's candidate had to get an estimated 134,460 signatures on petitions from registered voters; he or she would have needed 86,027 signatures to run as a new-party candidate in California, 43,680 in Oklahoma, and 39,094 in Georgia. In Florida, on the other hand, a new-party candidate could get on the ballot for Senate just by paying a filing fee, and in Mississippi, his or her party needed only to be "organized."[21] The sources of these state laws vary as well; some states tightened their requirements after World War II, due to a fear of subversive elements such as Communist parties receiving formal recognition from the government; others simply wanted to limit competition by keeping attractive candidates from filing under a third-party or independent label.[22]

The height of this ballot access hurdle seems to make a difference. Georgia, for instance, requires a new party to file petitions containing the signatures of at least 5 percent of registered voters (typically, almost 15,000 signatures per congressional district) to qualify for a place on the ballot for U.S. House of Representatives; the requirement was upheld by a U.S. court of appeals in 2002. The appeals court ruled that the 5 percent requirement did not impose a new qualification on candidates for federal office beyond those stated in the U.S. Constitution (which would have been unconstitutional), but simply ensured that prospective candidates have a substantial level of public support before getting on the ballot. In the sixty years since the law was passed, no third-party candidate for the U.S. House has ever been able to qualify.[23]

Because ballot access laws differ from state to state, a third party wishing to run in every state faces an especially difficult task. To get a presidential candidate on the ballot nationwide requires a minor party to research fifty different sets of state rules—a task that often requires paying for legal help— as well as the ways in which the rules might be misinterpreted by hostile state election officials. Ross Perot managed to overcome these hurdles and get on the ballot in all fifty states as the Reform Party's presidential candidate in 1996, but only after an unprecedented effort by paid workers and volunteers. Among the tasks his campaign faced was California's requirement that a third-party candidate submit more than 89,000 voter registrations for the party by October 1995—more than a full year before the actual election. The toughest state ballot requirements for presidential races are listed in Table 3.2.

Then there is the issue of remaining on the ballot. In South Carolina, a minor party needs only to run at least one candidate every four years in order to retain its ballot line. In Alabama, the same party would have to win 20 percent of the vote in the preceding election. The office named in this require-

Table 3.2   Getting on the Ballot for President: The Toughest State Ballot Access Laws for New Parties and Independents (2004)

	Requirements for Getting on the Ballot for a	
	Full Party Slate	Presidential Candidate
Louisiana	140,000 (est.) registered voters	must pay a fee
Minnesota	112,557	2,000[a]
California	77,389 registered voters	153,035
North Carolina	58,842	100,000 (est)[b]; 58, 842[c]
Oklahoma	51,781	37,027
Texas	45,540	64,077[b]; 45,540[c]
Tennessee	41,322	25
Alabama	41,012	5,000
Massachusetts	38,000 (est.) registered voters	10,000[a]
Georgia	37,153	37,153[a]
Ohio	32,290	5,000
Michigan	31,776	31,776
Florida	must be organized	93,024[b]; 0[c]

Source: Compiled from Richard Winger, *Ballot Access News,* http://www.ballot-access.org/2003/0901.html and personal communication, September 5, 2003.

Notes: Entries are the numbers of signatures on petitions (or, where indicated, the number of voters registered in that party) required to get on the state's presidential ballot.

a. A candidate who qualifies for the ballot can list his/her party label along with his/her name.

b. The number required for an independent candidate.

c. The number required for a new party's candidate.

ment matters as well; it is much easier for a minor party to get a certain percentage of the vote for secretary of state or some other less-visible office than to get the same percentage of the vote for president or senator in that state.[24]

Some states put restrictions on the types of people who can become party candidates. In California, for instance, you cannot be on the primary ballot unless you have been a registered member of that party for three months and not of any other party in the previous year. That makes it harder for minor than for major parties to recruit candidates.[25] Laws requiring new parties to pay filing fees in order to get their candidates on the ballot are also onerous for third parties. Thirteen states require fees of $200 or more for at least some offices, and there have been no minor party candidates elected in these states during the last fifty years.[26]

Other states slap restrictions on citizens who would support ballot access for new parties. In 1986, for instance, the West Virginia state legislature passed a law stating that anyone who circulated a petition to gain ballot access for a third-party or independent candidate must tell each potential signer that, as a result of signing the petition, he or she would lose the right to vote in the upcoming major-party primary elections. (Third parties don't normally hold primaries.) It was not until December 2003 that a U.S. district court judge granted an injunction to stop the law's enforcement; it still has not been ruled unconstitutional.[27]

Once a party has complied with these rules, the rules may change. To retain its place on the Indiana ballot through the 1982 election, for example, a party needed to win just half of one percentage point of the vote for secretary of state. But after the Libertarian candidate for that office surpassed that threshold in 1982, the state legislature raised the required minimum to 2 percent, and the Libertarians lost ballot access. In some states, deviating in the slightest from these strict rules leads to disqualification. The Natural Law Party had to sue the secretary of state of Kansas in 2002 to get rid of a law that limits party names to two words, one of which must be *party*. The law had prevented the Natural Law Party, with a three-word name, from getting its nominees on the ballot; they had to petition to be listed as independents.[28]

Parties hoping to qualify for a state ballot have to research questions such as these: Does the party need to file a separate petition for each office to get on the ballot, or just one petition overall? Eleven states require a new party to file a separate petition for each office.[29] How many signatures are required? Can anyone sign the petition, or only a registered voter? Do the petitions have to be notarized? Do the names have to be collected within a short period of time? How far in advance of the election do the petitions need to be completed (keeping in mind that interest in an election is at its lowest when the election is most distant in time)? Clearly, the more complicated the requirements, the more costly in time and money it will be to fulfill them—and third parties are not long on either.

Few would argue that there should be no restrictions at all on ballot access. Think of the 2003 special election to recall California's governor Gray Davis, in which the normal ballot access rules were set aside, and any candidate hoping to replace Davis needed only sixty-five signatures on a petition and a $3,500 filing fee to get on the ballot (or 10,000 signatures and no filing fee). A total of 135 candidates met those requirements, including a melon-smashing comedian, a twenty-three-year-old porn star, a sumo wrestler, and the publisher of *Hustler* magazine. Voters hoping to research each candidate would have needed to take vacation time. Ballot access rules, then, make a difference, whether they are open to all comers or whether they greatly advantage the major parties.

Some researchers contend that these laws are not insurmountable hurdles for third parties. One study found that ballot access laws do not account for much variation in the number of minor party and independent candidates who run for the U.S. House or in the percentage of the vote they receive.[30] Perhaps many third-party candidates are so driven by a commitment to a set of issues or by other motivations that they will work to meet whatever requirements exist, at least below a certain threshold.[31] And some might argue that stricter ballot access requirements can be a blessing in disguise, in that they force third-party candidates into introducing themselves to at least a certain minimum number of voters; asking people to sign petitions and to donate money for filing fees can lead to greater name recognition and support, just as television and newspaper ads do.

Yet other researchers have shown that as filing fees and petition requirements go up, the number of House candidates goes down.[32] Petition drives may not introduce the candidate's message and qualifications to a large number of voters efficiently and effectively—and in any case, the money spent on filing fees and petition drives clearly shrinks the budget that candidates have left for other campaigning. But because they must first get on the ballot in order to have a chance of winning, third-party candidates do not have the option of declining to meet these often-burdensome state requirements.

Court Rulings

In addition to ballot access rules, third parties and independent candidates face a stream of conflicting judicial decisions that affect the viability of their candidacies. Some Supreme Court decisions in recent years have undercut the standing of minor parties and helped to entrench the two-party system, even while some other decisions, especially by lower courts, have liberalized ballot access rules for third parties.

In some recent decisions, the U.S. Supreme Court has seemed to give states the right to protect the two-party system against minor-party assault. In the case of *Timmons et al. v. Twin Cities Area New Party,* for example, the Court ruled in 1997 that Minnesota could keep candidates from running on more than one party's label in an election (cross-filing).[33] Where cross-filing is allowed, a smaller party can list the candidate of another party, typically a major party, as its own candidate. These "fusion" tickets are thought to help sustain smaller parties by letting them link their names with attractive candidates and, sometimes, by gaining some influence over those candidates. A major-party candidate who won a close race, if that candidate had received enough votes on a smaller party's line to have tipped the balance, might be more attentive to the minor party's concerns as a result. New York's cross-filing law has helped sustain its Liberal and Conservative Parties for decades.[34]

The Court's majority opinion in *Timmons* rejected the minor party's argument that it had a First Amendment right to freedom of association and thus to select its own candidate, even if that candidate were also running on another party's ballot line. The Court majority instead supported the state's right to act on a belief that a two-party system provides needed stability and therefore should be protected. Most states do not permit fusion tickets. Those who do are more likely to encourage minor parties.[35]

And yet the Court has also upheld the parties' rights, under the First Amendment guarantee of freedom of association, to make their own choices about who can vote to select the party's nominees. It has, for instance, permitted the parties to decide whether they will open up their primaries to independents[36] and has banned the "blanket primary" established by a California voter initiative, and an appeals court decision struck down the blanket primary set up long ago by the Washington state legislature.[37] Blanket primaries let a voter choose candidates in both parties' primaries on the same ballot and therefore allow any voters, not just the party's supporters, to select its candidates (see Chapter 2 for a more thorough discussion of the blanket primary). Although the major parties are much better positioned than minor parties to take advantage of these First Amendment associational rights, the cases could prove to benefit third parties as well by strengthening their own authority over candidate selection relative to that of the major-party-dominated state legislatures.

In addition, since the late 1960s, both the Supreme Court[38] and lower courts have struck down a number of laws that discriminate against third parties in ballot access. Typically, though, they have done so in a conservative manner, with the ruling limited to the particular case and state, so that third parties must keep petitioning the courts to extend the ruling to other venues. That requires third parties and independent candidates to hire attorneys to challenge restrictive ballot access laws—a burden that the major parties do not bear.

Federal Funding for Presidential Campaigns

Most election law is state law. But one significant body of federal election law—the Federal Election Campaign Act (FECA) and its amendments on campaign finance—treats third party and independent candidates differently from Democrats and Republicans. The two major parties' presidential candidates can qualify for full federal funding of their general election campaigns as long as their party has won at least 25 percent of the vote in the previous presidential election—not much of a challenge for a major party. Other parties' candidates, however, receive federal funding only if they win at least 5 percent of the national general election vote. Even then, the federal money comes only after the election, when it can be used mainly to repay the loans that a minor party candidate has incurred during the campaign. Having won at least 5 percent of the vote, the party is then entitled to some funding for its candidate in the next general election. After Ross Perot won 8 percent of the presidential vote in 1996, his Reform Party qualified for public funding in 2000. But the Reform candidate got only about a fifth ($12.6 million) of that received by George W. Bush and Al Gore. No third-party candidate qualified for federal funding in 2004.

State Public Funding of Campaigns
About half of the states provide at least some public funds to statewide candidates, parties, or both. But only a few of these states permit minor party candidates, or the parties themselves, to qualify for the money. In Minnesota, for instance, candidates for statewide office, regardless of party, can qualify for full public funding as long as they raise a certain amount of money in small contributions and agree to accept spending limits.[39] Jesse Ventura qualified for public funding for his 1998 gubernatorial campaign in Minnesota after his Reform Party won 5 percent of the vote in the previous election. Ventura benefited as well from the fact that his opponents, who also accepted the state money, faced spending limits. That kept them from outspending Ventura as substantially as they might otherwise have been able to do (and might have chosen to do, if they had believed him to be a serious threat).

Third-party candidates in Vermont and Maine have also received public funding. But the money, while helpful, is often not enough to overcome other disadvantages faced by third-party candidates. In Minnesota's 2002 gubernatorial election, although both the Reform and Green Parties qualified for public funds, the Reform (now Independent) candidate got only 16 percent of the vote and the Green candidate won 2 percent—very impressive by third-party standards, but not enough for a plurality.[40]

Other Hurdles
Minor parties face many other challenges in American politics. States that permit a straight-ticket vote—in which voters can push a button or pull a lever that records their vote for every one of a given party's candidates on the ballot—have been found to yield a smaller share of the total vote for third parties and independent candidates than do states that lack this option.[41] Also,

candidate debates organized by commissions sponsored by the two major parties usually resist any efforts to include third-party candidates.

The behavioral hurdles are substantial as well. Public opinion is decidedly mixed about third parties. Polls show that increasing numbers of Americans would like more choices in elections and are dissatisfied with the hegemony of the Republicans and Democrats (see Figure 3.3). Yet we have seen that when other parties do get on the ballot, their candidates rarely receive many votes. One likely explanation is that although many Americans may be dissatisfied with what the major parties offer, their dissatisfaction is not a sufficient basis for agreement on any one particular third party or candidate.

Public dissatisfaction may also remain broad and diffuse, and not translated into votes for specific third-party candidates, because so few of these candidates can raise the money and get the media coverage to penetrate the consciousness of dissatisfied voters. Media coverage of campaigns is dominated by a focus on the "horse race"—who's ahead and who's behind—coverage that is thought to sell more newspapers and airtime because it conveys greater excitement and immediacy than does extensive discussion of issues and candidates' experience. But when coverage emphasizes the "horse race,"

Figure 3.3   Change in Public Opinion Toward Third Parties, 1944–1995

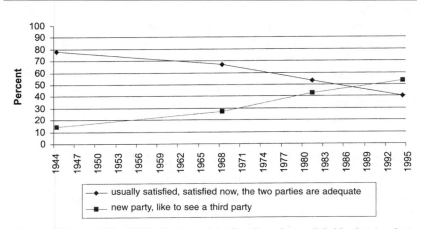

Source: Christian Collet, "Third Parties and the Two-Party System," *Public Opinion Quarterly* 60 (1996): 431–449. (See p. 443 for exact question wording.)

Note: The question (with some variation) was: "Do you find that you are usually satisfied with the stands taken by one or the other of the present big parties, or would you like to see a strong new party entirely different from either of the present parties?" The 1944 results come from a Roper poll (n=5,131); the 1968 results come from a Gallup poll (n=1,500); the 1981 data come from the U.S. Opinion Research Corporation (n=1,005); and the 1994 data come a CNN/*USA Today* poll (n=1,007).

it is easy to dismiss third-party candidates as sure losers; that makes it harder even for sympathetic citizens to consider voting for them. For candidates who receive little media coverage, the only other way to reach large numbers of voters efficiently is to buy media ads or other means of large-scale contact such as direct mail or phone banks. The cost of these types of campaigning, however, limits their use to parties or candidates with a great deal of money (or access to the personal wealth of others).

Perhaps the most important problem faced by third parties is the continuing influence of party identification. Asked whether they generally think of themselves as Republicans, Democrats, or independents, the majority of Americans say that they identify with a major party, and their party identification normally guides their voting behavior.[42] Most of the rest admit to "leaning toward" a Democratic or Republican identification; these "independent leaners" are often "closet" supporters of their party as well.[43] In 2002, only 9 percent of those surveyed claimed to be genuine independents or apoliticals—the lowest proportion recorded since 1964.[44] That doesn't give new parties much room to gain adherents.

All of these explanations for the weakness of third parties have their limits. If the major parties and their elected officials behave badly enough, or sidestep enough vital issues, then it is likely that potentially attractive candidates would run independently or under a third-party label, just as has happened at other times in American history. If such a candidate were appealing enough, he or she would probably get a lot of media coverage; media people are not as much in favor of the two-party system as they are in favor of attracting an audience. Campaign contributors and voter support would likely follow. The volatile voting patterns of recent years could, under the right circumstances, produce an opening for a minor party or independent alternative. Yet the legal and institutional obstacles in the path of third parties are substantial enough that the level of citizen discontent needed to provide this opportunity would have to be very high.

Should We Make It Harder for Third Parties?

This chapter has demonstrated that electoral law and institutions have built impressive barriers against third-party success in American elections. Do these barriers simply reflect the ability of the major parties to protect their dominant status, even after they have worn out their welcome?[45] Or are there reasons why we *ought* to make it hard for minor parties to gain and maintain strength?

To some, the debate may be no more consequential than the issue of where the bargaining and compromise in the political system take place. When many of the diverse interests in a nation are aggregated into two broad groupings, each of these two parties will need to engage in a lot of *internal* bargaining and compromise in order to set priorities. A multiparty system is likely to incorporate more of those diverse interests, but it divides them into a larger number of narrower parties. Each party will probably have to engage in less internal compromise in order to put forth its ideas. Yet because it is likely that no single party will be able to govern by itself, it will need to form relationships with other parties to create a majority coalition, and that requires compromise *among* the parties. To others the issue involved is no less than that of whether First Amendment rights apply to all the voices in a nation or just a majority.

It seems likely that a system in which minor parties compete on a more even playing field would change politics in the United States in important ways. The range of alternatives that are publicly debated would broaden. The major parties are likely to ignore or sidestep certain types of issues. To pay for increasingly expensive campaigns, major parties need to attract contributors as well as voters. So some ideas—even if they might prove appealing to large numbers of voters—may be unappealing to the dominant parties if those ideas repel the minority of citizens who donate money to candidates and the organized interests—corporate and trade political action committees, labor unions—that control important campaign resources. It is at least arguable that the policy stands of minor parties, who do not expect to win pluralities or raise big campaign budgets, may be less driven by the concerns of major moneyed interests. (On the other hand, a minor party or independent candidate who relies on big donors to mount ballot access drives and buy media ads could be just as much a captive of moneyed interests.)

Because the dominant parties need to appeal to majorities in order to win power, they may also "tend to ignore issues that concern only a minority of citizens and threaten the interest of the majority."[46] Issues such as discriminatory practices that target small minorities offer no electoral advantage to a major party. Third parties can be a form of insurance against a two-party system that is tempted to sidestep controversial or difficult issues, those that do not attract majority support, and those that offend powerful donors.

A system that encourages minor parties might also stimulate more citizen participation in politics. Voter turnout in the United States is among the lowest in the democratic world. Almost half of those eligible do not cast a ballot for president, and the turnout for other types of elections is even lower. There are many possible explanations; among them is that the dominant parties in a mature democracy have learned to maintain their "market shares" in the electorate as it stands. The Democratic and Republican Parties concentrate their turnout efforts on groups already likely to go to the polls in large numbers.[47] These parties are not likely to put many of their scarce resources into encouraging greater participation among alienated and disadvantaged groups. Minor parties may be more inclined to do so. In fact, the single recent increase in turnout levels occurred in the 1992 presidential race, when Ross Perot's independent candidacy seemed to provoke greater interest in the election.

But although a multiparty system may do a better job of placing a broad range of issues on the table and may encourage increased participation in politics, a two-party system offers time-tested benefits as well.[48] Whereas proponents of multiparty systems value innovation, supporters of two-party politics talk about the value of stability; they note that the American system of two dominant parties has remained relatively stable during times when other democracies have faced more rapid change in leadership, issue agendas, and parties. Because both of the major parties need to appeal to broad constituencies, they have an incentive to keep fringe groups and demagogues out of leadership positions in their organizations and campaigns.

A two-party system seems to have an advantage in legitimizing election results. Because the winner of a two-party contest will inevitably get a majority of votes, his or her ascension to power appears more legitimate and fair than it might in a multiparty election. This is not a trivial matter, of course; convincing the losers to accept the outcome of an election is one of the most basic needs in a democracy. In addition, multiparty systems often raise fears of serious fragmentation in governing, though many multiparty democracies avoid these concerns by adopting election rules such as thresholds for electing representatives, runoffs when no candidate gets a majority, and combinations of proportional representation and single-member districts.

Two-party systems may also be more consistent with the amount of effort most voters want to invest in political activity. It is rare for individuals to devote a great deal of time in their already-complicated lives for extensive research on candidates and political issues. Instead, to cut through the clutter of information that surrounds elections, voters often rely on shortcuts, or heuristics.[49] The limited range of alternatives that a two-party ballot provides may be a better fit with the low salience of politics in American society. Citizens who can simplify and clarify their choices may in fact be more likely to consider voting than if they were faced with a greater array of options.

There is no doubt, however, that in contrast to most other democracies, electoral laws and institutions in the United States pose significant disadvantages for third parties. As a result, especially since the mid-1900s, the Democratic and Republican Parties have established a level of dominance in elections and in voters' perceptions of politics that is found nowhere else in the democratic world. There is no shortage of "bees" in American political life, and at times their sting has been sharp enough to make the media and the major parties take notice. But as Brad Warren's experience suggests, electoral rules in the United States ensure that their impact will be fleeting.

Notes

1. Hershey, *Party Politics in America,* Chapter 2.
2. Warren is quoting Richard Hofstadter in *The Age of Reform*, p. 97.

3. See Rosenstone, Behr, and Lazarus, *Third Parties in America,* Chapters 3 and 4. Note that the present chapter uses the terms *third party* and *minor party* interchangeably.

4. Abramson, Aldrich, and Rohde, *Change and Continuity,* pp. 69, 127–128; Pomper, "The Presidential Election," pp. 133–135 and note 18. One should note that some scholars have argued that George W. Bush might have more easily won had Patrick Buchanan not run. See Burden, "Minor Parties."

5. Winger, "Minor Party and Independent Vote." The "top office" is the governor's race, or the U.S. Senate race in states where no gubernatorial election was held.

6. Out of thirty-six governors' races in the 1990 election, there were two third-party winners: Lowell Weicker of A Connecticut Party and Walter Hickel of the Alaska Independence Party. Jesse Ventura ran successfully on the Reform Party ticket to become governor of Minnesota in 1998, and Angus King won the governorship of Maine twice in the decade as an independent.

7. "Record Number of Libertarians Seeking Votes," *Hoosier Times,* p. B4.

8. See Reichley, *The Life of the Parties,* Chapter 6.

9. Rapoport and Stone, "Ross Perot Is Alive and Well," pp. 337–353.

10. Reichley, *The Life of the Parties,* pp. 147–148.

11. Gillespie, *Politics at the Periphery,* pp. 302–305. The figures were updated using relevant issues of *CQ Weekly.*

12. Lijphart, *Electoral Systems and Party Systems*, pp. 160–162.

13. Duverger, *Political Parties.*

14. See Klain, "A New Look at the Constituencies." Klain wrote that multimember districts had long been the norm in England, stemming from the days when it was considered safer for two or three representatives to protect one another's safety on the dangerous road to London; they could then serve as a check on one another's actions while in Parliament. Because of their familiarity with English elections, American colonists also adopted multimember districts; these continued to be used by the states after independence. Though Klain regarded the reasoning as faulty, he suggested that the switch to single-member districts was based on the argument that voters could cast their vote more thoughtfully and could better hold their representative accountable if they had to choose just one. In addition, reformers believed that representatives elected in multimember districts were more likely to be controllable by party bosses, whose power the reformers wanted to weaken.

15. Reichley, "The Future of the American Two-Party System," pp. 20–21. See also Schumaker and Loomis, *How Should We Elect Our President?*

16. Since 1900, the only candidate with a larger percentage of the electoral than the popular vote has been Strom Thurmond, the candidate of the States' Rights Democratic Party. Also known as the Dixiecrats, the party was an anti–civil rights offshoot of the Democratic Party in 1948. Because he won a plurality of votes in four southern states, Thurmond received 7.3 percent of the electoral vote, but only 2.4 percent of the popular vote.

17. Abramson, Aldrich, and Rohde, *Change and Continuity,* pp. 124–127.

18. See Epstein, *Political Parties in the American Mold*, pp. 129–132.

19. Bibby and Holbrook, "Parties and Elections."

20. See issues of the *Election Law Journal* and Richard Winger's Ballot Access News on the Internet at http://www.ballot-access.org.

21. Richard Winger, personal communication regarding 2000 ballot access for a new party candidate for U.S. Senate, 1999.

22. Rosenstone, Behr and Lazarus, *Third Parties in America,* pp. 22–23.

23. Bibby and Holbrook, "Parties and Elections," p. 63. See also Winger, "11th Circuit Upholds Georgia Law." The case is *Cartwright v. Barnes,* 02-10670 (U.S. Court of Appeals, 11th Circuit, 2002).

24. Winger, "Institutional Obstacles," p. 165.

25. Ibid., p. 162.

26. Ibid., p. 169.

27. Winger, "Injunction Issued Against West Virginia Restriction," p. 1.

28. The law was finally overturned by the Kansas state legislature in October 2003; it had been passed in 1901 by a Republican-dominated legislature threatened by the successes in the 1900 elections of Democrats and Populists who ran as the Peoples-Democratic Party. See "Briefly in Kansas."

29. White and Shea, *New Party Politics*, p. 314.

30. Collet and Wattenberg, "Strategically Unambitious," pp. 229–248. This comparative analysis is most interesting, but a definitive test would require us to find out the proportion of potential candidates who failed to file because of ballot access requirements—a very difficult task.

31. One of Nader's stated reasons for running, for example, was to help build the Green parties; see Berg, "Spoiler or Builder?" pp. 323–336.

32. Ansolabehere and Gerber, "The Effects of Filing Fees." See also Winger, "Institutional Obstacles," pp. 169–170.

33. 520 U.S. 351 (1997).

34. See Scarrow, *Parties, Elections, and Representation.*

35. Ryden, "'The Good, the Bad, and the Ugly," pp. 55–58. Currently, only about ten states permit fusion candidacies.

36. *Tashjian v. Republican Party of Connecticut,* 479 U.S. 1024 (1986).

37. *California Democratic Party v. Jones,* 530 U.S. 567 (2000), on the California blanket primary. The Washington primary was thrown out by the U.S. Ninth Circuit Court of Appeals in 2003.

38. See, for example, *Williams v. Rhodes,* 393 U.S. 23 (1968) and *Anderson v. Celebrezze,* 460 U.S. 780 (1983).

39. Bibby and Maisel, *Two Parties*, p. 65.

40. See Heyser, "Minnesota Governor," pp. 233–245.

41. Collet and Wattenberg, "Strategically Unambitious," pp. 240–241.

42. See, for example, Bartels, "Partisanship and Voting Behavior."

43. Keith et al., *The Myth of the Independent Voter.*

44. See National Election Studies data at http://www.umich.edu/~nes/nesguide/toptable/tab2a_1.htm.

45. Lawson, "The Case for a Multiparty System," p. 61.

46. Rosenstone, Behr, and Lazarus, *Third Parties in America,* p. 221. For an argument in favor of third parties, see Disch, *The Tyranny of the Two-Party System.*

47. Hershey, *Party Politics in America,* Chapter 8.

48. For an argument in favor of two-party politics, see Bibby, "In Defense of the Two-Party System," pp. 73–84.

49. See Sniderman, "Taking Sides."

4

Campaign Finance: Reform, Representation, and the First Amendment

Victoria A. Farrar-Myers

The concept of representation lies at the heart of the debate over campaign finance reform. The role of this concept often goes unstated, however, in large part because certain core principles are universally accepted:

- Fair and open elections are a cornerstone of the United States' form of representative democracy, and
- An elected official's providing a political favor as a quid pro quo for a campaign contribution is antithetical to his or her role as a representative of the people.

Although the *concept* of representation and its central role in the American political system are universally accepted, the *conception* of representation—what the term means and how representation can be enhanced—underlying each side of the campaign finance reform debate differs significantly. The conceptions of representation in the American political system are numerous and vary in terms of what aspects are accentuated and which parts are de-emphasized. Because various conceptions of representation are prevalent in American political thought, each side on the campaign finance reform debate can contend that its approach to the issue actually improves the representative nature of the American political system.

The campaign finance reform debate, however, is not solely about enhancing representation. Another fundamental component of the American political system is part of the debate—the protection of freedom of speech. The Supreme Court, in its decision in *Buckley v. Valeo* (1976), implicated the First Amendment when it ruled that the federal government's ability to regulate the flow of money in and around elections can be restricted. As a result,

43

these two tenets of American democracy—representation and the First Amendment—potentially could be placed at odds with each other.

So as we sit here at the crossroads of campaign finance reform, representation, and the First Amendment, we are left with the question of how to reconcile this conflict. Before this question can be addressed, we must first go back to the beginning and examine the law and subsequent Supreme Court decision that led to this enduring conflict of values. Further, we must explore the conception of representation that each side on the campaign finance reform debate employs as well as the assumptions that each side makes regarding the First Amendment.

The Origins of the Debate

The Federal Election Campaign Act

As a way to combat the influence of major donors that dominated political campaigns in the 1960s, Congress passed the Federal Election Campaign Act (FECA) of 1971[1] and the 1971 Revenue Act.[2] These two pieces of legislation created a structure to govern the campaign financing system. FECA went into effect in April 1972 and provided limitations on spending on media advertisements and from candidates' personal funds (although these latter limits were later repealed to conform with judicial pronouncements). FECA also permitted the creation of political action committees (PACs) for corporations and labor unions (among others) to participate lawfully in the federal electoral process. These PACs could solicit voluntary contributions from individuals and subsequently contribute funds to federal campaigns. The Revenue Act established the public financing system for presidential general elections, whereby citizens could check a box on their tax form that would give the federal government permission to use one of their tax dollars to finance presidential campaigns.

Amendments to FECA followed in 1974, 1976, and 1979. In a response to the Watergate campaign finance scandal, the 1974 amendments created an independent agency, the Federal Election Commission (FEC). The FEC was charged with overseeing whether FECA was being followed, given the authority to promulgate regulations to ensure compliance, and directed to provide information for the administration of elections. In addition to establishing the FEC, the 1974 amendments also expanded the scope of the presidential financing system by providing matching funds to presidential primary candidates and to the political parties to support their nominating conventions and allowed corporations and unions with federal contracts to create PACs. Further, the 1974 amendments created limitations on contributions and expenditures by all candidates and PACs in federal elections. These provisions sparked a lawsuit filed by Senator James L. Buckley (Conservative Party,

New York) and Eugene McCarthy (former Democratic senator from Min-
nesota) against the secretary of the Senate, Francis R. Valeo. The Supreme
Court handed down its ruling in the case on January 30, 1976, in *Buckley v.
Valeo.*

Buckley v. Valeo

Buckley was extremely important for two reasons. First, the *Buckley* decision
set the ground rules for our current campaign finance reform debate. The way
in which the Supreme Court framed and decided the issues brought before it
established the relevant vocabulary for the debate and set out the basis for
deciding which restrictions on money were permissible under the Constitution
and which were not. Second, the *Buckley* decision is routinely criticized by
both sides of the reform debate as being improperly decided. For those who
seek greater regulation on the flow of campaign-related money, *Buckley* starts
with faulty presumptions that block legitimate efforts to reduce corruption or
the appearance of corruption in elections. For those on the other side of the
issue, *Buckley* establishes an ill-conceived framework that results in impermissible restrictions on a person's First Amendment right to free speech.

The following discussion provides a narrow review of the *Buckley* decision and focuses only on those aspects that relate directly to the fundamental
tenets that are being addressed herein—representation and the First Amendment. In *Buckley*, regulation proponents posited three reasons in support for
the campaign finance restrictions set out in the 1974 amendments to the
FECA. First, and most important, was that the "primary interest served by the
limitations and, indeed, by the Act as a whole, is the prevention of corruption
and the appearance of corruption spawned by the real or imagined coercive
influence of large campaign contributions."[3] The other two interests, deemed
"ancillary" by the Court, were to "equalize the relative ability of all citizens
to affect the outcome of elections" and "to open the political system more
widely."[4] Of these, the Court considered the first one—stemming corruption
or the appearance of corruption—to be the only sufficient reason to potentially justify an infringement on First Amendment speech rights.

Among other provisions, the FECA amendments placed restrictions on
how much money people could contribute to candidates for office (what will
be referred to as "contributions"), how much candidates could spend either of
their own money or through their campaigns (collectively "candidate expenditures"), and how much money people could spend on their own in connection with an election but without coordinating such expenditures with any
candidate (known as "independent expenditures"). The Court went on to distinguish between contributions and the two types of expenditures. In regard to
contributions, the Court believed that the symbolic act of the contribution
itself was the important expression of political speech that could not be
infringed—not how much money was donated to a campaign. As a result, the

Court upheld limitations on the maximum amount of contributions that a person could make during any election cycle since they "entail only a marginal restriction upon the contributor's ability to engage in free communication."[5]

In regard to independent expenditures and candidate expenditures, however, the goal of seeking to limit corruption was insufficient to justify expenditure limitations. Here, the Court focused largely on the general principle that, in its view:

> A restriction on the amount of money a person or group can spend on political communication during a campaign necessarily reduces the quantity of expression by restricting the number of issues discussed, the depth of their exploration, and the size of the audience reached. This is because virtually every means of communicating ideas in today's mass society requires the expenditure of money.[6]

The Court further stated:

> It is clear that a primary effect of these expenditures limitations is to restrict the quantity of campaign speech by individuals, groups, and candidates. The restrictions, while neutral as to the ideas expressed, limit political expression at the core of our electoral process and of the First Amendment freedoms.[7]

Thus, since the government, through FECA and its amendments, placed restrictions on core First Amendment freedoms but did not have a sufficiently legitimate reason for doing so, the Court struck down the restrictions on candidate and independent expenditures. The effect of this aspect of the Court's decision, at least in the context of campaign expenditures, was to equate money with speech.

Competing Sides

As noted at the outset, both sides in the debate surrounding campaign finance since *Buckley* have certain assumptions regarding representation and the First Amendment underlying their positions. With the framework and issues from *Buckley* now laid out, we can turn to understanding what those assumptions are.

Regulation Supporters

As noted by the Supreme Court in *Buckley*, the primary interest being served by campaign finance restrictions is to stem corruption or the appearance of corruption in the electoral process. Also important is that such restrictions promote a sense of *equality* in the electoral process. In fact, Thurgood Marshall, both in his separate opinion in *Buckley* (concurring in part, dissenting in part) and in a dissenting opinion in a subsequent campaign finance case,[8] cited the concept of equal access to the political arena as being the primary reason for campaign finance regulations. When talking about equality in the electoral process, an important phrase comes to mind—one that underlies the conception of representation held by advocates of campaign finance restrictions: "one person, one vote."

The Supreme Court enunciated this premise—one person, one vote—in *Gray v. Sanders* (1963), with its roots in the seminal case of *Baker v. Carr* (1962). It stands for the proposition that each person's vote should and must be counted equally; that the dilution of one person's vote, with the resulting implication being the increased value of another person's vote, is impermissible in the American political system (see Chapter 10 for a greater discussion of *Baker v. Carr*).

In the campaign finance setting, the argument is that the great amounts of money that some people spend on political campaigns through contributions to candidates and/or as independent expenditures effectively give those people avenues to influence elections above and beyond their ability to cast a ballot. In addition, numerous organizations spend enormous sums of money in the electoral process, and those organizations do not have the right to vote (although, admittedly, their individual members do) or, in some instances, are prohibited from making contributions to candidates. Meanwhile, average voters, who do not have the money to participate in the electoral process in this way because they are spending their income on such items as housing and food, are left holding on to their one vote as the campaign process passes them by. The underlying goal of campaign finance regulations, thus, is to prevent the dilution of these individuals' votes.

How does this relate to representation? The electoral process is an important representational mechanism by which public officials are chosen and some sense of the public will is expressed. Underlying the views of regulation advocates are assumptions that each person in the nation has an equal interest in the public will and that the public will is an aggregation of those interests. The elected representative's job is to serve the interests of each of his or her electoral constituents equally. Regulation advocates' conception of representation, therefore, is, or may be, corrupted by individuals and groups that spend great amounts of money. Certainly, providing a quid pro quo in exchange for a campaign contribution distorts this representational process. But perhaps more significant is that the flow of money results in elected officials putting more emphasis, or at least appearing to put more emphasis, on the interests, wishes, and concerns of large contributors over other voters—that is, not all interests are served equally.[9] Thus, the notion of equality so crucial for representation in the American political system is lacking without constraints on money in elections.

This conception of representation is *dyadic* in nature. There is supposed to be a direct linkage between a public official and his or her electoral constituency in which the policy preferences of the legislator should reflect the policy preferences of the constituency. Representation is enhanced when that linkage is strong; but when the linkage is weakened by outside influences (for example, campaign contributions and independent expenditures), the nature of representation is distorted. Somewhat implied in this dyadic notion also is the idea that an elected official is supposed to be a *delegate* of the constituency. The representative should, to some degree, *mirror* the constituency's interests and desires and should reflect them in his or his decisions regarding governmental affairs.

But what of the third avenue of our intersection—the First Amendment? What assumptions do supporters of regulations make that would allow them to endorse campaign finance restrictions that the Supreme Court has said are impermissible infringements on the core liberty of freedom of speech? Quite simply, they have not agreed with the conclusion that money equals speech. This view already has made its way into several concurring and/or dissenting Supreme Court opinions. In *Buckley*, Justice White contended the FECA restrictions regulated the spending of money that could be used to defray the costs of speaking but did not limit speech itself. He added in another case that campaign expenditures produce speech but are not speech itself. Further, Justice Stevens in a case decided in 2000 stated succinctly, "Money is property; it is not speech."[10]

Such views of money eliminate the potential conflict noted at the beginning between the two tenets of democracy in the United States—representation and the First Amendment—because the First Amendment concerns are not triggered. The core principles of freedom of speech are not offended by campaign finance restrictions because direct infringements on speech are not involved. As a result, Congress should have greater flexibility in limiting the flow of money in political campaigns because the only fundamental issue at stake in doing so would be the representational nature of our government.

Regulation Opponents

We have examined the conceptions that underlie the positions held by supporters of campaign finance regulations; now, let us consider those of their opponents. For regulation opponents, the primary issue of concern is the infringement on political speech protected by the First Amendment. Both Justices Kennedy and Thomas have advocated that the Court overturn *Buckley* on the grounds that the distinction between contributions and expenditures (whether candidate or independent) is not of, in Kennedy's words, "constitutional significance." Money, regardless of form, generates speech and furthers the public dialogue of political issues. Therefore, restricting the amount of money permitted in political campaigns impermissibly results in restricting the quantity and quality of the information provided and the viewpoints advocated.

Although regulation opponents emphasize freedom-of-speech issues, that does not mean they subordinate concerns over representation to resolve the potential conflict between our two fundamental tenets. Instead, as noted before, they have a different conception of representation—one that focuses not on the equality of electoral constituencies but instead on the competition among interests in American society. This view is a pluralistic one, in which any individual, group, or set of related interests can work to promote its viewpoint in the hopes of persuading others, including elected officials, that their position is the best one. From out of this competition, the sense of the public will shall emerge. Thus, if a group spends money to elect an official supportive of its cause who helps implement that group's policy goals, that does not signify a corrupting presence in the political system; that, as Justice Thomas contended, "is successful advocacy of ideas in the political marketplace and representative government."[11]

Unlike regulation supporters, with whom we discussed the *dyadic* and *delegate* theories of representation, regulation opponents have underlying their position conceptions of representation that can be referred to as *collective* and *trustee* notions of representation. The notion of collective representation emphasizes the linkage between an elected body taken as a whole and the entire electorate as a whole.[12] Representation is enhanced when the proportion of interests in the elected body coincides with the proportion of such interests in the electorate. Restrictions on the flow of funds in elections would limit a person's or group's ability to advocate its positions in the political marketplace and to support a public official who would promote its cause, regardless of electoral constituency boundary lines, with the result being that its views would not be sufficiently represented.

Also underlying regulation opponents' views is a *trustee* notion of representation. This conception, with its roots in the writings of Edmund Burke, holds that an elected official should exercise his or her own independent judgment in determining what is best for the public. Justice Kennedy quoted Burke for the proposition: "Your representative owes you, not his industry only, but his judgment; and he betrays instead of serving you, if he sacrifices it to your opinion."[13] The theory behind this conception, as it relates to the issue of campaign finance restrictions, is that money in politics is not a corrupting force because the elected representatives, in their roles as trustees, are not persuaded to act against the public will based on the contributions they receive. Instead, they would continue to exercise their independent judgment; thus, representation would be served. Justice Kennedy admittedly stated that the reality of the situation is that not all representatives would act in such a manner. Thus, the citizenry must continually check their officeholders. The proper way to do so is not campaign finance restrictions, however, but instead "open, robust, honest, unfettered speech that the voters can examine and assess in an ever-changing and more complex environment."[14]

Recap of Fundamental Views on Campaign Finance
Table 4.1 summarizes the two fundamental views on campaign finance and how they relate to representation, speech, and money.

Table 4.1   Summary of Fundamental Views on Campaign Finance Reform

	Proponents	Opponents
Representation	Dyadic Delegate	Collective Trustee
Speech	Money is not speech	Regulations restrict quantity of speech
Money	Should be restricted	No—need unfettered speech

The Bipartisan Campaign Reform Act

In 2002, Congress passed the Bipartisan Campaign Reform Act (BCRA)—the first major overhaul of the nation's campaign finance laws since the 1974 FECA Amendments. This act culminated nearly seven years of continued efforts by congressional advocates of campaign finance regulation in keeping the issue on the congressional agenda and eventually passing the legislation. BCRA attacked what its proponents considered to be the "twin evils" of the campaign finance system: soft money and issue ads.

Soft money refers to unregulated funds not subject to FECA's hard-dollar limits on money collected by political parties. Originally conceived as a means to assist political parties in party-building activities, such as get-out-the-vote drives, soft money had become an increasingly prevalent factor in the world of campaign finance. For example, party committees might buy get-out-the-vote advertisements that would benefit both their federal and nonfederal candidates. In order to pay for these ads, the committee had to use federal funds for the portion that benefited the federal candidates but could use soft money to pay for the portion that benefited nonfederal candidates.

What began to happen was that more and more of the costs were shifted to the nonfederal portion. Further, these soft money contributions also provided an avenue for certain interests, such as corporations and labor unions, to make large political contributions even though they were otherwise forbidden from donating funds directly to candidates.[15] In addition, critics contended that, since soft money donations were not disclosed, corporations and labor unions (and all special interests for that matter) could wield significant influence as a result of large soft money contributions and that such influence would be virtually undetectable.

Although reporting of soft money was not done until 1991 (in order to comply with new rules promulgated by the FEC in 1990 requiring expanded disclosure of all funds raised and spent by national party committees), the statistics since then have demonstrated an increasing amount of soft money within the electoral system. As noted in Table 4.2, in the beginning both parties were able to raise soft money at roughly the same rate. But in 2001, the Republicans started to edge out the Democrats. Further, when Republicans and Democrats are compared in terms of hard dollar fund-raising, Republicans have historically been better at raising these contributions. Thus, when soft and hard money are added together, Republicans have had a decisive fund-raising advantage. Nevertheless, when examining which party is more dependent on soft money, it becomes evident that the Democrats, who by 2001 had just over half of their money collected from soft money, would be more harshly affected by a ban on soft money than would the Republicans. Both parties stood to lose a significant source of funds, however, if reform efforts banning soft money were enacted and upheld.

Table 4.2   Amount of Soft and Hard Money (in millions of dollars) Raised by Both Major Parties, 1991–2001

	Democrats				Republicans			
Election Cycle	Soft Money	Hard Money	Total	Percentage Soft Money	Soft Money	Hard Money	Total	Percentage Soft Money
1991–1992	36.3	177.7	214.0	17	49.8	267.3	317.1	16
1993–1994	49.1	139.1	188.2	26	52.5	245.6	298.1	18
1995–1996	123.9	221.6	345.5	36	138.2	416.5	554.7	25
1997–1998	92.8	160.0	252.8	37	131.6	285.0	416.6	32
1999–2000	245.2	275.2	520.4	47	249.9	465.8	715.7	35
2001	68.6	59.6	128.2	54	100.1	131.0	231.1	43

Source: Compiled by author from data available at www.opensecrets.org.

Issue ads are advertisements that appear strikingly similar to a campaign ad but do not use certain magic words such as "vote for" or "vote against" a certain candidate. Thus, they fail to reach the standard of express advocacy set forth in *Buckley v. Valeo* and other cases.[16] As a result, issue ads fell outside FECA's scope (see Chapter 5 for a greater discussion of issue advocacy ads).[17]

Among its most significant provisions, BCRA:

- Bans national parties from raising and spending soft money.
- Prohibits Federal officeholders and candidates from soliciting or raising soft money for political parties at Federal, state, and local levels, and from soliciting or raising soft money in connection with Federal elections.
- Prohibits state parties and local party committees from using soft money to pay for TV ads that mention Federal candidates and get-out-the-vote activities that mention Federal candidates. Permits state parties and local party committees to use contributions, up to $10,000 per donor per year, for generic GOTV activities and for GOTV activities for state and local candidates. Each state party or local committee must raise its own contributions and a portion of each expenditure must include hard money.
- Prohibits the use of corporate and union treasury money for broadcast communications that mention a Federal candidate within 60 days of a general election or 30 days of a primary and are targeted at the candidate's electorate. (Unions and corporations can finance these ads through their PACs.) Requires individuals and groups of individuals to disclose contributions and expenditures for similar broadcast communications.
- Raises limits on individual contributions to House, Senate and Presidential campaigns to $2,000 and indexes for inflation.[18]

By addressing soft money and issue ads, BCRA went beyond the mere mechanics of how the nation's campaign finance system works. It jumped straight to the heart of the issues of representation and freedom of speech that have resonated throughout the campaign finance reform debate since the days of *Buckley*. As a result, the debate in Congress throughout the seven-year period in which regulation advocates sought to pass campaign finance legislation tended to mirror the language we saw above from Supreme Court justices.

On the one hand, BCRA supporters focused on the damage to the integrity of the electoral system that corruption, or at least the appearance of corruption, has as well as the need to preserve some sense of equality in the expression of political ideas. Rep. Christopher Shays, one of the lead sponsors of BCRA in the House of Representatives, characterized BCRA in part as ending "the soft money system in which unlimited contributions from corporations and labor unions have drowned out the voice of individual Americans."[19] The act's opponents, on the other hand, concentrated on what they perceived as an impermissible restriction on free speech. As Senator Mitch McConnell, the self-proclaimed "Darth Vader" and leading opponent of campaign finance reform legislation, noted in an early debate over the bill that eventually became BCRA: "The proponents of this proposal seem to me to be dismayed at all of this speech out there polluting our democracy and our campaigns. The presumption underlying that, of course, is that we as candidates somehow ought to be able to control elections, as if only our voice should be heard."[20]

Shays's and McConnell's viewpoints demonstrate the interaction between representation and freedom of speech on the issue of campaign finance. Furthermore, they show how both sides have developed reasonable arguments of how their respective positions enhance both representation and freedom of speech. As discussed above, going back to *Buckley*, campaign finance regulation proponents have always emphasized the need for equality in the political process to enhance the representative nature of the electoral process. One premise underlying the quotation from Representative Shays is that elected officials cannot mirror their constituency if their constituency's interests are overtaken by other special interests. But Shays's statement regarding drowning out of the voice of individual Americans carries with it an interesting twist on the First Amendment arguments. Specifically, the First Amendment prohibits the government from infringing on a citizen's right to speech; the pre-BCRA environment effectively infringed upon individual voters' rights by leaving them with a diminished voice. Thus, one way to promote the quantity and quality of political discourse is to reduce the imbalanced presentation of ideas by restricting money in elections.

One problem that regulation proponents in Congress have encountered, both in passing BCRA in the first place and defending it since then, is the fact the *Buckley* tipped the First Amendment scales in favor of regulation opponents. Despite the views expressed above to the effect that money is property, the current governing law of the land is based on the *Buckley* premise that equates money to speech. Despite the regulation proponents' continued emphasis on equality, the only legitimate, constitutional reason the government could limit money in elections is to reduce corruption or the appearance of corruption. Despite the argument that can be inferred from Shays's statement above, McConnell's view of the First Amendment generally seems to comport well with *Buckley*'s standards for assessing what constitutes a permissible and impermissible restriction on speech. Until the Supreme Court says otherwise, if at all, the trustee and collective notions of representation favored by regulation opponents implicitly will underlie the nation's campaign finance laws. Regulation advocates attempted to swing the balance the other way with BCRA by promoting a view of representation focusing on equality, but even then they had to strive to ensure that the act's restrictions on issue ads, broadcast communications, and soft money were narrowly tailored to the legitimate interest of preventing corruption or the appearance of corruption in elections.[21]

Proponents and opponents knew that BCRA would not be the last word on the subject of campaign finance regulations and that the act would work its way into the judicial system. Promptly after BCRA became law, Senator Mitch McConnell, joined by the National Rifle Association and other groups,[22] initiated a lawsuit challenging the act's constitutionality. A three-judge panel in federal district court heard the case originally and issued its opinion in May 2003.[23] The result was a complex, lengthy opinion that seemed to add little clarity to (and more likely further clouded) the state of campaign finance. A summary chart of the panel's conclusions went on for four pages, covering twenty separate elements of BCRA and the combinations of judges who thought which provisions were constitutional and which were not. Following the district court panel, the case jumped immediately to the Supreme Court pursuant to a special provision in BCRA, which mandated that the Supreme Court take the case on expedited review. Although such a provision is seldom used by Congress, it reflects the sense of urgency that BCRA supporters felt in wanting to have the issues surrounding campaign finance resolved quickly.

In December 2003, the Supreme Court ruled in *McConnell v. Federal Election Commission*. Although the Court struck down some provisions of BCRA, it upheld the act's primary provisions banning soft money and regulating issue ads. These issues may have been new ones for the Court to address, but the fundamental concepts that have shaped the debate over campaign finance flowed through the various opinions offered by the justices.

Justices Stevens and O'Connor coauthored the Court's ruling with respect to the soft money ban and issue ads. In it, they relied heavily on the conception of representation based on equality—that a representative's job is to serve his or her constituents equally. In upholding the ban on soft money, the two justices premised their decision in large part on a view that the large sums of money flowing through the electoral system distort, or at least has the appearance of distorting, the legislative system: "The evidence connects soft money manipulation of the legislative calendar, leading to Congress' failure to enact, among other things, generic drug legislation, tort reform, and tobacco legislation. . . . To claim that such actions do not change legislative outcomes surely misunderstands the legislative process."[24] Underlying this statement is the belief, substantiated by statements of sitting and former senators regarding the effect of money on the legislative process, that the soft money contributions made by special interests halted legislation that Congress otherwise would have passed. Thus, not all constituents' interests were addressed or served equally; instead, the views of a select group of moneyed interests were given undue preference. As Stevens and O'Connor wrote, "Just as troubling to a functioning democracy as classic quid pro quo corruption is the danger that officeholders will decide issues not on the merits or the desires of their constituencies, but according to the wishes of those who have made large financial contributions valued by the officeholder."[25] By adopting this view, the Stevens/O'Connor opinion moves beyond the quid pro quo concerns raised in *Buckley* to incorporate the conception of representation-as-equality as a judicially accepted basis for campaign finance regulations.

As might be expected, Justices Thomas and Kennedy were highly critical of the Court's ruling handed down in the Stevens/O'Connor opinion. Justice Thomas reiterated his view that the effect on the legislative process highlighted by Stevens and O'Connor represents nothing more than the successful operation of the marketplace of ideas. "Apparently, winning in the marketplace of ideas is no longer a sign that the ultimate good has been reached by the free trade in ideas or that the speaker has survived the best test of truth by having the thought get itself accepted in the competition of the market. It is now evidence of corruption" (internal quotations omitted).[26] Justice Kennedy, however, tackled the Stevens/O'Connor conception more directly. He criticized them for their "quick and subtle shift, and one that breaks new ground"[27] by broadening the Court's conception of corruption:

> Favoritism and influence are not . . . avoidable in representative politics. It is in the nature of an elected representative to favor certain policies, and, by necessary corollary, to favor the voters and contributors who support those policies. It is well understood that a substantial and legitimate reason, if not the only reason, to cast a vote for, or to make a contribution to, one candidate over another is that the candidate will respond by producing those political outcomes the supporter favors. Democracy is premised on responsiveness.[28]

Although this statement would appear to conflict with Justice Kennedy's reference to the Burkean notion of representation discussed previously, the more important issue is that Kennedy was espousing a conception of representation in which representatives are not supposed to reflect their constituents' interests equally. Such imbalanced representation is expected and proper because it reflects the result of the competition among groups for Congress's attention.

As for the role of the First Amendment in the *McConnell* debate, the Stevens/O'Connor opinion upheld BCRA's disclosure requirements for issue ads over the contention that they constituted an impermissible restriction on the freedom of speech. But the opinion did not rely on a view that money is not the same thing as speech, a position that Stevens had previously enunciated. Instead, the opinion was based on a more narrowed interpretation of the *Buckley* decision's analysis regarding express advocacy (that is, that only express advocacy could be regulated). Stevens and O'Connor wrote, "the express advocacy restriction was an endpoint of statutory interpretation, not a first principle of constitutional law." They continued, "the unmistakable lesson from the record in this litigation . . . is that *Buckley*'s magic-words requirement is functionally meaningless. . . . *Buckley*'s express advocacy line, in short, has not aided the legislative effort to combat real or apparent corruption, and Congress enacted BCRA to correct the flaws it found in the existing system."[29] In other words, the regulations established by BCRA did not rise to the level of being a First Amendment issue and thus could be used to further the primary goal of reducing corruption and effectively improving the nature of representation in the political system. To further emphasize their point that the First Amendment concerns are not triggered, Stevens and O'Connor noted, "Curiously, Plaintiffs want to preserve the ability to run these advertisements while hiding behind dubious and misleading names. . . . Given these tactics, Plaintiffs never satisfactorily answer the question of how uninhibited, robust, and wide-open speech can occur when organizations hid themselves from the scrutiny of the voting public" (internal quotations omitted).[30]

Although the dissents (either in whole or in part) filed by each of Justices Rehnquist, Scalia, Thomas, and Kennedy all criticize the Stevens/O'Connor opinion on First Amendment grounds, Justice Thomas took particular offense to this last point. He argued,

> The historical evidence indicates that Founding-era Americans opposed attempts to require that anonymous authors reveal their identities on the ground that forced disclosure violated the freedom of the press. Indeed, this Court has expressly recognized that the interest in having anonymous works enter the marketplace of ideas unquestionably outweighs any public interest in requiring disclosure as a condition of entry, and thus that an author's decision to remain anonymous is an aspect of the freedom of speech protected by the First Amendment (internal quotations omitted).[31]

Thomas also warned that the logical extension of the Court's decision could lead to the "outright regulation of the press." This view brings home the issue that each of the four dissents referenced: the primacy of the First Amendment rights should trump the other goals Congress sought to promote in passing the regulations contained in BCRA. In this case, however, the dissenters ended up on the losing side of the Court's decision.

For the time being, there appear to be some inherent fund-raising disadvantages for Democrats, who had relied heavily on soft money to compete with the Republicans' advantage in raising hard money. In addition, special interests can still continue to influence the system through independent expenditures and the use of Political Action Committees. How the campaign finance system and the competing interests within it run their course under BCRA following the decision in *McConnell* will only be evident in the aftermath of the 2004 election season—leaving many to speculate as to what fundamentally will change under this new structure.

Conclusion

At a base level, campaign finance regulations merely provide the rules about who can give what kind of money, when they can do it, and how much they can give. Such rules in themselves are enough to generate significant debate in the political system because they can have an effect on which candidate, which parties, and which viewpoints win elections. But the issue of campaign finance also touches on our fundamental views of what we think this nation should be. Concerns over representation and the rights of individuals vis-à-vis the government were driving forces in the American Revolutionary War; the issues were hotly debated by the Federalists and Anti-Federalists during the ratification of the Constitution. These issues are fundamental matters in U.S.

political thought. Thus, neither side on the campaign finance debate is willing to relinquish its beliefs. Each side believes that it holds the proper conception of representation and freedom of speech and thus the correct position on the issue of campaign finance. From a theoretical perspective, campaign finance may be one of those issues on which, to some degree, both sides do have a correct position. But the reality of electoral politics dictates that one side win the debate. The side that loses, at least in the short term, can always promote its views in the marketplace of ideas to try to change the law.

Notes

1. P.L. 92-225.
2. P.L. 92-178.
3. *Buckley v. Valeo,* 424 U.S. 1, 25 (1976).
4. Ibid., p. 26.
5. Ibid., p. 20.
6. Ibid., p. 19.
7. Ibid., p. 39 (internal quotations omitted).
8. *Federal Election Commission v. National Conservative PAC,* 470 U.S. 480 (1985).
9. As Justice White argued in his dissent in *National Conservative PAC,* "The candidate may be forced to please the spenders rather than the voters, and the two groups are not identical." Ibid., p. 517.
10. *Nixon v. Shrink Missouri Government PAC,* 528 U.S. 377, 398 (2000).
11. *Colorado Republican Federal Campaign Committee v. Federal Election Commission,* 518 U.S. 604, 646 (1996).
12. Weissberg, "Collective vs. Dyadic Representation in Congress."
13. Quoted in *Shrink Missouri,* 528 U.S., p. 409.
14. Ibid.
15. The 1907 Tillman Act banned corporations and national banks from contributing to federal candidates' campaigns. The 1947 Taft-Hartley imposed a similar ban on labor unions.
16. In *Buckley,* the Supreme Court stated in footnote: "This construction would restrict the application of § 608 (e)(1) to communications containing express words of advocacy of election or defeat, such as 'vote for,' 'elect,' 'support,' 'cast your ballot for,' 'Smith for Congress,' 'vote against,' 'defeat,' 'reject.'" *Buckley,* p. 44. From this footnote, the "magic words" were born. The substantive proposition to which this footnote was tied stated, "that in order to preserve the provision against invalidation on vagueness grounds, § 608 (e)(1) must be construed to apply only to expenditures for communications that in express terms advocate the election or defeat of a clearly identified candidate for federal office." Ibid. For other Supreme Court cases related to this issue, see, for example, *Federal Election Commission v. Massachusetts Citizens for Life, Inc.* 479 U.S. 238 (1986), *Colorado Republican Federal Campaign Committee,* and *Federal Election Commission v. Colorado Republican Federal Campaign Committee,* 533 U.S. 431 (2001) (follow-up litigation to *Colorado Republican I*). For cases in lower federal courts, see the distinctions between *Federal Election Commission v. Furgatch,* 869 F.2d 1256 (9th Cir. 1987) on one side and *Faucher v. Federal Election Commission,* 928 F.2d 468 (1st Cir. 1991), *Maine Right to Life Committee v. Federal*

Election Commission, 914 F. Supp. 8 (D.Me. 1996), and *Federal Election Commission v. Christian Action Network*, 110 F.3d 1049 (4th Cir. 1997) on the other.

17. For a fuller description of the perceived "twin evils" of soft money and issue ads, see Dwyre and Farrar-Myers, *Legislative Labyrinth*, pp. 21–28.

18. Offices of Congressmen Shays and Meehan. "Short Summary of Shays-Meehan." February 14, 2002. www.house.gov/shays/hot/CFR/ssum2-2356.htm. For a more complete analysis of how BCRA differed from prior law, see Cantor and Whitaker, "Bipartisan Campaign Reform Act of 2002."

19. Shays, "Statement on Today's Campaign Finance Reforms Supreme Court Oral Arguments."

20. *Congressional Record*, 105th Cong., 2nd sess., 25 February 1998, S.997.

21. Representative Shays believed that "the Act was written to work within the Constitution and the guidelines the Court has laid out in numerous campaign finance rulings over the last 27 years." Shays, "Statement on Today's Campaign Finance Reforms Supreme Court Oral Arguments."

22. The parties involved in the consolidated case decided by the federal judge panel include Senator Mitch McConnell, National Rifle Association of America, Emily Echols (a minor child through her next friends, Tim and Windy Echols), Chamber of Commerce of the United States, National Association of Broadcasters, American Federation of Labor and Congress of Industrial Organizations (AFL-CIO), Congressman Ron Paul, Republican National Committee, California Democratic Party, Victoria Jackson Gray Adams, and Representative Bennie G. Thompson.

23. *McConnell v. Federal Election Commission*, 253 F. Supp. 2d 18 (D.D.C. 2003).

24. *McConnell v. Federal Election Commission*, 124 S.Ct. 619 (2003), p. 664.

25. Ibid., p. 666.

26. Ibid., p. 735.

27. Ibid., p. 747.

28. Ibid., p. 648.

29. Ibid., p. 689.

30. Ibid., p. 691.

31. Ibid., p. 736.

5

Issue Advocacy Electioneering: The Role of Money and Organized Interests

Allan J. Cigler

Political campaigns have long been a focal point for interests that understood that their fortunes were linked to electing public officials favorable to their policy positions. Organized interest involvement has typically ranged from simple endorsements to internally mobilizing their membership in support of chosen candidates to aiding campaigns with money and other resources. Organized interests have historically been subservient to parties and candidate campaign organizations in elections, providing support but typically not engaging in independent electioneering.

Recent decades have witnessed a change in such a pattern. Since the early 1960s the nation has experienced not only an impressive increase in the number of organized interests involved in electoral campaigns but also an expansion in the nature and breadth of their involvement.[1] A variety of factors has contributed to the new trend. Fundamental has been the expansion of government lawmaking and regulatory activity that has raised the stakes of politics, creating incentives for interests of all kinds to become involved in elections. The electoral process has also become more penetrable, creating an opening for organized interests to participate in almost all aspect of electoral politics, from well before the formal party nomination process begins to the postelection funding of gubernatorial and presidential inauguration galas.

In this new context some interests have become far more than indirect participants or merely resources for parties and candidates to tap during election years. Taking advantage of certain loopholes in federal campaign finance laws that enable them to circumvent the disclosure and spending limitations imposed, a number of organizations have learned to operate on their own as electioneering entities, without either the cooperation of or collaboration with political parties or candidate campaign organizations. By the mid-1990s one of the major tools in their arsenal had become issue advocacy electioneering.

Issue Advocacy or Express Advocacy? The Court Decides

Issue advocacy, in its purest sense, simply refers to "communications whose major purpose is to promote a set of ideas, not particular candidates."[2] The targets of issue advocacy ads are ordinarily the citizenry at large or elite opinion leaders rather than elected officials; such targets are usually reached through sponsored advertisements on radio or television or in newspapers, periodicals, or other printed material. Although organized interests prefer to think of their efforts as "public education campaigns," issue advocacy ads might be best thought of as a form of "outside lobbying," in which sponsors hope the targets of the ads will come to support the group's position and communicate their feelings to elected policymakers.

Issue advocacy advertising by organizations has a history in U.S. politics stretching back over three-quarters of a century,[3] but special interest advertising efforts on policy issues have become much more prevalent over the past two decades. Perhaps the most extensive and expensive effort of all occurred during the 1993–1994 deliberations over the Clinton administration's comprehensive health care plan, during which it has been estimated that 650 organizations spent $100 million to influence the debate; roughly $60 million of the spending involved various forms of issue advocacy ads, including $14 million spent by one organization, the Health Insurance Association of America (HIAA). In a series of television ads that showed a middle-aged couple discussing alleged weaknesses in the Clinton plan (nicknamed the "Harry and Louise" ads), the group may have been instrumental in raising the public skepticism that ultimately led to the defeat of the legislation.[4] More recently, the American Association of Retired Persons (AARP) advertised extensively on network prime time during the 2003 debate over a Medicare prescription drug benefit for seniors, breaking ranks with its Democratic allies in Congress and supporting the proposal pushed by President Bush. Such advertising by interests to push their policy agendas, although annoying critics worried about the disproportional influence of moneyed interests, is considered a fact of contemporary political life protected by the First Amendment of the Constitution. No one seriously questions the legality or right of groups or individuals to engage in such activity.

Much more controversial has been the use of issue ads during elections, which has enabled some organizations to invest large sums of money to influence campaigns outside of the confines of the federal campaign finance regulations. The opening for the use of interest group issue ads as electioneering devices can be found in a Supreme Court decision dealing with legislation designed to limit the role of money in campaigns.

Recognizing that existing campaign finance laws were ineffective and not enforced and that the influence of big money on elections created, at a minimum, the impression of corruption, Congress passed the Federal Election Campaign Act (FECA) in 1971 and, in the wake of the Watergate scandal, its 1974 Amendments. The broad-sweeping law was designed to limit the influence of "fat cats" (individuals and organizations with extensive resources) in elections and affected both candidates and those who supported them. The statute constrained the behavior of organized interests by putting a ceiling on all contributions and election-related expenditures. Such interests were now required to raise and spend election-related money through political action committees (PACs), administrative vehicles set up specifically for those purposes. At the core of the new campaign finance law was the requirement for full disclosure to the Federal Election Commission (FEC), an appointed body charged with enforcing the law.

Unfortunately for the reformers, as Victoria Farrar-Myers notes in Chapter 4, FECA was substantially modified in the landmark 1976 Supreme Court case of *Buckley v. Valeo*.[5] The Court viewed FECA as a serious threat to freedom of expression, with the potential to have a chilling effect on political debate. The Court made a fundamental distinction between the constitutionality of limiting direct political contributions and limiting political expenditures.[6] The judges did uphold the power of Congress to regulate campaign contributions in federal election campaigns, letting stand both contribution ceilings and the requirement of public disclosure. From the Court's viewpoint, contributors to political committees retained no control over the money once donated, and a contribution signified only who it supported, not any underlying rationale or motivation for the support that might contribute to political discussion. Restrictions on free expression were, as a consequence, relatively minor.

Limiting expenditures by individuals and organized interests on elections was an entirely different matter, however, since expenditures by individuals or groups may "convey *why* the spender supports or opposes a particular candidate, and limiting them would necessarily restrict the quality and quantity of political discourse."[7] In the Court's view the linkage between money and political expression was clear—"virtually every means of communicating ideas in today's mass society requires the expenditure of money."[8] As a consequence, limiting expenditures limits speech. Further, according to the Court, government attempts to restrict expenditures in order to equalize the influence of various interests by expenditure ceilings had no constitutional basis.

The vagueness of many of FECA's provisions dealing with expenditures was especially problematic for the Court. For example, the judges ruled that FECA's central expenditure limitation provision—"[n]o person may make any expenditure relative to a clearly identified candidate during a calendar year which, when added to all other expenditures relative to a clearly identified candidate during a calendar year which, when added to all other expenditures made by such person during the year advocating the election or defeat of such a candidate, exceeds $1000"[9]—would have the effect of prohibiting all individuals, except either candidates themselves or media owners, from voicing their views in meaningful ways. The use of the phrase "relative to" was vague, failing to set a precise boundary between allowable and nonallowable speech; it created an impossible basis upon which to separate protected true issue advocacy from advocacy endorsing the election or defeat of a candidate. With no meaningful boundary, people would be unsure what was permissible and what was not; government officials (in this case the FEC) would be left to be the final arbiter, a dangerous precedent.

The Court went on to offer its own specific demarcation line between the kind of issue advocacy that could be regulated and that which could not, presenting what has come to be called its "express advocacy" guidelines: any legal limitations on independent spending to influence elections could only apply to communications containing express words of advocacy, such as "vote for," "elect," "support," "cast your ballot for," "Smith for Congress," "vote against," "defeat," or "reject."[10] In practical terms, these "magic words" meant that express advocacy is any communication that advocates the election or defeat of a candidate for federal office using these words; issue advocacy represents a residual category of all communication that does not use the specific words. Only express advocacy could come under the rubric of the FECA. But there are a lot of ways to advocate the election or defeat of a candidate besides express advocacy. A loophole undermining the reformers' intentions was born.

Organized Interest Behavior After *Buckley v. Valeo*

The issue advocacy loophole was not utilized in the immediate aftermath of *Buckley,* and groups continued to largely operate within confines of a weakened FECA. Organized interests did find themselves limited in their direct contributions (the sources of funds and group contributions that had to be reported to the FEC in a timely fashion) to candidates and political committees, but the Court's hesitation in limiting more autonomous forms of electioneering activity afforded groups additional ways to influence campaigns without ceilings on spending. For example, PACs were permitted to spend unlimited funds expressly advocating the election or defeat of a candidate as long as such efforts were made without consultation or coordination with a candidate or a representing agent. Such activity is known as "independent spending"; the sources of funds and spending activity did have to be reported to the FEC. Further, organizations through their PACs could spend any amount they desired on internal communications expressly advocating the defeat or endorsement of any candidate to their membership; the amount of any expenditures over $2,000 per election had to be reported to the FEC.[11]

Generally speaking, until the early 1990s, FECA guidelines worked relatively well as groups, especially unions and business interests, participated in elections largely through direct contributions from their PACs or through internal communications dealing directly with their membership. But for a limited number of organizations, express advocacy communications through the device of independent spending became increasing important. The so-called nonconnected PACs (organizations unaffiliated with unions, businesses, or trade associations and organized solely for the purpose of influencing elections) quickly became major actors in a number of political campaigns. By the late 1970s and early 1980s several nonconnected PACs with a conservative political orientation, the National Conservative Political Action Committee (NCPAC) being the most prominent, became notorious for spending large sums on express advocacy against a number of senators, some of whom were defeated in close votes.[12] In 1982, NCPAC was the leading fund-raiser among all PACs and spent more than $3 million in independent expenditures against six incumbent liberal senators. Besides greatly irritating the targeted candidates, the typically negative focus of these early independent spending efforts received strident criticism from the media and even from the candidates who were the supposed benefactors of the advertising. Supported candidates worried whether the electorate would be confused about the sources of such ads and that the candidates might be blamed for the negative campaigning. By the end of the 1980s independent spending on express advocacy in campaigns was becoming less important, however, especially for nonconnected PACs that had difficulty raising funds in an increasing competitive environment; many contributors had become reluctant to be publicly disclosed as supporting organizations associated with negative advertising.

The Rise of Issue Advocacy Electioneering

It was not until the early 1990s that many organized interests started to engage in electoral activity well beyond the boundaries found in federal election law. Individual corporations or unions could contribute unlimited sums of money to political party committees, so-called soft money, by taking advantage of another campaign finance loophole originally intended to raise money for "party building" purposes, much of which was used to influence campaign outcomes through party issue advocacy. As Victoria Farrar-Myers notes in Chapter 4, soft money contributions to the parties grew at an incredible rate in the 1990s; by the 1999–2000 election cycle it had reached nearly a half a billion dollars, far outstripping even PAC contributions to candidates.[13] Soft money contributions to party committees could come directly from union or corporate treasuries. Until the 1992 election soft money contributions were not even disclosed.

The "express-advocacy standard had little noticeable effect on the conduct and financing of campaigns for almost 20 years after it was set by the courts."[14] But groups did eventually learn they could participate in more direct ways in elections by campaigning for or against a candidate if they simply avoided using the so-called "magic words" spelled out in the *Buckley* decision in any of their political communications. As long as such words were avoided, sponsoring organizations could claim the ad was merely an issue ad, unregulated by the campaign finance laws.

In practice, issue advocacy ads in elections have been shown to be virtually indistinguishable from campaign ads run by the parties or candidates through television or radio commercials or by phone messages or flyers.[15] Such ads often provide a picture of one or both of the candidates, usually mentioning their names, sometimes in a positive, but often in a negative way. Issue ads can be directed toward all federal election candidates, including those seeking the presidency. The identity of the group sponsoring the ad may be unclear, and donor identities do not have to be disclosed, providing a great advantage in raising money for often hard-hitting, negative ads. Rather than encouraging viewers to vote for a particular candidate, ads typically ask viewers to write or call a candidate to register their support or opposition to the candidate's policy actions or pronouncements. Two examples from the 2000 election campaigns vividly illustrate the nature of issue advocacy electioneering by groups that had become increasingly common in competitive elections during the 1996 election.

During the last week of October, just prior to the 2000 elections, the NAACP National Voter Fund, a 401(c)(4) tax exempt "social welfare" organization created by the National Association for the Advancement of Colored People (NAACP), whose donors were not identified, ran a television ad in a number of areas. The ad criticized Republican presidential contender George Bush for vetoing a hate crimes bill while he served as governor of Texas. While the video showed a chain being dragged from the back of a pickup truck with a Texas license plate, a voice on the audio portion said:

> I'm Renee Mullins, James Byrd's daughter. On June 7, 1998, in Texas, my father was killed. He was beaten, chained, and then dragged three miles to his death, all because he was black. So when Governor George Bush refused to support hate crimes legislation, it was like my father was killed all over again. Call George Bush and tell him to support hate crimes legislation. We won't be dragged away from our future.

Other ads may reflect thinly veiled efforts to support a candidate, so-called thank you ads. One group that typically prefers to engage in positive issue ad electioneering is the 750,000-member National Association of Realtors. For example, in a commercial run in a 2000 California congressional race, the group named Democratic congressman Cal Dooley "a leader in helping Americans buy their very first home," going on to ask viewers to call the congressman's office and thank him "for his hard work."[16] Both the NAACP National Voter Fund and the National Association of Realtors ads represent ways of exploiting the magic words standard to fund ads designed to influence voters legally outside of the regulations of the campaign finance laws.

Not surprisingly, issue advocacy electioneering by special interests became a topic of wide concern as soon as it started appearing. The mainstream press and public interest lobbies such as Common Cause and Public Citizen were particularly outraged about this innovative way to avoid public disclosure and FEC regulation. Although other forms of issue advocacy electioneering, such as communicating through printed material including voter guides, also picked up in volume, it was the ability of groups to spend large amounts of unlimited and undisclosed funds on issue ads on television and radio during the last few weeks of a campaign that particularly drew the ire of politicians and the media.

Taking its cue from the Democratic Party's use of the express advocacy loophole starting in 1995 to publicize the accomplishments of the Clinton administration,[17] the American Federation of Labor–Congress of Industrial Organizations (AFL-CIO) and a number of its affiliated unions became the first organized interest to engage in issue advocacy electioneering on a massive scale. In an attempt to reverse the 1994 Democratic loss of Congress, the group spent $35 million in 1996 to influence federal elections, the greatest proportion of which was used to buy nearly 27,000 television ads in forty congressional districts.[18] In twenty-one of the most competitive districts, roughly $10 million was spent on advertising during the last few weeks of the campaign.[19] By the 1998 elections, issue advocacy electioneering was practiced by a wide range of political groups from both ends of the political spectrum, from the Business Roundtable and the Christian Coalition to the NAACP and the Sierra Club.

Because of the undisclosed aspect of issue advocacy electioneering, only estimations can be made concerning the extent of the activity. But it was clear after the 1996 elections that issue advocacy electioneering expenditures were growing faster than any of the regulated expenditures tracked by the FEC. In the 2000 election cycle, one group of researchers estimated that parties and groups combined spent $509 million on broadcast issue advertising, three times the amount spent in 1996.[20] Another group of researchers monitoring interest group advertising estimated that groups spent between 10 and 21 percent of all candidate-centered advertising in House and Senate races in seventy-five of the largest media markets in 2000.[21] These percentages likely underestimate the electoral impact of such advertising, since the same researchers found that group spending was concentrated in a rather limited number of competitive congressional districts or states.

It should come as no surprise that supported candidates often welcomed groups independently involved in issue advocacy electioneering on their behalf. A large proportion of issue advocacy electioneering by groups essentially parallels the campaign agenda of the candidate campaigns, in many ways helping candidates leverage their campaign resources. At times it may even appear that coordination between groups, parties, and candidates is taking place (which is disallowed by campaign laws). For example, a researcher studying a 1998 competitive congressional race in Kansas found that the AFL-CIO ran television ads in the district in early September depicting Republicans as seeking to undermine Social Security and health care by their proposed tax cuts.[22] The union commercials were run even before ads for the two candidates started to appear in early October. The group ads set the campaign agenda in a manner quite compatible with the Democratic contender's campaign. While "officially" not coordinated with the Democrat's campaign, some of the ads appeared almost to be lead-ins to the challenger's advertising efforts. One invited viewers to call the Republican incumbent and protest the Republican stance on Social Security and health care. A short time later an ad by the Democratic challenger appeared proclaiming his support for Social Security and health care. The union's activity might have been the difference in a close contest in which the incumbent was defeated in a heavily Republican district.

Typically, however, the outcry over the exploitation of the issue advocacy electioneering loophole did not focus upon high profile groups such the AFL-CIO, the Business Roundtable, or the Sierra Club. Such groups have well-known positions on issues and are commonly associated with one of the two major parties in the public's mind; their names are indicators of the interests they represent. More troublesome is issue advocacy electioneering by groups that are not easily identifiable (often not even by the candidates) or that list a misleading name as the sponsor of the ad, yet spend huge, unlimited sums on campaign advertising. Such ads often are negative in tone and are aired during the last days of a campaign, not affording attacked candidates time to respond.

In the 2000 election, by far the largest practitioner of issue advocacy electioneering was an organization listed on its ads as Citizens for Better Medicare (CBM). The group spent between an estimated $40 million and $65 million on issue ads attempting to influence federal elections.[23] Using the more conservative $40 million estimate, issue ad expenditures by this one group alone were equivalent to 15 percent of the total amount of hard money contributions by all PACs to candidates in the 1999–2000 election cycle and roughly 16 percent of all the soft money funds contributed to either the Democratic or Republican Parties during the same period![24] CBM's advertising expenditures helped make health care the dominant topic of issue ads in the election, representing nearly a quarter of all electioneering ads by groups in the period.[25]

Despite the group's name, no doubt chosen so voters would associate CBM with perhaps a senior citizens group pushing for prescription drug coverage under Medicare, the group produced ads very critical of the highly publicized Democratic plan to expand Medicare coverage. The organization clearly preferred the Republicans' more private sector alternative, which called for government reimbursement to private insurance firms for expanded drug coverage.

CBM ran negative issue ads nationally against Democratic incumbents in competitive races who had embraced the Clinton health care plan while sponsoring positive issue ads in support of Republicans who had taken the lead against the plan. Some Democratic challengers got special attention, including Brian Schweitzer, a Senate candidate from Montana.[26] Schweitzer, a political newcomer on a crusade against big drug companies, had received national media coverage in early 2000 for organizing senior citizen bus trips to Canada to purchase drugs that were manufactured in the United States but were cheaper across the border. CBM ran attack ads throughout Montana accusing Schweitzer of wanting "Canada-style government controls on medications here in America." Schweitzer was forced to begin his television advertising much earlier than he planned in order to answer the charges. Interestingly, Republican incumbent Conrad Burns opposed CBM's activity in the state as well, not wanting to be associated with a negative advertising campaign, but also because of his feeling that the CBM ads altered his campaign agenda by putting far too much attention on the prescription drug issue. Requests to the CBM that the ads be stopped fell on deaf ears.

Whom exactly did CBM represent? Early in the campaign it was impossible to tell. It was later revealed that CBM claimed to represent a coalition created in 1999 by the Pharmaceutical Research and Manufacturing Association of America (PhRMA), a drug industry trade group, and the Healthcare Leadership Council, which speaks for fifty drug companies, hospitals, and healthcare providers. No information was ever revealed, however, concerning the group's specific financial supporters.

CBM considered itself to be a 527 committee under the Federal Tax Code, thanks to obscure provisions incorporated in 1974 that enabled political groups to benefit from certain tax advantages without any public disclosure. Section 527 organizations did not have to report in any way to the FEC, nor was there even any approval process necessary for Internal Revenue Service (IRS) certification (groups simply claimed they met the provisions of Section 527). As long as such groups refrained from express advocacy in their communications or any hard money activity (such as contributing money through a PAC) while still claiming to be a political organization that existed to influence federal elections, they were exempt from federal taxation and campaign finance regulation. The one stipulation was that collected funds from donors had to be in non–interest bearing accounts. In short, 527 committees like CBM were unregulated political organizations whose donors were undisclosed and unlimited in the amounts they could raise and spend. And, as long as they refrained from express advocacy, such committees could spend unlimited amounts to influence elections, earning them the title in the media of "Stealth PACs."[27]

The explosive growth in soft money contributions to the parties (much of which went to pay for party-sponsored issue advocacy electioneering) and the increasing reliance upon issue advocacy electioneering by organized interests made clear to most observers that the campaign finance regulation system established in the 1970s had little meaning. With its focus on hard money activity, the FEC "could no longer restrain most of the financial activity that takes place in modern elections."[28]

Campaign Reform Again

Soon after the 1996 election, campaign finance reform was again on the legislative agenda, and the two major targets were issue advocacy electioneering and soft money contributions to the parties. Doing something about the issue advocacy electioneering loophole appeared to be the most difficult challenge for any reform efforts, since the federal courts had consistently held fast to *Buckley*'s "magic words" standard as a matter of binding precedent. A number of FEC efforts to charge groups with violating the requirements on express advocacy on the basis of implied support or opposition to particular candidates, even if it was unequivocal, were overturned by the federal courts. Although the courts acknowledged that the magic words test may miss what are deliberate efforts to support or oppose a candidate, they were most adamant in the belief that free expression is best protected by determinate standards that allow citizens to know in certain terms what is permissible and what is not.[29]

Campaign finance reformers were not dissuaded from their efforts. They took solace from the fact that in *Buckley* the Court did acknowledge that Congress could, under certain circumstances, limit free expression in order to prevent "corruption and the appearance of corruption spawned by the real or imagined coercive influence of large financial contributions."[30] In a later Court case, Chief Justice Rehnquist even invited the Congress to attempt to create a different standard, noting that "we [the Court] are obliged to leave the drawing of lines such as this [the specific express advocacy words] to Congress if those lines are within constitutional bounds."[31] Reformers argued that the Court's decision in *Buckley* did not say the "magic words" express advocacy test was exhaustive and permanent, only that the original FECA's test for defining campaign ads was too vague and indeterminate. Further, the pervasive role of soft money and issue advocacy electioneering was unanticipated by the Court at the time of the *Buckley* decision. In the modern context, in which campaigning was increasingly outside of existing government regulation, the new challenge was to design a set of unambiguous standards that would distinguish between a campaign ad and true issue advocacy and to defend the standard as necessary to protect the electoral process from corruption or the appearance of corruption.

Ironically, despite the widespread public cynicism about money and politics so prevalent in the 1990s, there was no groundswell among the public to pressure public officials into taking action.[32] But even though campaign finance reform was a distant issue to voters, to certain reform-minded political elites and elements of the press it had become a major issue. The spiraling costs of campaigns and reliance upon unregulated interested money were viewed as contributing to political cynicism, helping to undermine citizen participation, and making a mockery of the nation's claim to be a genuine democratic polity.

Congressional interest in campaign finance reform picked up momentum after the 1996 elections. The increasing influence of money outside of the regulatory system for political communication challenged the very fundamentals of the candidate-centered campaign system, entering uncertainty into the process, something incumbents seek to avoid. In a number of close contests, party and organized-interest spending even outpaced candidate spending. Perhaps even more disquieting to elected officials, outside money "framed the debate and shaped the closing arguments in some 1996 House and Senate races."[33] Officials feared losing control of their ability to set the issue agendas of their campaigns.

It was not until 2002 that a comprehensive campaign finance reform bill was finally passed by Congress. The legislation was unceremoniously signed by a reluctant President Bush in late March 2002, who called the bill "flawed" but did not want to be labeled as being against campaign finance reform.[34] The new law was to be put into effect after the November 2002 congressional elections.

The fight to pass the new law, the Bipartisan Campaign Reform Act of 2002 (BCRA), had been long and difficult.[35] Efforts to set new standards for campaign ads were especially controversial and opposed on First Amendment grounds by a diverse coalition of groups ranging from those philosophically opposed to any form of government intrusion upon free expression, such as the Cato Institute and the American Civil Liberties Union (ACLU), to groups that had been avid practitioners of issue advocacy electioneering from all ends of the political spectrum, such as the AFL-CIO, the National Rifle Association (NRA), the U.S. Chamber of Commerce, the Christian Coalition, and National Right to Life. Like incumbent politicians, groups do not like uncertainty either, and many had come to view issue advocacy electioneering as essential to their strategies to influence public policy. Support for change came from a reform coalition led by public interest groups such as Common Cause and Public Citizen. It was only through a set of very fortuitous circumstances, particularly the Enron scandal that highlighted the unsavory connection between political money and elected officials, that the first comprehensive campaign finance reform bill since the early 1970s was able to become law.[36]

Among BCRA's many provisions (see Chapter 4 for further discussion of BCRA), the act set a new standard concerning the *content* of election-related political communications and *when* organized interests could engage in issue advocacy electioneering.[37] "Electioneering communication" was defined as any ad that used the magic words at any time or as a broadcast, cable, or satellite communication that referred to a clearly identified federal candidate within thirty days of a primary or within sixty days of a general election and was "targeted." An ad is considered "targeted" if it can be received by 50,000 or more persons in a district or state where a federal election is taking place.

Under BCRA, unions and corporations, although they were still able to form PACs and engage in hard money expenditures including independent spending regulated by the FEC, were strictly forbidden to either directly or indirectly finance "electioneering communications." Nonprofit corporations and incorporated political committees defined by section 527 of the Tax Code were covered as well.

Disclosure to the FEC of those involved in "electioneering communication" was made mandatory. Those engaging in such communications were required to file a disclosure report within one day of having spent an aggregate of $10,000, with a new report having to be filed each time an additional $10,000 was spent. Disclosure is thorough, including not just all donors contributing $1,000 or more; organizations also had to list the actual spender and any person(s) who in some way had some control over any of the electioneering communications.

For all intents and purposes, issue advocacy electioneering by organized interests near an election, and outside of the hard money regulations of the campaign finance laws, would become a thing of the past. But BCRA still had to face a constitutional test.

The Courts, BCRA, and Issue Advocacy Electioneering

Because fundamental First Amendment issues were the focus of much of the debate over BCRA, a provision in the new law provided for a quick review of its constitutionality, first by a three-judge panel of the U.S. District Court for the District of Columbia and subsequently by an appeal directly to the Supreme Court. Senator Mitch McConnell (R-KY), the longtime leader of congressional opposition to BCRA, filed suit in district court within a day after the president signed the legislation, contesting the constitutionality of much of the new law, including the "electioneering communications" provisions. Eighty-eight special interest groups as well as a number of party committees filed suit as well; all the suits were eventually consolidated into one case, *McConnell v. Federal Election Commission*.[38]

In early May the district court announced its decision in a 1,638-page opinion. The panel was divided 2–1 on many of the BCRA provisions and struck down nine of twenty challenged provisions in the act. In terms of electioneering communications, the court's decision did support the reformers' efforts to broaden the express advocacy test beyond merely the use of specific magic words to include ads that are "suggestive of no plausible meaning other than exhortation to vote for or against a specific candidate."[39] The court panel also found disclosure constitutionally acceptable, as well as the ban on funding of ads from union, business, and most nonprofit group treasuries. But what was perhaps the key provision, forbidding electioneering communication within thirty days of a primary and sixty days of a general election, was not upheld.

The district court panel's decision was immediately appealed. The Supreme Court was to have the final word on the matter. Most observers believed that a majority of the nine judges would be even less sympathetic to BCRA provisions than was the district court.

Many were surprised when the Court majority, in an obviously contentious 5–4 decision announced December 10, 2003, upheld all of the key provisions of BCRA, including those dealing with electioneering communication. The majority opinion, written by Justices John Paul Stevens and Sandra Day O'Connor, with Justices Souter, Ginsburg, and Breyer supporting, reflected an overwhelming concern with the corrosive effects of soft money in politics; the rationale for upholding BCRA was more from a practical than philosophical perspective. Although the abuse of "soft money" seemed to be of paramount concern (see Chapter 4 for more discussion), the majority opinion indicated the five judges were convinced by the arguments and evidence offered by the reformers that issue advocacy electioneering in practice was "functionally equivalent" to express advocacy advertising and helped undermine public confidence in the electoral process.[40] The Court majority, which spent only six pages of its 119-page opinion on electioneering communication, declared the subject "as to be almost perfunctory."[41]

On the other hand, minority dissent on the matter of restricting electioneering communications was not cloaked in pragmatism and reality but in a passionate defense of a constitutional principle. The dissenting judges did not believe that there was enough good, hard evidence of the corrupting influence of money on the political system that would warrant the suppression of free expression, and the decision, in the words of Justice Kennedy, "breaks faith with our tradition of robust and unfettered debate."[42] Justice Scalia's dissent was the most biting of all:

> This is a sad day for the freedom of speech. Who could have imagined that the same court which, within the past four years, has sternly disapproved of restrictions on such inconsequential forms of expression as virtual child

pornography, tobacco advertising, dissemination of illegally intercepted communication, and sexually explicit cable programming would smile with favor upon a law that cuts to the heart of what the First Amendment is meant to protect: the right to criticize the government. For that is what the most offensive provisions of this legislation are all about. We are governed by Congress, and the legislation prohibits the criticism of members of Congress by those entities most capable of giving such criticism loud voice.[43]

But even those in the Court majority did not believe BCRA would solve the problem of the insidious role of money in elections—"Money, like water, will always find an outlet. What problems will arise, and how Congress will respond are concerns for another day."[44]

Conclusion: Interest Group Electioneering After BCRA

It is difficult to predict with any precision how groups will be affected by BCRA. Fundamentally, the law returned federal campaigns to the status quo of the period before the 1990s when neither soft money nor issue advocacy electioneering played important roles. Some organized interests may actually gain in political influence with the restrictions on electioneering communications. One of the inherent dangers of the act, according to longtime campaign finance scholar Herbert Alexander, is that "it reduces the number of voices relating to issue advertising, magnifying those remaining, particularly those of the media."[45] Political commentary and endorsements by the press, at any time during an election, are unaffected. The head of the NRA, Wayne LaPierre, called the court's ruling on BCRA "the most significant change in the First Amendment since the Alien and Sedition Acts of 1798, which tried to make it a crime to criticize a member of Congress."[46] He indicated that the group was toying with the idea of buying television stations to become a media owner, which would again enable the group to engage in broadcast communications promulgating its views about candidates unrestricted by BCRA.

More likely than not most organized interests will take far less drastic steps in their efforts to adapt to BCRA's electioneering communications restrictions. Some may decrease their indirect involvement in electioneering, concentrating their efforts on hard money contributions to the candidates. Some will simply begin their broadcast electioneering earlier in the campaign process, outside of the timing window of BCRA. More important, BCRA only affects radio and television communication. It does not pertain to voter mobilization efforts through phone contact, canvassing, or direct mail. For groups with large membership bases a shift from an "air war" to "ground war" strategy is likely to take place, concentrating on grassroots efforts.

The shift for many groups was already starting even before the passage of BCRA. The AFL-CIO, which had invested so heavily in issue advocacy electioneering in 1996, in subsequent elections started reallocating its election resources in the direction of GOTV (get-out-the-vote) efforts targeted to union households.[47] In the 2000 elections, three-quarters of the $46 million allocated was targeted for such efforts, with only one-quarter to be used for mass media campaigns, a reversal of the organization's 1996 proportional allocations. Labor leaders had formed the impression that the 1996 union ads were not cost-effective because they were just as capable of activating opponents as they were in getting their own supporters to the polls. The Christian Right has learned a similar lesson and is heavily reliant upon grassroots electioneering targeting supporters.[48]

BCRA may also spawn a wealth of new, innovative efforts by groups to influence elections.[49] As Lee Goodman discusses in Chapter 7, the Internet, unregulated by BCRA, may become more important. For example, the NRA has indicated that in 2004 it plans to run a series of pure issue ads on television, followed up by information that would instruct viewers to seek more specific information on the group's website.[50] And groups such as MoveOn.org., an online organization that touts that it has 2.3 million members and a large war chest based largely on small contributions, has already been active in the winter of 2003–2004 airing a series of anti-Bush ads on network television.

Although the law targeted political parties and other organized interests, wealthy individuals with strong viewpoints, who are willing to be publicly identified, may forgo operating through groups altogether. Individuals can spend unlimited amounts on electioneering communication as long as they disclose amounts above a threshold of $10,000.[51]

If the past is any indication, organized interests have proved quite creative in circumventing periodic efforts to change the campaign finance laws in a privately funded system. We should expect such creativity this time as well.

Notes

1. See, for example, Cigler and Loomis, "The Changing Nature of Interest Group Politics," pp. 1–33; Rozell and Wilcox, *Interest Groups in American Campaigns*.

2. West, "How Issue Ads," p. 149.

3. West and Loomis, *The Sound of Money*, p. 51.

4. Ibid., p.83.

5. 424 U.S. 1 [1976].

6. Ortiz, "Constitutional Restrictions," p. 63.

7. Ibid.

8. 424 U.S. 1 [1976].

9. The Federal Election Campaign Act Amendments of 1974 (Public Law 93-443), Section 608 (e)(1).

10. 424 U.S. 1 [1976], n. 52.

11. There is also a large internal communications loophole. If the primary reason for the communication is not an endorsement, no reporting is necessary. See Magleby, "Executive Summary," p. 6.

12. Sabato, *PAC Power*.

13. In 1992 the two national parties together raised and spent nearly $100 million; by the 2000 election cycle $495 million was raised. See Dwyre and Kolodny, "Throwing Out the Rule Book," pp. 133–162.

14. Mann, "Linking Knowledge and Action," p. 74.

15. Magleby, *Dictum Without Data*. For television ads specifically, see Holman and McLoughlin, *Buying Time 2000*.

16. From the University of Pennsylvania, Annenburg Public Policy Center Ads Collection (www.appcpenn.org/issueads/NAR.htm [March 21, 2001]).

17. In the fall of 1995, nearly a year before the 1996 general election, the Democratic National Committee aired a number of television ads that labeled the Republicans in Congress as radical extremists in an effort to enhance President Clinton's reelection possibilities. Since the ads all avoided using the "magic words" of issue advocacy, the party claimed they represented generic party ads. The ads were not challenged by the FEC and opened the gates for similar activity by organized interests. See Mann, "Linking Knowledge and Action," p. 74.

18. Herrnson, *Congressional Elections*, pp. 123–124.

19. Corrado, "Financing the 1996 Election," pp. 162–163.

20. www.appcpenn.org/issueads/estimate.htm (June 3, 2001). Totals are probably understated since not all ads were identified by the researchers, and many groups would not reveal spending totals.

21. "2000 Presidential Race First in History."

22. Cigler, "The 1998 Kansas Third Congressional District Race," pp. 77–92.

23. Estimates vary because the CBM did not release expenditure data. The conservative estimate comes from Mintz and Schmidt, "Stealth PACs Report Campaign," p. A17. The high estimate comes from Magleby, "Executive Summary," p. 28. A detailed discussion of the CBM case can be found in Cigler, "Interest Groups and Financing the 2000 Elections," pp. 180–182.

24. Total PAC contributions in the 2000 election cycle totaled $259.8 million. See Cigler, "Interest Groups and Financing," pp. 167–173. In terms of soft money, the Democratic National Party committee raised $245.2 million in the same cycle; Republicans raised $249.9 million. See www.FEC.gov/press/051501partyfund.htm1 (June 1, 2001).

25. The CBM and eight other health care groups spent more than $86 million in the primaries or 24 percent of the total spent on issue advocacy electioneering. Spending on environmental issues was next with 15 percent. See Falk, "Issue Advocacy Advertising through the Presidential Primary 1999–2000," pp. 11–12.

26. Wilson, "The 2000 Montana Senate Race," pp. 92–105.

27. Trister, "The Rise and Reform of Stealth PACs," pp. 32–39. Although it did not substantially affect the behavior of most 527 committees in the 2000 election, the behavior of groups like CBM in the spring 2000 primaries led to a law's being passed in the summer that added more regulations. The new law required such committees to register within one day of their formation; donations and spending over certain sums had to be disclosed if the group had intentions of spending more than $25,000 on federal elections. CBM was not affected; the group simply stopped receiving contributions after the law was passed and later formally registered with the IRS as a 501(C)(4) "social welfare organization," a classification in which donors are not publicly disclosed.

28. Corrado, "Financing the 1996 Election," p. 120.

29. A summary of the leading cases is found in Potter, "Issue Advocacy and Express Advocacy," pp. 227–239.

30. 424 U.S. 1 [1976].

31. *Federal Election Commission v. Massachusetts Citizens for Life, Inc.*, 479 U.S. 248 [1986].

32. Polls consistently indicated that although a large proportion of the public believed campaign finance was in need of reform, the issue never ranked high as a political priority compared to issues such as employment, health care, and taxes.

33. Herrnson, "Parties and Interest Groups in Postreform Congressional Elections," pp. 145–167.

34. Foerstel, "As Groups File Lawsuits," p. 868.

35. Corrado, "The Legislative Odyssey of BCRA," pp. 21–39.

36. Cigler, "Enron," pp. 231–250.

37. A summary of the key provisions law is found in Malbin, "Thinking About Reform," pp. 8–11.

38. *McConnell v. Federal Election Commission*, no. 02-1674.

39. Although the district court did strike down BCRA's primary definition of "electioneering communication," it did accept this secondary definition. This would still leave the law with a much broader standard than the "magic words" test.

40. 124 S.Ct. 619 (2003), p. 13 of the majority opinion.

41. Greenhouse, "The Supreme Court," p. A24.

42. 124 S.Ct. 619 (2003), p. 59 of Justice Kennedy's dissent

43. Ibid., p. 3 of Justice Scalia's dissent.

44. Ibid., p. 118 of the majority opinion.

45. Alexander, "The Political Process After the Bipartisan Reform Act of 2002," p. 53.

46. Van Drehle, "McCain-Feingold Ruling Angers Activists on Both Left and Right," p. A1.

47. Swoboda, "AFL-CIO Plots Push for Democratic House," p. A1.

48. Guth et al., "A Distant Thunder?" pp. 161–184.

49. Kuhnhenn, "Election Financing Turns Creative," p. A16.

50. CNN News, "MoveOn.org Becomes Anti-Bush Powerhouse," www.cnn.com/2004/TECH/internet/01/12/moveon.org.ap/index.html, (January 13, 2004).

51. The amounts some individuals intend to spend on the 2004 elections far surpass any amounts spent prior to the enactment of BCRA. For example, one of the nation's richest men, George Soros, has pledged $10 million to the liberal activist group America Coming Together (ACT) to be used for voter mobilization drives in seventeen competitive states in an effort to defeat President George Bush. See Blumenfeld, "Soros's Deep Pockets vs. Bush," p. A3.

6

Media Coverage:
The Local Effects of Deregulation

Brian F. Schaffner

It was about 1:00 AM on a cold January night in 2002 when a train derailment sent toxic fertilizer into the air around Minot, North Dakota. In responding to the emergency, police attempted to contact the local radio station, KCJB, to request an emergency broadcast about the danger from toxic fumes. At the time, however, KCJB was airing a national satellite feed from its parent company, Clear Channel Communications, and the police were unable to contact anyone at the station to air the emergency broadcast. Eventually, station employees were reached at their homes and ran the emergency broadcast, but only after a lengthy delay.[1]

The story from Minot called attention to the increasing centralization of media outlets across the United States. When authorities were unable to reach anyone at KCJB, they knew they would run into the same problem at other stations, since Clear Channel Communications owned all six commercial stations in town. In fact, Clear Channel is the largest operator of radio stations in the nation, owning 1,225 of the nation's roughly 11,000 radio stations.[2] As part of this consolidation, Clear Channel has cut costs by reducing the local staff at its radio stations and using more programming from national satellite feeds. This often means a reduction in both the quantity and quality of local news, particularly in Minot, where Clear Channel employs just one full-time news reporter for all six of its radio stations.[3]

The recent consolidation of local broadcast stations is not unique to radio. In fact, large companies have also been consolidating holdings of television stations and newspapers. This leads one to question: how do such trends affect the way news media cover political campaigns? Critics of consolidation argue that as Congress and the Federal Communications Commission (FCC) continue to deregulate the media industry, local political news may suffer as a result. After all, if the people of Minot were unable to get news about the danger of toxic fumes on that January night, what prospect do they have for getting a reasonable amount of local political news?

In 2000, the Seattle area witnessed a competitive congressional campaign between incumbent representative Jay Inslee and challenger Dan McDonald. Although the candidates spent a combined $3.5 million contesting the election, residents who regularly watched the area's Fox affiliate, KCPQ, for local news would have heard little, if anything, about the campaign. In fact, according to transcripts from Video Monitoring Service, KCPQ aired its first story on the contest on November 6, the day before the election. On the other hand, KING-TV, Seattle's NBC affiliate, provided modest coverage of the contest with five stories during the month of October, totaling nearly twenty-five minutes in length. Critics of deregulation would be quick to point out that KCPQ is owned by one of the nation's largest television owners—the Tribune Company—whereas KING-TV is a subsidiary of the much smaller Belo Corporation. Yet, examples such as this one provide only tenuous evidence of a connection between media ownership and the quality of local campaign coverage.

In this chapter, I consider the relationship between media ownership regulations and campaign coverage in the United States. I begin by discussing why citizens find local news to be an important source of news about political campaigns. I then examine the laws and court decisions that created and shaped the power of the FCC over time and follow by examining recent decisions by Congress and the FCC to loosen many of the restrictions on media ownership in the United States. Finally, I conclude by examining evidence on whether the consolidation of media outlets has affected the quality of campaign coverage that citizens may receive from local news outlets.

The Importance of Local Media Coverage in Political Campaigns

Citizens are often criticized for having little knowledge about politics.[4] A great deal of research has identified a number of factors that lead some people to have more political knowledge than others. Among these factors is the attention a citizen pays to news media.[5] People who pay more attention to the media have greater knowledge about politicians and political parties, even when controlling for other factors such as education and income. Furthermore, local news outlets tend to be much more popular with the public than national news. Table 6.1 presents results from a survey that asked respondents which types of media they used most for news. According to the survey, more than half of the American public watched local television news on a daily basis, compared to just one-third of the public that watched network or cable news regularly. In addition, more than 40 percent of Americans listened to a local radio station or read their local newspaper each day.[6] Thus, when citizens turn to the news media for political information, they tend to turn to local news outlets.

Table 6.1   News Consumption by the U.S. Public

News Outlet	Percentage of Public Using Regularly
Local television news	57
Local radio station	41
Local newspaper	41
National network news	32
National cable news	33

Source: "Public's News Habits Little Changed by September 11," Pew Research Center for the People and the Press (http://people-press.org, 9 June 2002).

One reason that citizens turn to the local news more often is that they tend to be interested in news that directly affects their lives. For example, in 1993 news about Department of Defense base closures was a recurring example of a national story with distinct relevance for local communities. When the national media outlets covered the story, reporters focused on base closings because of the conflict they produced in Congress. The national media often neglected the local impacts of the base closures, however. "As a national story, it's a blur," remarked Leonard Schwartz, founder of States News Service. "Cut it up locally and it will force its way onto Page One."[7] Across the nation, local newspapers and television stations reported on the danger that closures presented to communities. The focus was on the local impact of the closures rather than the institutional conflict they caused at the national level. In many ways, this was the more important story for most Americans. Regardless of whether base closures caused partisan conflict in Congress, they had a real impact on many local communities across the nation.

Indeed, campaign events often have significance to local communities that would be lost on national news outlets. For example, during the second debate of the 2000 presidential campaign, George Bush and Al Gore briefly discussed the tragic school shootings that occurred in 1999 at Columbine High School in Colorado. This discussion was almost completely ignored by the national network news programs, but each television station and a news radio station in Denver discussed that portion of the debate on their news programs. Although the national media found little importance in the Columbine discussion, the news was much more important for citizens in Denver who were still dealing with the repercussions of the tragedy. National network news and local Denver news covered the same event in different ways because that event had different meanings for their audience.

Thus, even when national and local news outlets are covering the same story, each outlet may bring a unique and important perspective. Yet, many fear that the local perspective will begin to vanish as an increasing number of local newspapers and broadcast stations are owned by national news organizations. After all, it is more cost effective for a large company to produce one story for all of its news outlets rather than to produce a different local story for each station. Will consolidated news organizations pay as much attention to campaigns for local offices, or will coverage focus increasingly on the national campaigns? Likewise, will this coverage focus on how campaigns are important for issues in local communities? These questions have led many activists to call on the FCC to stem the tide of consolidation of broadcast outlets across the United States. Before we can answer these questions, however, we must understand the FCC. Why does the FCC have the authority to regulate the extent of media ownership in the United States? Why did Congress find it necessary to create an executive agency primarily charged with governing the communications industry in the United States? To answer these questions about the FCC and its authority to regulate broadcast communications in the United States, we must begin with the dawn of broadcast communications a century ago.

The Creation of Broadcast Media

In 1901, Guglielmo Marconi introduced the first wireless telegraph device, the "radiotelegraph," so that merchant ships could be reached while out at sea.[8] It was a remarkable invention, but the feature that made the wireless telegraph so appealing was also a feature that posed a problem for those attempting to use the device—it relied on an open communications network. Although access to a wire telegraph was limited, anyone with a transmitter and receiver could communicate over the wireless telegraph. Thus, as the number of ships outfitted with the wireless device increased, interference became a problem—if multiple ships tried to transmit over the same frequency, none of the messages would be discernible. It was comparable to attempting a conversation with someone standing on the other side of a loud and crowded room at a party.

In response to the problem of interference, Congress passed the Radio Act of 1912. This law required all wireless companies to transmit only on frequencies that were approved by the Commerce Department. Thus, a company had to get a license to broadcast over a particular frequency. This licensing requirement lent a bit of order to what might otherwise have been chaos over the radio waves. At the time, this mostly applied to the shipping industry, which used the radio to communicate with ships at sea. It was not long, however, before companies such as General Electric, Westinghouse, and the Radio Corporation of America (RCA) realized that the radio could have an appeal among the public. These companies manufactured and sold radio receivers, and the prospect of selling more of those receivers was very appealing. To generate demand for the receivers, the companies began transmitting regular broadcast programs over the radio waves—programs that any citizen with a radio could listen to. These programs became the nation's first radio broadcasts for general consumption.

During the 1920s, the household radio became increasingly common, and the number of radio stations quickly rose. As a result, it was becoming difficult to keep stations from interfering with each other's signals. Congress addressed the issue again with the Radio Act of 1927. This legislation created the Federal Radio Commission, which would administer licenses to stations whose broadcasts served the "public interest."[9]

Seven years later, Congress readdressed the issue of communications over the airwaves with the Communications Act of 1934. With this legislation, Congress replaced the Federal Radio Commission with the Federal Communications Commission and charged the new organization with regulating radio broadcasting as well as the burgeoning telephone industry. The FCC was given trusteeship over the airwaves and instructed to license frequencies, maintaining the requirement that stations be licensed to companies broadcasting in the public interest. The FCC quickly asserted its authority and began closely regulating the airwaves, but many saw the agency's power as potentially unconstitutional. This was a question that the Supreme Court would have to settle just nine years later.

The First Amendment and Licensing of the Airwaves

In the FCC, the federal government created an agency that had the authority to determine who was able to broadcast their messages over the radio (and eventually the television) airwaves and who was not allowed to do so. This raised the question of whether the FCC had essentially been given the authority to restrict freedom of speech, a right guaranteed in the First Amendment. After all, if the FCC denied a license to a particular individual, the right of that individual to use the airwaves to freely express him or herself had been abridged.

Two Supreme Court rulings clearly laid the framework for granting the FCC the power to selectively license the television and radio spectrum. The Court first ruled on this issue in 1943 in the case of *National Broadcasting Company v. U.S.*[10] In 1941, the FCC put into effect new regulations stating that only a certain portion of a radio station's time could be programmed by the network that station was affiliated with. If a local station aired more network programming than allowed, the FCC could refuse to renew that station's license, effectively putting that station out of business. The two major radio networks at that time, the National Broadcasting Company (NBC) and the Columbia Broadcasting System (CBS), found the new restrictions detrimental to their operations, since they were actively trying to expand the reach of their national broadcasts. Accordingly, the networks sued the FCC to keep the agency from enforcing the new regulations, arguing that they infringed on a station's First Amendment rights.[11]

It is important to note that the networks did not directly challenge the authority of the FCC to license the airwaves. Rather, the main argument of the networks in this case was that the FCC's jurisdiction should only extend to the prevention of signal interference. The networks argued that the FCC should not be allowed to issue licenses based on the "public interest" standard established by the Radio Act of 1927 and reinforced by the Communications Act of 1934. Yet, in a unanimous opinion, the Court upheld the FCC's regulations and affirmed that the FCC had the power to regulate the airwaves according to the "public interest." In writing the decision, Justice Felix Frankfurter refuted the networks' argument that the FCC's regulations violated the First Amendment:

> Freedom of utterance is abridged to many who wish to use the limited facilities of radio. Unlike other modes of expression, radio inherently is not available to all. That is its unique characteristic, and that is why, unlike other modes of expression, it is subject to governmental regulation. Because it cannot be used by all, some who wish to use it must be denied. . . . The right of free speech does not include, however, the right to use the facilities of radio without a license.[12]

The Supreme Court's opinion in this decision addresses the unique nature of the radio spectrum. Because there are a limited number of entities that can broadcast without interfering with other radio signals, the government must restrict the use of the spectrum. Since the government must restrict access to the airwaves, broadcasting is a privilege, not a right, of the broadcaster, and it must be regulated to assure that the public's interest is taken into account. Indeed, the final sentence quoted above was the Court's clearest position on the relationship between licensing of the airwaves and free speech. This was an unequivocal statement from the Court that free speech was not infringed on by the FCC's authority to license the airwaves.

Thus, the Supreme Court's decision in *National Broadcasting Company v. U.S.* recognized the right of the federal government to restrict access to the airwaves and to do so based on criteria related to the "public interest." The Court reaffirmed this need for regulation in its unanimous decision in *Red Lion Broadcasting v. Federal Communications Commission* (1969).[13] In this case, the court upheld the FCC's decision to force a radio station to offer equal time to a writer who was personally criticized in a review of his book aired on the station. Justice Byron White wrote the majority opinion that echoed the principles of the *National Broadcasting Company v. U.S.* ruling:

> Where there are substantially more individuals who want to broadcast than there are frequencies to allocate, it is idle to posit an unbridgeable First

Amendment right to broadcast comparable to the right of every individual to speak, write, or publish. If 100 persons want broadcast licenses but there are only 10 frequencies to allocate, all of them may have the same "right" to a license; but if there is to be any effective communication by radio, only a few can be licensed and the rest must be barred from the airwaves. It would be strange if the First Amendment, aimed at protecting and furthering communications, prevented the government from making radio communication possible by requiring licenses to broadcast and by limiting the number of licenses so as not to overcrowd the spectrum. . . . But the people as a whole retain their interest in free speech by radio and their collective right to have the medium function consistently with the ends and purposes of the First Amendment. It is the right of the viewers and listeners, not the right of the broadcasters, which is paramount.[14]

In this opinion, the Court again referred to the importance of scarcity when considering First Amendment issues with regard to radio broadcasting. In fact, Justice White even suggested that the First Amendment supports the FCC's power to license the airwaves because the amendment's purpose is in "protecting and furthering communications." Thus, not only did this decision favor the power of the FCC to regulate the broadcast industry, but it also explained the justification for this regulation "even more clearly and forcefully than it had been described in the earlier Supreme Court decision."[15]

FCC Regulations

Throughout much of its history, the FCC has used its licensing power to govern two aspects of radio and television—content and ownership. Regulation of media content has taken many forms over time. For the most part, the FCC has attempted to assure that programming was at least partially devoted to the public interest. For example, the FCC instituted the Fairness Doctrine in 1949 to require stations to give time to any individual who was criticized on a radio or television station. The rule was often difficult to enforce, however, and it was eventually repealed in 1987. The FCC also instituted an Equal Time Provision that still stands. This rule states that if a station gives a political candidate time on the air, then it must give that candidate's competitor(s) equal time. The Equal Time Provision also states that if a station sells advertising to one candidate during a campaign, that station must sell advertising to all candidates during comparable time slots and for comparable rates.

Although the Equal Time Provision is not often a concern during campaigns, there are some notable exceptions. When Ronald Reagan, a former actor, ran for president in 1976, 1980, and 1984, television stations did not air his movies during the campaigns. If they had done so, the FCC could have required those stations to give equal time to the other candidates in the race. More recently, Arnold Schwarzenegger, an actor famous for his role in the *Terminator* movies, won California's gubernatorial recall election in 2003.

During that campaign, many stations and networks were careful about airing movies or entertainment shows that included Schwarzenegger. With 135 candidates running in that election, providing equal time to each would have been unfeasible, so stations did not air his movies during the campaign. Yet, the important exception to the Equal Time Provision is that it does not apply to legitimate news programs. Thus, Howard Stern successfully petitioned the FCC to have his show classified as a news program so that he could interview Schwarzenegger during the campaign without having to provide equal time to the other candidates.

Although the Equal Time Provision is occasionally an issue during a campaign, the FCC does not presently devote much of its resources to regulating the political content of television and radio broadcasts. Rather, it is the commission's regulation of media ownership that has a more significant impact on political coverage.

Since its inception, one of the FCC's primary concerns has been to regulate media ownership closely. Since radio and television airwaves are scarce resources, it has often been the FCC's goal to make certain that a large share of those airwaves are not owned by the same individual or corporation. In setting regulations, the FCC has focused largely on fulfilling three different goals: maintaining viewpoint diversity, competition, and localism. To accomplish these goals, the FCC instituted a number of regulations on media ownership over the years:[16]

> *Local Radio Ownership Rule (1941)*—To assure the diversity of programming in markets across the nation, the FCC instituted a limit on the number of radio stations that could be owned by a single company in each market. This limit varied with the size of the market.
>
> *National Television Ownership Rule (1941)*—To maintain diversity and localism in markets across the nation, the FCC instituted a regulation that prohibited a single company from owning more than seven television stations nationwide.
>
> *Dual Network Rule (1946)*—To maintain diversity and competition at the national level, the FCC prohibited more than one of the major networks (NBC, CBS, or the DuMont network) from being owned by the same company. This rule was expanded to later include the American Broadcasting Companies (ABC) and Fox Television Stations.
>
> *Local Television Ownership Rule (1964)*—The FCC limited a single company from owning more than one television station in a single market, unless there were more than eight stations in that market. This rule was intended to maintain competition and diversity at the local level.

Television-Radio Cross-Ownership Rule (1970)—The FCC began regulating television and radio ownership together rather than separately with this regulation. Again, this regulation was intended to maintain competition and diversity in local markets by limiting the number of radio and television stations that a single company could own in any market. As a company owned more radio stations, it was allowed to own fewer television stations.

Broadcast-Newspaper Cross-Ownership Rule (1975)—The FCC expanded its view of cross-ownership to include print media in the mid-1970s. This regulation banned a company from owning both a television station and a newspaper in the same market, unless the company had such holdings before the rule was instituted.

FCC limits focused both on nationwide ownership as well as ownership in different local markets. With the election of Ronald Reagan in 1980, however, and the new members he appointed to the commission, the direction of FCC policy began to shift toward deregulation—a relaxing of the restrictions on media ownership. For example, the National Television Ownership Rule was modified in 1984 to allow a company to own television stations that reached up to 25 percent of the national audience. Nevertheless, most of these restrictions remained essentially the same, even with the shift in FCC policy during the 1990s. But things changed drastically when Congress passed, and President Bill Clinton signed, the Telecommunications Act of 1996.

The Telecommunications Act of 1996

When Congress drafted the Communications Act of 1934, nobody owned a television, much less had cable or a satellite dish. Yet, although the act was revised and amended a number of times by Congress, it remained as the primary legislation governing the broadcast communications industry in the United States. One reason for its longevity was that the act gave the FCC a great deal of discretion in drafting regulations dealing with the communications industry. For instance, the act was passed before the invention of television; yet, the FCC was able to adapt its restrictions on radio ownership to govern the growing television industry in the 1940s and 1950s. Thus, because the FCC had been relatively successful in adjusting regulations to meet technological innovations and shifting realities, congressional action was not required for quite some time. By the mid-1990s, however, fast-paced changes in the reality of the communications industry finally caught up with the Communications Act of 1934, and Congress sought to draft one of the most significant pieces of legislation of the decade.

The Telecommunications Act addressed a number of issues, including the substantial deregulation of the telephone industry.[17] When it came to regulation of media ownership, the act provided "significant regulatory relief" to companies who wished to expand their holdings of broadcast stations.[18] First, the FCC increased the length of licenses to broadcast stations. Previously, radio stations had to apply to renew their licenses every seven years, and television stations did so every five years. Under new provisions in the Telecommunications Act, both radio and television stations would only be required to renew their licenses every eight years. By increasing the length of the license, stations now had to face FCC scrutiny less frequently.

The second and most sweeping change in broadcast regulations applied to radio ownership. In addition to removing the national limit on the number of radio stations that a single company could own, the Telecommunications Act also loosened the limitations on station ownership within a market. The new limits gave a company the ability to own as many as eight stations in a large media market (they could previously only own four). However, the change in ownership limits most drastically affected small markets—those with fourteen or fewer commercial radio stations—where a single company could now own five stations.[19]

The third change in broadcast regulations instituted by the Telecommunications Act affected regulations on television ownership in the United States. Since the National Television Ownership Rule was enacted in 1941, the FCC had limited the number of television stations that a single entity could own nationwide. In 1985, the limit on stations was modified to allow a single company to own stations reaching up to 25 percent of the national audience. This rule was changed again with the Telecommunications Act, which opened the door for companies to own stations reaching up to 35 percent of the national audience. The act did not change the limitations on ownership within a similar market, but it did instruct the FCC "to conduct a rulemaking proceeding to determine whether to retain, modify or eliminate" those regulations.[20]

Thus, the Telecommunications Act was a major step toward removing limitations on media ownership in the United States. No longer constrained by national limits, a handful of companies began purchasing radio stations across the United States. The largest of these companies, Clear Channel Communications, increased its holdings from just forty-three radio stations in 1995 to approximately 1,225 radio stations in 2002—an increase of 2,749 percent in just seven years. Many have responded to this consolidation by arguing that a company as large as Clear Channel cannot possibly serve the local needs of each market. Since passage of the Telecommunications Act, the size of the typical radio news staff has fallen from an average of 4.5 employees in 1974 to just 1.6 in 2001.[21] As staff sizes shrink, radio stations may need to rely more on national wire services and network affiliates for their news content. On the other hand, Clear Channel's creed states that the company has "an obligation for the well-being of the communities in which we live," and its large size does not necessarily mean that it is incapable of serving those communities.[22] In fact, according to Video Monitoring Service, Denver's KOA radio news station devoted far more coverage to the 2003 mayoral campaign compared to coverage produced by its rival, KNUS. The Denver example demonstrates that the size of the parent company does not always affect the amount of coverage devoted to local campaigns—KOA is one of Clear Channel's 1,225 radio stations, whereas KNUS is one of just ninety-two stations owned by Salem Communications.

Thus, it is still unclear how the consolidation of radio stations has affected local coverage of political campaigns. It is also important to note that similar levels of consolidation did not occur in the television industry following the Telecommunications Act, since limits remained in place to prohibit companies from reaching more than 35 percent of the national television audience and to limit the number of stations companies could own in a single market. Yet, the Telecommunications Act of 1996 did instruct the FCC to conduct a review of its ownership regulations every two years. In 2003, this review led the FCC to institute sweeping and controversial changes that removed many of the television ownership restrictions in the United States.

The FCC's Deregulation of Television Ownership Restrictions

In 2003, the FCC conducted the biennial review of ownership regulations as mandated by the Telecommunications Act. This review took place against the backdrop of two recent changes—a shift toward more conservative membership on the FCC and a court decision casting doubt on the status of current ownership rules. When George W. Bush won the presidential election in 2000, he also won the right to appoint individuals to the FCC (subject to approval from the Senate). In 2001, Bush's appointments to the commission changed the balance from three Democrats and two Republicans to a 3–2 Republican majority. Since Republicans were more likely to favor deregulation, a change in FCC rules became increasingly likely in 2003.

Along with a change in the balance on the FCC came an important decision from the U.S. Court of Appeals that called into question the legitimacy of the FCC rules limiting national ownership of television stations. In 1998, the FCC had decided not to modify the restriction on the percentage of the national audience that a single company could reach (the National Television Ownership Rule). This decision was particularly harmful to Fox and Viacom (which owns CBS), which had recently completed mergers that increased their holdings above the 35 percent cap. In addition, the National Television Ownership Rule was preventing Fox from purchasing another corporation whose television stations would increase Fox's reach to beyond 40 percent of the national audience. Facing FCC action for violating the 35 percent cap, Fox sued the FCC to have the cap removed.

The Twelfth Circuit Court's (District of Columbia) decision in *Fox Television Stations Inc. v. Federal Communication Commission* was issued early in

2002, the same year that the FCC was scheduled to review its ownership restrictions again.[23] For those favoring deregulation of ownership restrictions, the timing of the decision could not have been better. The opinion from the court largely sympathized with Fox, determining that "the Commission's decision to retain the rules was arbitrary and capricious and contrary to law."[24] The court remanded the decision back to the FCC for review, instructing the commission to repeal the rule or provide significant justification for its existence.[25]

Thus, in 2003 the FCC announced that it would review all existing restrictions on broadcast ownership. Chairman Michael Powell later called this review "the most exhaustive and comprehensive review of our broadcast ownership rules ever undertaken."[26] The result of this sweeping review, announced on June 2, was a decision to revise a number of existing regulations on media ownership. In particular, this ruling affected the above-mentioned National Television Ownership Rule, Local Television Ownership Rule, and the Cross-Ownership rules:[27]

> *National Television Ownership Rule*—This rule was relaxed again, as any single entity can now own television stations that reach up to 45 percent of the national audience. This was particularly important for Fox and Viacom, since their recent mergers had increased their share of the national audience above the old cap of 35 percent.
>
> *Local Television Ownership Rule*—The FCC also made it easier for a company to own multiple television stations in the same market. In small markets (one–four television stations), a company can only own a single station. A company may own two stations in medium-size markets (five–seventeen stations), however, and three stations in large markets (eighteen or more stations).
>
> *Cross-Ownership Rules*—Cross-ownership of television stations, radio stations, and newspapers is still prohibited in small markets (one–three television stations). Some cross-ownership is now allowed in markets with four–eight stations, however, and there are no limits on cross-ownership in markets with nine or more stations.

These new regulations would allow major media companies to own more stations nationally and in a number of local markets. To illustrate this point, Table 6.2 shows the companies reaching the largest share of the national television market before the FCC ruling and the number of stations each company owned. Note that Fox and Viacom had been in violation of the previous national cap of 35 percent, but under the new 45 percent limit, both companies still had room to expand, and many companies had room for significant growth.

The FCC decision was very controversial among both lawmakers and the public, especially in rural areas were consolidation was likely to have the biggest effect (see the Minot example at the beginning of the chapter). There

**Table 6.2   Percentage of the National Audience Reached by Top
10 Television Station Groups (prior to 2003 FCC ruling)**

Station Group	Number of Stations	Percentage of Audience Reached
Viacom	40	39.5
Fox	34	38.1
Paxson	68	33.7
NBC	24	30.4
Tribune	23	28.7
ABC	10	23.8
Univision	32	21.0
Gannett	22	17.5
Hearst-Argyle	34	15.9
Trinity Broadcasting	23	15.8

Source: Alec Klein and David A. Vise, "Media Giants Hint That They Might Be Expanding,"
Washington Post, 3 June 2003, A6.

was a great deal of protest from interest groups before June in anticipation of
the ruling. Interest groups running the ideological spectrum were concerned
that consolidation would mean less competition among media outlets, thereby
driving up the cost of advertising or, worse, limiting where groups could
advertise. Adding to the controversy was the fact that the vote on the new regulations was split along party lines, with the two Democratic commissioners
objecting to the loosening of regulations. Although the issue did not originally
resonate with the public, after the ruling, polls showed that a majority of the
nation's citizens thought the new regulations would have a negative impact;
only 10 percent thought the effect would be positive.[28] The objection from the
public was particularly notable given the typical disinterest with which most
executive agency regulations are met. To some extent, this objection was
fueled by reports of the lobbying activities of media companies leading up to
the ruling. Between 1999 and 2002, the twenty-five largest media companies
in the United States spent over $82 million lobbying Congress and the FCC.[29]
When the FCC changed its regulations to allow these companies to increase
their size, many questioned the role that the lobbying activity had played in
influencing the decision.

As public opinion became more vocal after the decision, the courts and
lawmakers seemed to take notice. In early September 2003, the U.S. Court of
Appeals for the District of Columbia ruled that the new regulations could not
take effect until court cases challenging the new rules had ended. At the same
time, Congress seemed to be expressing its dissatisfaction with the new rules.
In July, the House passed legislation that included a provision that would keep
the FCC from implementing the new regulations. In mid-September, the Senate went even further by passing legislation that would repeal all of the new

rules. President Bush promised to veto any legislation that would affect the FCC's decision, however. Ultimately, Congress and the White House agreed to amend the National Television Ownership Rule in 2003. The FCC had increased the share of the national population that any one company's television stations could reach from 35 percent from 45 percent in 2002, but Congress rolled the limit back to 39 percent with an appropriations bill passed in January of the following year. With a limit of 39 percent, Fox and Viacom were no longer violating the rule, but they had little room to expand beyond their current holdings. Yet, regardless of the actions by Congress and the president, a number of court challenges will still move forward.

In June 2004, the U.S. Court of Appeals for the Third Circuit in Philadelphia ruled that the FCC did not provide sufficient justification for amending the Local Television Ownership and the Cross-Ownership Rules. As a result, the court ordered the FCC to rewrite these rules while providing more evidence and reasoning for any changes. The FCC may choose to appeal this decision to the Supreme Court, but this decision and the action taken by Congress have challenged or amended most of the major changes the FCC implemented in June 2003. Furthermore, these challenges indicate that the public and politicians have begun to take an interest in the deregulation of the media industry. Proponents of deregulation argue that it is necessary and harmless because of the continuing technological innovations that affect the amount of information available to citizens. Chairman Powell defended the changes as "modern rules that take proper account of the explosion of new media outlets for news, information and entertainment."[30] A *Washington Post* editorial published the day before the June 2 decision argued that some of the previous rules were "a relic of a time when consumer choice was far more limited than it is today."[31] In the past, citizens were only able to watch a handful of television stations, listen to a few radio stations, and read their local newspaper. Now, however, most people get hundreds of television stations via cable or satellite, and they can read nearly any newspaper on the Internet. Thus, many consider regulations designed to assure that consumers have choices when it comes to broadcast media unnecessary.

Opponents of deregulation fear that the increasing centralization of ownership by a small number of companies may affect the quality and quantity of news citizens may have access to. FCC Commissioner Jonathan Adelstein voted against the rule changes, warning:

> This is a sad day for me, and I think for the country. I'm afraid a dark storm cloud is now looming over the future of the American media. This is the most sweeping and destructive rollback of consumer protection rules in the history of American broadcasting. The public stands little to gain and everything to lose by slashing the protections that have served them for decades. This plan is likely to damage the media landscape for generations to come. It threatens to degrade civil discourse and the quality of our society's intellectual, cultural and political life.[32]

The primary contention of opponents is that the increasing consolidation of broadcast stations will inevitably lead to a decline in the diversity of programming. Many people are quick to cite Clear Channel's rapid growth and consolidation following the Telecommunications Act of 1996 as a model for what could happen with the television industry. The *St. Louis Post-Dispatch* expressed its reservations before the decision with fears that "the new rules would inevitably reduce competition, concentrating power in fewer hands and fewer voices."[33]

Thus, both sides make compelling arguments about this issue. One cannot debate the point that citizens have at their fingertips a more diverse array of information sources than ever before. Yet, as noted earlier in this chapter, a majority of Americans still use their local television news broadcast as their primary source of news despite the choices available to them. Thus, consolidation of television stations may affect the news that Americans are most exposed to. Then again, consolidation does not have to result in newscasts that are of lesser quality. Indeed, as I discuss in the following section, it is not entirely clear yet what impact media consolidation has on local campaign coverage.

Centralization of Ownership and the Quality of Campaign Coverage

With the recent shift toward deregulation, fewer companies are beginning to own more of the broadcast media in the United States. But does this centralization of ownership matter, as opponents claim? Some political scientists and mass communications scholars have considered the effect of consolidation on the quality of local news coverage. One area in which some research does exist examines the effect of centralized ownership on the quality of newspaper reporting. Although the FCC regulates broadcast ownership in the United States, it has no direct authority when it comes to newspaper ownership. Thus, national consolidation of local newspapers has been occurring for a much longer period than the consolidation of broadcast media.[34] Some research has indicated that coverage does suffer because of newspaper consolidation, but other research is less conclusive.[35] At the very least, it appears as though political coverage produced by chain-owned newspapers is less locally oriented than coverage produced by newspapers that are independently owned.[36]

Studies examining the impact of consolidation on broadcast news are less common. One of the most comprehensive examinations of this question comes from the Project for Excellence in Journalism (PEJ).[37] It analyzed 23,000 news stories from 172 news programs over the course of five years to compare the quality of coverage by stations owned by small companies to those owned by larger companies. The PEJ found mixed results when it came to the quality of news coverage. There was some evidence that consolidation did not have any effect, and in some cases may have actually produced better coverage. In particular, companies that cross-owned a television station and a newspaper in the same market produced higher quality newscasts. On the other hand, the PEJ concluded that consolidation also had its drawbacks. Television stations owned by smaller companies tended to produce better newscasts than those owned by larger companies, and stations owned by the national networks also tended to have lesser quality newscasts than locally owned stations.

The above research addressed overall news quality, but it is important to consider how consolidation affects coverage of political campaigns. After all, a majority of Americans use the local television news as their primary source of information about political campaigns. In 2002, the Lear Center at the University of Southern California analyzed campaign coverage in the news broadcasts of 122 television stations in the top fifty media markets.[38] As part of this study, the Lear Center ranked the coverage according to several criteria, including the percentage of news time devoted to campaign coverage and the percentage of locally oriented campaign stories. In Table 6.3, I use this data to examine the impact of consolidation on the quality of campaign coverage. I divided the stations from the Lear Center's study into two groups—one included stations owned by one of the ten largest television ownership groups and the second included all other stations. The table compares these two groups of television stations on the measures of news quality mentioned above.

The first two rows of the table show the percentage of stations in each group that provided the best (those ranked in the top third) and worst (those ranked in the bottom third) amount of coverage of the 2002 campaigns. Interestingly, the pattern here seems to be opposite of what one might expect.

Table 6.3   The Relationship Between Media Ownership and Campaign Coverage

News Quality	Stations Owned by One of Ten Largest Companies	Stations Not Owned by One of Ten Largest Companies
Coverage Devoted to Campaign	Percentage	Percentage
Top Third[a]	44.26	21.31
Bottom Third[b]	26.23	40.98
Campaign Coverage Devoted to Local Issues		
Top Third[a]	31.15	34.43
Bottom Third[b]	34.43	32.79

Source: Compiled by author from "Local TV News Coverage of the 2002 General Election," Lear Center Local News Archive and Center for Public Integrity. www.localnewsarchive.org.

Notes: a. The best ranking out of 122 television stations, according to Lear Center criteria.
   b. The worst ranking out of 122 television stations, according to Lear Center criteria.

Although over 44 percent of stations owned by one of the ten largest companies were ranked among the top third in the amount of campaign coverage they provided, only 21 percent of stations owned by smaller companies were ranked in the top third. Thus, stations owned by larger companies were more likely to provide more coverage of the 2002 campaigns. Similarly, stations owned by smaller companies were far more likely to be ranked in the bottom third (41 percent)—to produce less coverage—compared to those owned by the ten largest companies (26 percent). Thus, from this evidence, it appears as though stations owned by larger conglomerates actually produced more campaign coverage.[39]

Of course, the concern is not necessarily that these stations will produce less coverage, but that the coverage will be similar across all media markets. In other words, when stations are owned by one large national company, they may be less likely to produce campaign coverage that focuses on how politics and campaigns affect the local community. The data in Table 6.3 suggest that, so far, there is little difference between the local nature of coverage produced by stations owned by large national companies and those owned by smaller groups. Stations owned by smaller companies were slightly more likely to be ranked among the top third in this category (34 percent compared to 31 percent for stations owned by large companies), whereas those owned by the ten largest companies were slightly more likely to be ranked in the bottom third (34 percent versus 33 percent). These differences were small, however, and may or may not be an accurate portrayal of reality among all television stations.[40]

How do we put the findings from Table 6.3 into perspective? First, it is important to realize that this is just one piece of evidence that we can use to address a very complicated issue. Thus, it is important not to make too much of these findings. Second, it may be too soon to gauge the effects of consolidation on campaign coverage. With regard to media consolidation, FCC Commissioner Adelstein warned, "It may take a while for the public to feel the full effects."[41] For this reason, it is important for scholars and researchers to continue to revisit comparisons such as this one as time passes. Third, the patterns in Table 6.3 may be a bit misleading. From this evidence, it is impossible to know whether stations provided more news coverage because they were owned by one of the ten largest media companies, or if those companies purchased those stations because they produced better newscasts. A more stringent test of the effects of media ownership should be undertaken by evaluating whether news coverage changes, for better or worse, after a large company has purchased a station. Research of this nature may provide better evidence of the impact that ownership has on campaign coverage.

Despite the above warnings, we may draw some conclusions from the information in Table 6.3. Indeed, it is interesting to note that although stations owned by the largest media companies tend to dedicate more time to campaign coverage, they are no more likely to produce coverage that focuses on how campaigns affect local issues. It is this localism that many fear will be lacking if national corporations continue purchasing local television stations. Although the evidence here suggests that there may be a tendency for stations owned by the largest media companies to produce less locally oriented coverage, the evidence is by no means conclusive. Indeed, we are still very uncertain as to how the consolidation of broadcast outlets will affect the local news coverage that so many Americans rely on as their primary source of political news.

Conclusion

For nearly a century, the U.S. government has regulated broadcast communications in order to preserve the local and diverse nature of that medium. Yet, the recent deregulation of the communications industry brings into question whether campaign coverage will continue to be locally oriented and diverse. Will stations continue to impart a local perspective on political coverage when they are owned by large national corporations? Can citizens expect to continue receiving news about campaigns for mayor, city council, and other local offices under these circumstances? Will news about national campaigns focus less on the local importance of those contests? Presently, there is no definitive evidence of how the recent consolidation of local news outlets affects coverage of political campaigns. Although there is some indication that stations owned by larger companies produce more campaign news, that coverage may also be less centered on the local community. Regardless, the issue remains an important one. A majority of citizens in the United States use the local media as their primary source of campaign news, and it remains to be seen whether the deregulation of the media industry will affect what citizens find when they tune in.

Notes

1. Lee, "On Minot, N.D," p. C-7.
2. This information comes from Clear Channel's website: www.clearchannel. com.
3. Lee, "On Minot, N.D.," p. C-7.
4. For example, see Converse, "The Nature of Belief Systems."
5. Patterson and McClure, *The Unseeing Eye*; Clarke and Evans, *Covering Campaigns*.
6. Pew Research Center for the People and the Press, "Public's News Habits."
7. Kurtz, "Local News Heroes," p. W16.
8. For the complete story on the invention, see Jolly, *Marconi*.
9. Ford, "The Meaning of the Public Interest."
10. *National Broadcasting Company v. U.S.*, 319 U.S. 190 (1943).
11. Tillinghast, *American Broadcast Regulation and the First Amendment*.
12. *National Broadcasting Company v. U.S.*, p. 226.
13. *Red Lion Broadcasting v. Federal Communications Commission*, 319 U.S. 367 (1969).

14. Ibid., pp. 386, 390.

15. Teeter and Le Duc, *Law of Mass Communications*, p. 92.

16. Federal Communications Commission, "FCC Sets Limits on Media Concentration."

17. Aufderheide, *Communications Policy and the Public Interest*.

18. Meyerson, "Ideas of the Marketplace," p. 277.

19. The legislation defines radio markets very liberally, often grouping together multiple communities into the same market. Therefore, Clear Channel Communications can own all six commercial radio stations in Minot because that community is included with Bismarck into a single radio market. Clear Channel owns all six stations in Minot, but only two 100 miles away in Bismarck.

20. Telecommunications Act of 1996, P.L. No. 104-104, 110 Stat. 56, § 202(c)(2).

21. These figures come from surveys of television and radio stations conducted by the Radio-Television News Directors Association. The report is available at www.rtnda.org/research/staff_2001.shtml.

22. This information comes from Clear Channel's website: www.clearchannel.com.

23. *Fox Television Stations, Inc. v. Federal Communications Commission*, 280 F.3d (2003).

24. Ibid., p. 3.

25. It should be noted that the Court rejected Fox's arguments that the FCC's rule violated the First Amendment. Once again, the Court maintained the right of the government to regulate ownership of broadcast stations through licensing restrictions.

26. Powell, "Press Statement."

27. Labaton, "Deregulating the Media"; Federal Communications Commission, "FCC Sets Limits on Media Concentration."

28. Pew Research Center for the People and Press, "Strong Opposition to Media Cross-Ownership Emerges."

29. Figures reported by the Center for Responsive Politics according to lobbying reports submitted to Congress. Information online at http://opensecrets.org.

30. Quoted in Ahrens, "FCC Eases Media Ownership Rules," p. A-1.

31. "Who Can Own Media?" p. B-6. Newspapers are not necessarily uninterested observers on this matter (the *Washington Post* owns several television stations too).

32. Adelstein, "Press Statement."

33. "Soapbox Monopoly," p. D-6.

34. At one point, hundreds of cities (including many medium-size cities) had several newspapers. Today, fewer than thirty cities have more than one paper.

35. For research claiming that newspaper consolidation does adversely affect coverage, see Bagdikian, *The Media Monopoly*. For research providing less conclusive results, see Demers, "Corporate Newspaper Bashing."

36. Schaffner and Sellers, "Structural Determinants."

37. Rosenstiel and Mitchell, "Does Ownership Matter in Local Television News."

38. "Local TV News Coverage of the 2002 General Election."

39. A Chi-square test for independence indicated that these differences were statistically significant at the .05 level. In other words, we can be fairly confident that these differences will exist among all stations in the United States.

40. A Chi-square test for independence indicated that these differences were not statistically significant at the .05 level. In other words, we cannot be confident that these differences will exist among all stations in the United States.

41. Adelstein, "Press statement."

7

The Internet: Democracy Goes Online

Lee E. Goodman

On November 4, 1972, one day before President Richard Nixon trounced George McGovern to win reelection, Hamilton Jordan, a twenty-seven-year-old aide to Georgia governor Jimmy Carter, drafted a memo outlining what it would take for Carter to be elected president four years later. The memo read like a catechism, a litany of political and organizational "to do's." It included the names of foreign policy experts Carter should consult and rivals he should watch. The memo also addressed specific strategic challenges Carter would have to overcome if he were to catapult from being an obscure former governor (Carter would leave the Georgia governorship in 1974) to becoming a nationally recognized presidential contender.[1]

The lynchpin to Jordan's strategy was the imperative of establishing national name identification through favorable coverage by national media. Jordan concluded that Carter could go nowhere without favorable coverage by the nation's media elite, and his memo was very explicit about this first major hurdle to national credibility:

> [I]t is necessary that we begin immediately to generate favorable stories and comments in the national press. Stories in the *New York Times* and *Washington Post* do not just happen, but have to be carefully planned and planted. . . . Once your name begins to be mentioned in the national press, you will not lack for invitations and opportunities to speak in major groups and conventions. . . . [W]e should begin immediately to (1) generate favorable stories in the national press on the accomplishments of your administration, (2) develop and/or maintain a close personal relationship with the principle national columnists and reporters, and (3) take full advantage of every legitimate opportunity for national exposure as long as it is couched in terms of what you have accomplished in Georgia.
>
> We should compile a listing of regional and national political editors and columnists who you know or need to know. You can find ample excuse for contacting them—writing them a note, complimenting them on an arti-

cle or column and asking that they come to see you when convenient. Some people like Tom Wicker or Mrs. Katherine Graham are significant enough to spend an evening or a leisurely weekend with. . . .

Like it or not, there exists in fact an eastern liberal news establishment which has tremendous influence in this country all out of proportion to its actual audience. The views of this small group of opinion-makers in the papers they represent are noted and imitated by other columnists and newspapers throughout the country and the world. Their recognition and acceptance of your candidacy as a viable force with some chance of success could establish you as a serious contender worthy of financial support of major party contributors.[2]

Jordan's memo went on to spell out in excruciating detail the efforts Jimmy Carter would have to expend to cultivate national and regional media leaders, all in an effort to get mentioned favorably in their publications. Jordan's "to do" list highlighted other key challenges facing Carter as well, such as the difficult task of identifying campaign contributors on a national scale and recruiting a national fund-raising chairman to meet the huge projected cost of a national campaign.

Following Jordan's game plan, the pleasant New South governor assiduously courted the national media and embarked upon the effort to leverage press attention into national credibility. By 1974, he had begun to build a national but targeted network of key supporters in the early primary states of Iowa, New Hampshire, and Florida. And his campaign staffers (many unpaid) were jotting down the names and addresses of new contacts on note pads wherever Carter traveled, and he traveled everywhere.

Still, after two years of intensive efforts and incessant travel, Jimmy Carter entered 1975 as a formally declared candidate for the U.S. presidency facing two intractable problems: "Not many people knew who he was. And not many cared."[3] The latest polls of 1974 did not even rate him in the cast of likely candidates. And a popular refrain was emerging in political parlance: "Jimmy who?" According to press secretary Jody Powell, even Carter's supporters in various states "had no idea—and saw no evidence—that we had anything going on anywhere else. They each thought they were the only ones working for Jimmy in the whole country."[4] The national media appearances were simply not forthcoming.

Fund-raising remained an obstacle, too. Carter started his campaign with a direct mail list of a little over 500,000 names—about 30,000 of them Georgia political supporters, the rest borrowed from other national lists.[5] It took Carter over a year to generate a list of 1,800 donors who gave more than $100, and by the end of 1975, one year before the election, he had raised only $850,000. Through continuous and expensive mailings, Carter was able to push this list of loyal donors to contribute another $250,000 and eventually to build a national list of donors that gave more than $1 million.

The presidential campaign of Jimmy Carter demonstrated just how difficult—and indeed improbable—it historically has been for a nonestablishment candidate to rise from obscurity and build a national network of support, a fund-raising base, and recognition in the media age. In the media age, a candidate who cannot earn media coverage often cannot afford to buy media to promote his name, either. That Carter achieved these twin objectives is what makes his successful bid for the presidency in 1976 such a remarkable story of twentieth-century politics.

The Jimmy Carter experience stands in stark contrast, however, to the way in which each of the "to do's" in Hamilton Jordan's 1972 memo would be achieved today. Three decades later, in early 2002, another obscure former governor from a small state set out to win the Democratic nomination and the 2004 presidential race. His name was Howard Dean, a former physician who had served as governor of Vermont for twelve years. Like Carter, Dean started his run for the presidency four years before the election with no national name recognition and no national network of supporters. Every inch of his drive to national credibility would have to be earned in a field crowded by better-known senators, congressmen, and even a former military general.

But Dean's twenty-first century bid benefited from new technological campaign tools not available to Jimmy Carter in 1976. Most prominent among them were the personal computer and the Internet, two innovations that had hit the scene in the mid-1990s. By 2002, it was estimated that half of all Americans had access to the Internet in their homes.[6] Campaigns in the late 1990s had started to employ the communications power of the Internet to post websites, collect donations, and generate support. Senator John McCain gave everyone a glimpse of the Internet's potential during his unsuccessful primary race for president in 2000.[7] But no candidate had marshaled the new technology as effectively as the virtually unknown Howard Dean in galvanizing a national network of activist supporters and raising tens of million of dollars from thousands of modest financial contributions.

Like most campaigns since the late 1990s, the Dean campaign entered 2003 with a website that posted information about the campaign and the former Vermont governor's positions on issues. These passive websites could be analogized to nothing more than an electronic brochure that sits on a server until someone clicks by and picks it up. But the Dean campaign was soon to launch an electronic communications strategy that would make political history.

Beginning in March 2003, the campaign initiated an aggressive communications strategy utilizing cutting-edge techniques and software over the Internet.[8] Almost overnight, the Dean campaign raised over $11 million online between April and September 2003.[9] That was half of the campaign's total funds raised at very little cost per dollar.

More significantly, the Dean campaign successfully deployed Internet technologies to build and expand a national network of supporters. According to the company that provided the Dean campaign's technology, in six months Dean registered more than 450,000 people to receive regular online campaign messages, sent 6.5 million e-mails to supporters to keep them engaged and to solicit contributions, and downloaded to thousands of supporters an electronic volunteer fund-raising system that empowered the supporters to open their own websites for the purpose of recruiting additional supporters and raising funds from their personal friends and contacts online. In just three months, individual supporters employing the Dean campaign's fund-raising software raised $625,000—money that would have gone uncollected if the Dean website had passively accepted contributions only from the supporters who located it. The website facilitated recurring contributions from donors' credit cards so effectively that the Dean campaign received 110,786 contributions online from 84,713 supporters (an average of $61.14) in one three-month period.[10]

Dean support on the Internet took on a phenomenal life of its own. People from around the country started communicating to each other about the Dean campaign on "web logs," also known as "blogs," which are personal websites people post to express their own opinions or advertise local events of interest. Many of these blogs were generated with software downloaded from the Dean campaign website; others were established and hosted by inveterate "bloggers." The blogs operated across the country like local bull-horns, advertising Dean events and connecting people to the larger national events. Using this system, Dean supporters around the country held "meet ups" at local restaurants and house party fund-raisers, often on a synchronized schedule, including Dean Halloween parties, Generation Dean debate-watching parties on October 26, 2003, and Governor Dean's Birthday Bash on November 17, 2003. The system also facilitated the participation of 10,000-plus people on nearly 3,560 telephones at more than 1,440 house parties across the country for a massive conference call with the candidate known as "Dr. Dean's House Call."[11]

"He's really leveraging the medium, putting it in the hands of the people," one Internet expert was quoted as saying. "What he's done is substantiated a community."[12] That's certainly a community Jimmy Carter initially lacked. His local volunteers felt isolated, and they sought affirmation that their efforts in their communities somehow contributed to a broader national movement. They begged for national press appearances for that affirmation—appearances that more often than not were not forthcoming in 1974 and 1975. And, because Dean's Internet skills were instrumental in vaulting him past his Democratic rivals in both funding and following, as well as national polling, the candidate who once had begun to hear "Howard who?" quickly found himself headed into the primary season with the national media recognition Jimmy Carter earned only after winning several primaries. Like Carter, Dean had a message. Unlike Carter, Dean had at his disposal a technological tool to spread the word quickly and efficiently.

Howard Dean did not ultimately win the Democratic Party's nomination in 2004. Nevertheless, the technological strategy he implemented to vault himself from obscurity to the front cover of *Time* magazine will go down in history as the trailblazer of Internet campaigning—as the campaign that proved that the Internet has truly changed political campaigns and democracy. Henceforth, virtually all candidates and advocacy organizations in the United States will deploy an Internet strategy, not just as a passive informational website, but as an assertive campaign tool to disseminate their message, raise contributions, and, most important, engage people in their cause and build a national network of loyal supporters. A common refrain of the late 1990s had been *"The Internet changes everything!"* In six months of 2003, the campaign of Howard Dean proved that the Internet indeed had changed U.S. politics and public advocacy quite profoundly.

Background: The Law of Campaign Finance, Free Speech, and the Internet

Although effective political communication in the United States is still dominated by mass media and will remain quite expensive for decades to come, Internet-based communication is quite inexpensive and, as Howard Dean's campaign has shown, is competing with television, radio, and print media in effectiveness. Its effectiveness is expected only to increase over the next decade, especially as broadband and software technologies advance, more Americans log on, and a new generation of citizens acclimated to the Internet comes of age and becomes more politically active. A decade from now the personal computer and television set might even merge into one electronic device, diminishing even further television's competitive advantage.

This transformation in information and communication technologies strains campaign finance rules and regulations conceived and designed in the 1970s for political communication via expensive media. That stress illuminates profound theoretical and constitutional questions regarding the government's authority to restrict much political speech over the Internet.

In the fall of 1999, the Federal Election Commission (FEC), the federal agency in charge of regulating federal campaigns and enforcing federal campaign finance laws, issued a call for public comments regarding a range of political activities on the Internet.[13] Among the questions put to the public was whether the FEC should devise a new set of regulations specifically tailored to Internet political activity or, instead, adapt existing rules to new political applications of the Internet on a case-by-case basis. Several years passed without any systemic revision to the FEC's regulations. Meanwhile, the FEC began to issue fact-specific advisory opinions regarding particular uses of the Internet, leading most of the regulated community to conclude that the FEC had decided on the latter approach (adaptation of existing rules). Some of the

FEC's decisions revealed a regulatory schizophrenia, as if the FEC were holding a wolf by its ears—on the one hand recognizing that this new technology
should be set free, while on the other hand nervous about what havoc the technology might wreak on the rest of the regulated world of campaign expenditures. The FEC's approach has been to try to fit Internet activity into traditional regulatory paradigms.

The question the FEC implicitly raised in its 1999 call for public comment, which is the same question for any serious student of campaign finance
regulation today, is whether the Internet and its low-cost technologies have
eclipsed a complex cobweb of laws and regulations conceived for the high-cost
media-centered politics of the late twentieth century. An informed answer to
that question requires a thorough consideration of competing democratic values—those justifying the old restrictions versus those promoted by the new
technologies. In other words, what was the government's compelling rationale
supporting restrictions on free political speech under the First Amendment, and
does that rationale sustain restrictions on free speech over the Internet?

The Constitutional Rationale for Restricting
Campaign Contributions and Expenditures

As part of his "trust-busting" reforms, President Teddy Roosevelt sought new
restrictions on the influence of business corporations in elections. The result
was the Tillman Act of 1907, the first campaign finance law on the books,
which banned corporations from making political contributions to federal
campaigns.[14] The second major reform era started in the 1930s in reaction to
abuses of the federal workforce by President Franklin Roosevelt. After many
years of trying, a Republican Congress extended the ban against corporate
contributions to labor unions in the Taft-Hartley Act of 1947.[15]

But it was not until 1971 and then again in 1974 that Congress enacted a
sweeping set of restrictions on campaign finance in the Federal Election
Campaign Act (FECA).[16] As discussed in Chapter 4, the law was amended
following the Watergate scandal and revelations of campaign "slush funds"
provided by wealthy donors. Among other restrictions, the law restricted the
amount of money each citizen could contribute to a campaign for federal
office to $1,000 per election. It restricted how citizens could spend their own
money to voice their opinions about federal candidates and, in some cases,
even public policy. The law also tightened restrictions on business corporations and labor unions in how they could spend their funds, short of contributing them to campaigns, to advocate the election or defeat of federal candidates. Regulatory authority and enforcement power for the new FECA was
vested in a new agency, the Federal Election Commission (FEC).

The new law was quickly challenged in court on the basis that the new
restrictions violated each citizen's First Amendment rights of free speech and

association. What could be more expressive, those who challenged the law argued, than each citizen's right to contribute time and resources to candidates of his or her choice in a democracy? Restrictions on campaign finances directly limited the ability of federal candidates to communicate via modern media and press channels, which charged significant sums of money to disseminate political advertisements and messages. Even brochures and flyers cost money to print and distribute.

In 1976, the United States Supreme Court issued a seminal decision in the case of *Buckley v. Valeo*.[17] Again, see Chapter 4 for a more thorough discussion of *Buckley*, but I review it briefly here because one must understand the reasoning of that decision to address whether Internet-based speech can or should be restricted too. In *Buckley*, the Supreme Court held that money—both contributions to campaigns and expenditures to fund one's own political speech—is indeed synonymous with free speech in a market in which the communication of one's ideas and political advocacy costs significant sums. According to the Court, "The expenditure limitations contained in the [FECA] represent substantial rather than merely theoretical restraints on the quantity and diversity of political speech."[18] Of most significance to today's Internet aficionados is the Supreme Court's focus on the necessity of money to communicate by expensive mass media channels. What would the Court say today when informed that a single individual can speak to millions of voters on a website that costs less than $200 to post on the Internet?

Having concluded that legal restrictions on campaign funding curtail free speech, the Court then turned its attention to what legitimate government interests might justify such restrictions. The Court concluded that Congress could restrict political speech protected by the First Amendment in order to serve only the most "compelling" of governmental interests and only so long as the means it chose to achieve its asserted interest was the least restrictive alternative.[19] The federal government advanced three interests to justify its new restrictions: restrictions on campaign contributions and expenditures were necessary (1) to "equalize" the ability of each citizen to speak and be heard, (2) to reduce the "skyrocketing cost of political campaigns," and (3) to prevent political corruption in which federal officials might become beholden to large donors.[20]

As to the first asserted interest, the Supreme Court rejected the notion that the "equalization" of speech could serve as a permissible governmental interest, much less a compelling one. The Court reasoned that "the concept that government may restrict the speech of some elements of our society in order to enhance the relative voice of others is wholly foreign to the First Amendment, which was designed to secure the widest possible dissemination of information from diverse and antagonistic sources."[21] Although this holding is often overlooked, its significance has reemerged in modern-day discussions over Internet speech because everyone has roughly equal access to post opinions on the Internet.

The Court also rejected the second asserted justification. The Court stated that the government has no business trying to reduce the overall amount of political speech by capping how much campaigns and citizens may spend to communicate their ideas.

As to the third asserted interest, the Supreme Court recognized that large contributions of money to candidates, and large expenditures spent on behalf of candidates, had the potential to influence candidates to lend official support in return to the same big contributors and spenders. In other words, donors could secure a political quid pro quo from candidates. The Court noted that "large individual financial contributions" raised an "appearance of corruption" and tended to erode "confidence in the system of representative Government."[22]

Important to the discussion of low-cost Internet speech—which will be discussed in more detail below—is the fact that the Court expressed no concern over the expense of campaigns for public office or the oft-mentioned generality that there is "too much money" in the political system. To the contrary, the Court made clear that the expenditure of large sums of money advances our "profound national commitment to the principle that debate on public issues should be uninhibited, robust, and wide-open."[23] What the Supreme Court articulated was a very particular concern over one potential evil in the U.S. political system—the potential for "quid pro quo" arrangements in which official favors would be exchanged for large contributions and expenditures. But one must query whether this concern is present when thousands of campaigns, interest groups, media entities, and individual citizens post opinions and information on a virtual free market of speech on the Internet for a mere fraction of the communication costs contemplated by the Supreme Court in *Buckley v. Valeo*.

The Supreme Court has issued numerous decisions on the topic of campaign finance since the *Buckley* decision in 1976. Two decisions are particularly worth mentioning in a discussion of how the Internet may have eclipsed twentieth-century laws regulating campaign finance. Both address the First Amendment rights of business corporations to speak in a democracy. In *First National Bank of Boston v. Bellotti* (1977), the Court held that business corporations in the United States have a First Amendment right to spend corporate funds to express their views on matters of public policy.[24] Since issues are just that—issues—there is no public official to be corrupted, and there is no justification for muting a corporation's viewpoint from the debate. Indeed, citizens benefit from hearing as many viewpoints as possible to form their opinions.

Years later, the Court had occasion to address whether corporations could be banned from spending corporate funds to advocate the election or defeat of *candidates* for public office in *Austin v. Michigan Chamber of Commerce* (1990).[25] The Court held that Congress could prohibit corporate speech expressly advocating the election of a candidate because such a restriction is necessary to prevent "the corrosive and distorting effects of immense aggregations of wealth that are accumulated with the help of the public forum."[26] The Court reasoned that the large treasuries corporations bring to political campaigns could purchase enough communications to drown out the voices of candidates and individual citizens. Again, however, it is not the actual *viewpoint* or *speech* by corporations that was deemed distortive of democracy (to the contrary, citizens could benefit from hearing these viewpoints), but the *amount* of communication corporations might be able to buy relative to individual citizens and candidates.

In sum, throughout the Supreme Court's jurisprudence on political speech, the Court never has expressed concern over too much speech or the content of public advocacy itself. To the contrary, robust speech containing a wide array of viewpoints is the cornerstone of the First Amendment protection and essential to a healthy democracy. Nor have the Court's decisions ever expressed a preference for any particular source of public advocacy, except in the case where corruption is a possibility. Even legal requirements for speakers to disclose their identity have been upheld for the sole purpose of enforcing potentially corruptive contributions and expenditures. The Court has upheld the paramount First Amendment right of speakers to publish and disseminate their views anonymously in the absence of corruptive potential, such as where a citizen passed out leaflets urging voters to vote against an issue referendum and did not mention candidates.[27]

For those who view the Internet as the most democratic and ubiquitous medium for political communication ever invented, these legal principles are particularly significant. If the Internet allows an average citizen to communicate as loudly and widely as a major corporation, interest group, or candidate for public office, and each source of information can speak as effectively as the next using a website and software that costs less than about $200, then where is the potential for corruption? What federal candidate will sell his conscience in return for a $200 expenditure on a supportive website and mass e-mail message? Since Congress already has concluded that federal officeholders cannot be corrupted for contributions or expenditures of up to $4,000 ($2,000 in a primary election and $2,000 in a general election from a single donor), then $200 should present no legally cognizable threat at all.

The FEC has exhibited some ambivalence on this theory. For example, the FEC has endorsed the right of corporations to post press releases announcing their support for federal candidates on their corporate websites, but only if corporations post such releases discreetly among all other press releases and actual costs to post are *de minimis*—meaning so small as to not have an effect.[28] But the FEC drew the line at press releases, otherwise prohibiting corporations from posting any other kind of favorable or critical advocacy on their websites.[29] Following this principle, the FEC has severely punished a corporation that provided a link to a favored candidate's website, even though the cost to post the link imposed no demonstrable financial cost to the corporation.[30] The ambivalence arises because the FEC is, on the one hand, recognizing that corporations, otherwise prohibited from spending corporate treasury funds to communicate their support or oppose federal candidates, can at least express themselves so long as there is no marginal cost to doing so. On the other hand, restrictions on placement of a press release and a prohibition against any other advocacy, including a link that costs nothing to post, strain the FEC's own logic.

Of course, none of this discussion is intended to suggest that the FEC must ignore large expenditures of money just because they are directed at the Internet audience. Large amounts of money may be spent to build and advertise a website devoted solely to the election or defeat of a candidate, and the FEC already has ruled that its regulations apply to such expenditures.[31] But the focus of the FEC's regulation, it seems, should target an *actual expenditure*, not the speech itself. And if posting an endorsement or a link on an existing website costs nothing more than the time it takes to type the link's code, then regulation of this comes very close to restricting speech and only speech.

Some advocates of stronger government regulation of political activity would go a step further, however. They urge the FEC to assign a "fair market value" to each Internet communication, regardless of the absence of any out-of-pocket expenditure.[32] The FEC has dipped its foot into this pool of thought as well. The FEC has opined, for example, that if a website owner does not ordinarily charge for links, he may provide viewers free links to a campaign's website without regulation.[33] But if a website owner ordinarily charges others for links, he is required to charge a campaign the same price—even though the provision of a link may cost him nothing.[34] Putting an agency of the federal government with no expertise in the free market or in technology in charge of assigning "fair market values" to each political posting, link, and "blog" on the World Wide Web, however, likely would bog down in an unworkable system of "assigned values." More important, such a system might exceed the government's legitimate regulatory purview as articulated in *Buckley* and might not stand up to constitutional scrutiny under the First Amendment.

Some observers wonder, however, whether that kind of case-by-case "market equivalence" logic might break down by comparison to the underlying purpose of campaign finance regulation—namely, the prevention of financial corruption. What is corrupting, they argue, about a free link that objectively costs nothing to post on a website? It might be effective, helpful, and influential in an election, for sure, but without carrying any financial cost.

If that is the case, then the government's restrictions target the postings themselves, not expenditures for the postings.

Media Exempted from Campaign Finance Restrictions

Another provision of the 1974 amendments to the Federal Election Campaign Act of 1971 carries important relevance for today's Internet-driven democracy—the "media exemption." The law provides that the media and press are entirely exempted from the financial restrictions on public advocacy and speech: "The term 'expenditure' does not include any news story, commentary, or editorial distributed through the facilities of any broadcasting station, newspaper, magazine, or other periodical publication, unless such facilities are owned or controlled by any political party, political committee, or candidate."[35] Legislative history indicates that Congress was concerned about not interfering with the media's core First Amendment right to comment upon political matters when it adopted the FECA and that this concern led it to adopt the "media exemption": "[I]t is not the intent of the Congress in the present legislation to limit or burden in any way the first amendment freedoms of the press and of association. Thus the exclusion assures the unfettered right of the newspapers, TV networks, and other media to cover and comment on political campaigns."[36]

In the past, the FEC has interpreted this exemption quite broadly. It includes, for example, the provision of free and unfettered airtime to actual candidates and political parties to expressly advocate their candidates. The FEC has applied the "commentary" exemption to cable, satellite, and broadcast television stations donating free television time to federal candidates and the national political parties to expressly advocate their candidacies and solicit financial contributions unfiltered by journalists.[37] The FEC has applied the exemption to a Webcaster's gavel-to-gavel coverage of the national party conventions[38] as well as to a Webcaster's "electronic town hall" linking presidential candidates directly to the Webcaster's subscribers.[39] The FEC has afforded the exemption to a newspaper that provided free space to federal candidates to promote their candidacies.[40] The FEC has applied the media exemption to Garry Trudeau's *Doonesbury* cartoon,[41] *The Rush Limbaugh Show*,[42] CBS's *60 Minutes*,[43] *Flower and Garden* magazine,[44] and Northwest Airlines's in-flight magazine *WorldTraveler*.[45] As the FEC has noted in the past, "[t]he statute and regulations do not define the issues permitted to be discussed or the format in which they are to be presented under the 'commentary' exemption nor do they set a time limit as to the length of the commentary."[46]

Federal courts that have addressed the "media exemption" have adopted a two-step analysis in the case of media organizations not controlled by political parties or candidates. The initial inquiry is whether the entity is a bona fide press or media organization. If so, the second inquiry is whether the political communication is disseminated or distributed within the media organization's ordinary course of media activity or press function (including solicitations to advertise and sell its publications).[47]

The only limitation the Supreme Court has ever imposed upon the "media exemption" is that a newsletter be published and distributed in the ordinary course of the publisher's regular activities.[48] In other words, a publisher that ordinarily mails each successive edition of its newsletter to 10,000 recipients cannot, on the eve of an election, mail one million "special editions" of its newsletter to every registered voter in a state urging voters to vote for the incumbent senator in next week's election. But the publisher could do so in a regularly scheduled edition mailed to 10,000 subscribers. More recently, however, in *McConnell v. Federal Election Commission*, the Supreme Court suggested in passing that the media exemption might protect only the "institutional press" from regulation by the FEC.[49]

In the Internet age, the question that immediately comes to mind is: *What*—or *who*—qualifies as a bona fide press organization? And just what is the *institutional press* in the Internet age? How the media exemption applies to online publications by individuals, advocacy organizations, and business corporations is still the subject of some confusion and debate, particularly by those who believe more regulation of campaign speech is needed. On the one hand, the FEC has extended the media exemption to cover Bloomberg and other online media outlets. On the other hand, the FEC is conflicted over what constitutes a bona fide press publication when published by nontraditional media entities.[50] The specter of a government agency sitting in case-by-case judgment over the bona fides of thousands of websites and weblogs portends a highly dubious regulatory system.

Individual Volunteer Efforts Exempted
from Campaign Finance Restrictions

FEC regulations permit individual citizens to volunteer their time and to use the resources of their homes and vehicles on behalf of political campaigns without triggering regulated contributions or expenditures.[51] To date, the FEC has opined that the "personal volunteer activity" exemption protects an individual's personal website and advocacy on a home computer.[52] That ruling acknowledges the growing ubiquity of personal computers in American homes. So long as that hands-off regulatory approach prevails, there is great promise for the empowerment of individual people in the U.S. political system.

That is not to say, however, that personal political activity on the Internet may always be safe from regulation. Legal theories in other contexts abound that individual activity using centralized technology or software is not personal activity, but group activity. There is nothing in current law that prevents the FEC from rethinking its current paradigm in the future when individual citizens find ways to bond together in common causes online—as Howard Dean and his ardent followers did so effectively.

The Future of Democratic Engagement on the Internet

Scholars and practitioners of U.S. politics are split on the degree to which the Internet will supplant traditional media such as television and radio for effective political communication. One camp advocates "reinforcement" theory, which holds that the Internet will merely reinforce existing media and institutions but not otherwise revolutionize political communication over the next few decades.[53] Others, known as "mobilization" theorists, predict far more profound transformations.[54] Mobilization theorists view the Internet as the latest development in a long line of political and technological advances, from the Populist movement of the 1820s to the Nineteenth Amendment (women's suffrage) in 1920 and the Voting Rights Act of 1965 to the referendum movements of the 1980s and 1990s, that have democratized the political system in the United States.[55]

The true effects may actually fall somewhere in the middle—the effects upon political communication will be profound and discreet but will not wholly revolutionize the U.S. government. Institutional players such as political parties, interest groups, incumbents, and the establishment press will harness the Internet to maintain their traditional roles, whereas individuals, new publishers, and upstart political movements and candidates (such as Jimmy Carter and Howard Dean) will utilize the Internet to challenge the institutional players with unprecedented communications power. Indeed, almost all observers of U.S. politics agree that the Internet increasingly will empower individual people at the expense of large established institutions. And nobody can overstate the palpable benefits the Internet promises American people as citizens and voters in the form of greater access to diverse sources of information (both original sources as well as interpretive news), immediate information, power to communicate and organize, and greater opportunity to join and engage in political causes across old geographical and political boundaries and despite limited financial resources. The promise is as infinite as the development of new more-powerful and cost-effective technologies.

It suffices to conclude, in the first decade of the twenty-first century, that the Internet will serve as a powerful "democratizer" of American politics. The question for students and scholars of democracy in the United States today is not necessarily how much it will democratize the polity but the extent to which government will allow it to fulfill its inherent potential.

The Internet Reduces the Cost of Political Speech

Former political consultant Dick Morris, an avid proponent of political action on the Internet, has outlined the following comparison of campaign costs:

[W]ere one to mail all voters in an inexpensive television market like Jackson, Mississippi, one would spend about $80,000 to reach all 200,000 voters in that market. Even a targeted mailing aimed at swing voters would cost upwards of $30,000. On television, $30,000 in Jackson, Mississippi, will buy about one thousand points of television advertising—enough to reach every voter eight to ten times with a thirty second advertisement, a far better buy than sending out one mailing.

But with e-mail, the mathematics changes dramatically. With no cost for postage or handling and instant delivery, e-mailing is far more immediate, intimate, and inexpensive than any other form of electoral communication. Once a candidate has an e-mail list for her district, she can reach her voters as often as she wishes with whatever content she wants. As broadband Internet access increases, she can even send streaming video, very much like the political ad of today, all with no cost.[56]

Candidates also will be able to send each voter an advertisement tailored to his or her personal interests—not just one, but one a day—for pennies per advertisement. Although no politician today would be well advised to abandon television, radio, and print audiences, the day when those candidates can reduce their budgets on those media may be as close as a generation away. In the meantime, virtually every candidate for federal office and most candidates for state and local office are launching aggressive Internet communications strategies for little more than the cost of one radio ad. In 1998, third-party gubernatorial candidate Jesse Ventura reportedly launched a highly effective website—credited with motivating enough voters to push his margins over two opponents—for less than $600.[57] In 1997, Virginia gubernatorial candidate Jim Gilmore launched an innovative campaign website that, among other things, incorporated a highly popular tax-savings calculator that allowed each voter to log on and determine precisely how much he or she would save under Gilmore's campaign-defining "No Car Tax" proposal.[58]

It is precisely the reduced cost of transmitting mass-customized messages over the Internet that challenges a regulatory system fixated upon large expenditures of money. This will remain an important issue to resolve for policymakers, political practitioners, and scholars over the next decade, especially as technologies improve, more Americans log on the Internet, and campaigns as well as citizens innovate creative and effective political applications for the medium.

The Internet Permits Ordinary
Americans to Join Grassroots Movements

Before the Internet, cause-oriented organizations faced many of the same challenges that Jimmy Carter faced in 1974. Building a national network and reputation required expensive and time-consuming travel by a charismatic leader and significant media attention to generate and communicate the movement's credibility. In the 1960s, Reverend Martin Luther King Jr. traveled across the country for the better part of a decade catalyzing local, grassroots civil rights movements. At least Rev. King started with local church and community networks. But, still, his national movement necessitated years of hard work, intensive time, and King's own physical presence in march after march, speech after speech. Many local acolytes lacked confidence that they could achieve change in their local institutions, but televised news reports of successes elsewhere fed the faith of local organizers in small isolated towns. Rev. King understood the need for free media attention, and much of his strategy was aimed at attracting national media attention to small cities across the South. It took publication of a letter to the editor of the Birmingham, Alabama, newspaper in 1963 and a nationally televised speech on the stairs of the Lincoln Memorial in Washington, D.C., in 1964 to establish Rev. King's national credibility.

Today, thousands of national and local cause-oriented groups organize people around the country electronically. They use the Web to accomplish everything from fund-raising to message dissemination to generating mass numbers of letter and e-mails to turning out supporters to speak at public hearings or march in protest. These philosophically charged organizations may spread the word about their respective policy causes to the entire world without restriction by the FEC so long as they do not expressly advocate the election or defeat of specific federal candidates.[59] They may say anything they want about policy and philosophy, and they can even urge citizens to contact public officeholders to seek their support for the cause. There are many conservative (for example, ClubForGrowth.com) and liberal (for example, MoveOn.org) websites that have sprung up out of nowhere and enlisted millions of Americans to engage in their respective causes.[60] These are in essence political movements that did not exist before the Internet empowered such small groups to grow into national networks of citizens. They are proof that the prospect for greater civic engagement is tremendous on the Internet.

Every Citizen Is "Citizen Kane" on the Internet

Just a decade ago, a commentator considering the media's special legal right to speak, write, and publish opinions on campaigns and candidates posed this rhetorical and legal quagmire:

> If it is a First Amendment violation to tell Rupert Murdoch that he cannot publish an editorial in the *New York Post* supporting or opposing a candidate, by what logic is it permissible or even appropriate to tell Murdoch's next door neighbor that she cannot purchase an advertisement in the *New York Times* in order to express support for or opposition to a candidate? The distinction cannot turn on the fact that Murdoch owns a printing press while the next-door neighbor does not. But once you allow Rupert Murdoch to spend as much as he chooses to support or oppose candidates—as apparently we must do under the First Amendment—the entire regime of spending limits begins to unravel.[61]

The Gutenberg press was invented in the fifteenth century. That invention revolutionized the world by providing a powerful new technology for the dissemination, indoctrination, and institutionalization of ideas. Yet, despite continuous improvements in the printing press over the next 550 years, even today a printing press is expensive to own, rent, and operate, and practical distribution limitations prevent ordinary citizens from publishing their ideas and delivering the written word across a broad geographical readership. Likewise, even brief communications via television, radio, and direct mail can cost tens of thousands of dollars. Therefore, only wealthy publishers have been able to speak as the "media."

All that changed in the early 1990s with the invention of an affordable personal computer and the Internet. For the first time in history, individual citizens can join the ranks of the American press. In the first decade of the twenty-first century, new online publications are springing up overnight. Some characterize themselves as electronic "newspapers," others as "magazines" or "editorials" or "newsletters." They include influential online dailies such as DrudgeReport.com, PoliticsNY.com, and PoliticsNJ.com, and they are attracting wide readership totaling in hundreds of thousands each day by breaking major news stories of the kind once broken only by their establishment predecessors. They are low-cost online publications available to hundreds of millions readers worldwide. And they are challenging long-established media monopolies.

Today, every citizen has the ability to publish a regular newsletter, editorial page, or even a news daily for the entire world to read on the Web. Indeed, thousands of American citizens are doing so on low-cost "blogs," and dozens have attracted a regular and prolific readership. In short, the Internet has completely democratized the American press as well as, arguably, the ability of all citizens to speak about federal candidates without regulation by federal campaign finance laws. Whether this new freedom is permitted to thrive has yet to be determined.

Enhanced Access to Political Information and Government: Sunshine on the Internet

The Institute for Politics, Democracy, and the Internet at George Washington University interviewed 271 political journalists in 2002 about how the Internet changed their reporting.[62] Among the findings: 74 percent of reporters said they could find more sources of information about the political campaigns they cover than before the Internet became a widespread source of political information, and 64 percent said the sources they found were more diverse than before.[63] A world of information at your fingertips is indeed the essence of the Internet. For centuries reporters have thrived upon information. Indeed, they have enjoyed greater access to public officials and records since the profession began. But no class of citizens has a monopoly on the information made available on the Internet, and now individual citizens may bypass information intermediaries and interpreters by going straight to the original sources themselves.

The importance of the Internet for affording citizens greater access to information cannot be gainsaid. The FEC has ruled that organizations desiring to publicize nonpartisan political information about policy issues as well as candidates for public office may do so on the Internet without government restriction.[64] As a result, the Web has supercharged the ability of citizens to obtain information about politics and government. Popular informational websites include Dnet.org (sponsored by the League of Women Voters) and Vote-Smart.org, both of which compile biographical and related information about candidates and issues.

As a result, information that just a decade ago was beyond the reach of an ordinary citizen, today is at every person's fingertips. Voting records of officeholders, for example, were embedded in congressional records located in libraries or filtered through interest groups that rated only a dozen or so votes each year. Now, voting records on all issues are readily available on numerous websites.

Candidates' disclosures of campaign contributions and expenditures were originally touted as the public's primary check against corruption and "vote-buying" by large contributors,[65] but few citizens could locate each candidate's voluminous finance reports that were archived in filing cabinets and microfiche reels in out-of-the-way election board offices. Voters only occasionally learned about who donated to whom through random news articles. Today, a citizen can look up all contributions to a candidate as well as each contributor's total donations at sites such as PoliticalMoneyLine.com (collecting all federal contributions in a searchable database) and VPAP.org (collecting all state contributions in Virginia elections).

In short, the Internet has made a plethora of information available to the average citizen, and this information will make government more accountable to citizens in the new century.

Voting Online

Although "butterfly" and punch-card ballots received all of the attention in the 2000 presidential election, the Internet made its own remarkable debut as a voting machine. In March 2000, the Arizona Democratic Party sponsored the first presidential primary election that permitted citizens to cast their ballots via the Internet. Of the 85,970 primary voters, 39,942, or 41 percent, cast their votes on their personal computers.[66] Another 32,747 voters, or 38 percent, voted from home by mailing their ballots.[67]

The notion of a wide-scale democratic election's being conducted over the Internet is probably decades off in the United States (see Chapter 9 for more discussion of Internet voting). Practical obstacles include the fact that fewer than 60 percent of American households currently have access to the Internet.[68] Senior citizens, minorities and less affluent Americans comprise a disproportionate percentage of those without access.[69] This situation raises significant issues of equity.[70] Another challenge is ballot integrity. Although Arizona employed admirable security measures, including personal identification numbers (PINs) and personal questions to validate each voter's identity,[71] the trend in other states has been to require voter identification in person at the polls.[72] Still, the prospect of this technology's facilitating more elections like the Arizona Democratic primary of 2000 is well within the realm of the possible. Absentee balloting via the Internet, in lieu of voting by mail, might present the best proving ground for Internet voting in the coming years.

How Will the Internet Change Democracy?

The short answer to this question is: *However we let it.* In so many ways the Internet has eclipsed the current system of campaign finance regulation. The challenge for political scientists and civic-minded citizens is how to rethink an old regulatory regime as applied to a ubiquitous new technological medium and the political speech and association it facilitates.

There are different avenues through which a disconnect between old law and new cultural or technological developments can be reconciled. One way is the way the FEC appears to be proceeding today—on a case-by-case, incremental basis. This may present a safe approach and allow regulators time to assess the many new technological advances and practical uses of the Internet before inadvertently opening a gaping regulatory loophole. It also avoids a medium-specific regulatory approach some find shortsighted. But the incremental approach sows years of confusion in the field and chills much legitimate political activity while regulators study and plod. Alternatively, Congress or the FEC could conduct a systematic overhaul of existing laws or regulations with particular reference to the Internet. At least the FEC could lay down some bold new principles regarding when Internet speech is subject to regulation and when it is not, and the FEC could base that principle in the notion of expenditures of dollars instead of leaving everyone confused over market "values" or other values attributed to otherwise free communication. And yet another way that legal disconnects often are revealed through litigation is in courts. But litigation to vindicate constitutional rights is expensive, slow, and often too incremental.

Regardless of the process by which legal change occurs, the Internet's unique ability to empower candidates, citizens, and organizations to speak and associate on behalf of political causes should be embraced by public policy. Moreover, the low cost of Internet communication should challenge an old regulatory paradigm fixated on large expenditures of money sufficiently to justify a new paradigm: that government will regulate only large and identifiable expenditures for speech, but otherwise not seek to regulate the speech itself. That is, the FEC should make clear that it does not regulate speech on the Internet, only expenditures for speech on the Internet. Since the vast majority of political speech and activity on the Internet costs very little, such a new paradigm would leave the Internet largely a regulatory free zone for democratic engagement and speech.

What one hopes may emerge is a virtual free market of ideas and political causes. Ideas for public policy and elections would rise or fall on their merit and popular appeal without regard to whether they were published by established politicians and political parties, or the wealthiest corporations and established press, or the humblest of community activists, or even an individual citizen posting her opinions from a personal computer sitting on top of a kitchen table. And even the most obscure candidates—whether former governors or ordinary citizens—might find they can communicate their ideas and attract a national following as effectively as the most established and well-funded politicians. Is this kind of democratization possible? It just may be.

Notes

1. Schram, *Running for President 1976*, pp. 55–61.
2. Ibid., pp. 56–57.
3. Carter officially declared his candidacy on December 12, 1974. Ibid., p. 64.
4. Ibid.
5. Ibid., p. 72.
6. Pew Internet and American Life Project, *The Ever-Shifting Internet Population*; United States Department of Commerce, *A Nation Online*; CyberAtlas, *Population Explosion!* (citing Central Intelligence Agency and Nielsen data and available online at www.cyberatlas.com).
7. True, "Presidential Candidates Cast for Votes in Cyberspace."
8. Cummings, "The E-Team—Behind the Dean Surge," p. 1A.
9. Convio, Inc. "Howard Dean Uses Convio."
10. Ibid.
11. Ibid.
12. Weiss, "Democrat Howard Dean Strikes an Online Chord with Campaign" (quoting Carol Baroudi, author of *Internet for Dummies*).
13. 64 Fed. Reg. 60360 (Nov. 5, 1999).
14. Tillman Act of 1907, 34 Stat. 864 (1907).
15. Labor Management Relations Act of 1947 (codified at 29 U.S.C. § 141 *et seq.*).
16. 2 U.S.C. § 431 *et. seq.*
17. *Buckley v.* Valeo, 424 U.S. 1 (1976).
18. Ibid., pp. 14, 19.
19. Ibid., p. 25.
20. Ibid., pp. 25–26.
21. Ibid., pp. 48–49 (internal quotations omitted).
22. Ibid., p. 27.
23. Ibid., pp. 14, 19.

24. *First National Bank of Boston v. Bellotti*, 435 U.S. 765 (1977).

25. *Austin v. Michigan Chamber of* Commerce, 494 U.S. 652 (1990).

26. Ibid., pp. 659–660.

27. *McIntyre v. Ohio Elections Commission*, 514 U.S. 334 (1995).

28. 66 Fed. Reg. 50358, 50365-66 (Oct. 3, 2001) (codified at 11 C.F.R. § 117.3).

29. Ibid.

30. FEC Matter Under Review 4340 (1998) (Tweezerman).

31. See, for example, FEC Advisory Opinion 1999-37 (X-PAC) (regulating only out-of-pocket expenditures "directly attributed to a particular communication" over the Internet); FEC Advisory Opinion 1998-22 (Leo Smith) (regulating only the actual costs incurred to create and maintain a website).

32. See, for example, Comment, "Election Law and the Internet" ("postings are a direct grant to the candidate of something with economic value"), p. 723.

33. FEC Advisory Opinion 1999-7 (the "issue would turn on whether or not the owner of the web page providing the link would normally charge for the providing of such a link").

34. Ibid.

35. 2 U.S.C. § 431(9)(B)(i). The Federal Election Campaign Act and FEC regulations contain several corollary statements of the "media exemption." For example, the Bipartisan Campaign Reform Act of 2002 added a new restriction against certain kinds of "electioneering communications" but explicitly exempted the media: "The term 'electioneering communication' does not include a communication appearing in a news story, commentary, or editorial distributed through the facilities of any broadcasting station, unless such facilities are owned or controlled by any political party, political committee, or candidate." 2 U.S.C. § 434(f)(3)(B)(i). For other statements of the "media exemption," see 11 C.F.R. §§ 100.33(c)(2), 100.73, & 100.132.

36. H.R. Rep. No. 93-1239, 93d Congress, 2d Sess. at 4 (1974).

37. FEC Advisory Opinions 1998-17 (Daniels Cablevision), 1982-44 (Turner Broadcasting and WTBS).

38. FEC Advisory Opinion 2000-13 (EXBTV and iNEXTV).

39. FEC Advisory Opinion 1996-16 (Bloomberg media affiliates).

40. FEC Matter Under Review 486.

41. FEC Matter Under Review 3500.

42. FEC Matter Under Review 3624.

43. FEC Matter Under Review 3931.

44. FEC Matter Under Review 3660.

45. FEC Matter Under Review 3607.

46. FEC Advisory Opinion 1982-44.

47. See *Federal Election Commission v. Phillips Publishing*, 517 F.Supp. 1308, 1312-1313 (D.D.C. 1981); *Readers Digest Association v. Federal Election Commission*, 509 F.Supp. 1210, 1214 (S.D.N.Y. 1981).

48. *Federal Election Commission v. Massachusetts Citizens for Life, Inc.*, 479 U.S. 238 (1986).

49. *McConnell v. Federal Election Commission*, 540 U.S. 102 (2003).

50. Compare FEC Matter Under Review 3607 (where the FEC ruled Northwest Airlines, a nontraditional media corporation, was afforded the "media exemption" for its in-flight magazine) to FEC Matter Under Review 5315 (where FEC commissioners split over the question of whether Sam's Club's monthly magazine would qualify).

51. 11 C.F.R. §§ 100.74 (personal volunteer time), 100.75 (personal residences), and 100.79 (personal vehicles).

52. FEC Advisory Opinion 1999-17 (Bush for President Exploratory Committee).

53. Garrett, "Political Intermediaries and the Internet 'Revolution,'" p. 1055 ("[T]he Internet will not so transform our system that it will look radically different in the next ten, fifteen, or twenty years.").

54. Morris, "Direct Democracy and the Internet," p. 1033 ("The Internet offers a potential for direct democracy so profound that it may well transform not only our system of politics but also our very form of government.").

55. Ibid., pp. 1036–1038.

56. Ibid., p. 1042.

57. Milbank, "Virtual Politics," p. 22.

58. I served as policy director to the Gilmore for Governor campaign and was instrumental in creating the website's content and tax-savings calculator in 1997.

59. *Buckley*, 424 U.S., pp. 43–44 and n. 52.

60. Taylor and Tumulty, "Internet Politics," p. 32.

61. Eisenberg, "Buckley, Rupert Murdoch, and the Pursuit of Equality in the Conduct of Elections," pp. 451, 459–460.

62. Institute for Politics, Democracy, and the Internet, *The Virtual Trail*.

63. Ibid., p. 71.

64. FEC Advisory Opinion 1999-25 (Democracy Net); FEC Advisory Opinion 1999-24 (Election Zone).

65. *Buckley*, 424, pp. 65–67.

66. Alvarez and Nagler, "The Likely Consequences of Internet Voting for Political Representation," pp. 1115, 1135–1137.

67. Ibid., p. 1138.

68. Pew Internet and American Life Project, *The Ever-Shifting Internet Population*; United States Department of Commerce, *A Nation Online*.

69. Ibid.

70. See Alvarez and Nagler, "The Likely Consequences of Internet Voting for Political Representation," pp. 1144–1148 ("the results . . . demonstrate clearly that these people on the wrong side of the digital divide—women, the elderly, the nonwhite, the unemployed, and rural residents—were less likely to use the Internet to vote in the 2000 Arizona Democratic Presidential Primary").

71. Ibid., p. 1137.

72. See, for example, Va. Code § 24.2-643 (Virginia law requiring voters to appear at the polling place, have their names called out loud, and present a valid identification card).

8

Defining Voters' Rights: Equal Protection and the Impact of *Bush v. Gore*

Evan Gerstmann

The Supreme Court's decision in *Bush v. Gore* blocked a crucial electoral recount in Florida and effectively made George W. Bush the winner of the 2000 presidential election. It has been, by far, the most controversial judicial decision since the Supreme Court ruled that the Constitution protected a woman's right to an abortion. Not even the recent decision protecting the sexual privacy of gays and lesbians or the case challenging the constitutionality of including "under God" in the pledge of allegiance has generated the volume of angry response that greeted *Bush v. Gore*. A leading political journal offered one of the tamer critiques of the decision, calling it a "disgrace." A prominent commentator argued that the only way the decision might have been justified would be if the case had been called "*Bush v. Hitler*." Another constitutional scholar called the Supreme Court majority responsible for the decision "absolute, utter, contemptible fools."[1] Alan Dershowitz, a Harvard law professor and perhaps the best known legal scholar in the country, none too subtly titled his book on the decision *Supreme Injustice: How the Court Hijacked Election 2000*. Even the more polite critics of the decision have described it as "astonishingly egregious," among other things.

On the other side of the argument, there are those who defend the Court's decision and accuse the critics themselves of becoming too enraged over the controversy. One of the country's leading conservative legal scholars, Richard Posner, has said:

> The precipitance and shallowness of many of these criticisms cast a shadow over constitutional law as a subject of law school teaching and research. As an academic field, constitutional law is both overpoliticized and underspecialized. . . . Professors of constitutional law have little command of the full range of subjects encompassed by modern constitutional law. Their reaction

to a subject within that range that eludes their understanding tends to be driven by their politics rather than by their expertise.[2]

Although Posner may be correct in stating that the majority of constitutional law experts are more likely to be on the liberal end of the political spectrum, it should be noted that even the defenders of the decision, often political conservatives, have been less than enthusiastic about it. Even Posner himself admitted that the reasoning given by the Court for its decision "is not a persuasive ground."[3] Noted conservative constitutional law expert Richard Epstein defended what the Court did, but as for the reasons the Court gave for its decision, Epstein said, "Quite simply, I regard that argument as a confused nonstarter at best, which deserves much of the scorn that has been heaped upon it."[4] The conservative legal scholar and former law school president Terrance Sandalow called the decision "incomprehensible."[5] John Yoo praised the Court for putting "an end to the destructive partisan struggle . . . that . . . threatened to spiral out of control."[6] Paul A. Gigot commended the Court for having "saved the country another month of fighting before reaching the same result."[7] Charles Krauthammer argued that the Court saved the election from being turned "into a lawyers' contest."[8] Nonetheless, "few conservative commentators have undertaken the onerous burden of defending *Bush* on its merits."[9]

The degree of vitriol by all of these constitutional heavyweights indicates the importance and controversial nature of the decision. The purpose of this chapter is to help the reader understand exactly what happened in Florida during the 2000 election, what the Court did, and why it was so controversial and important. First, however, we begin with some legal and historical context so that we may better understand what happened.

Our Not-So-Democratic Constitution

Most people are aware that our nation's founding fathers were ambivalent about democracy and popular empowerment. They were leery of monarchy, of course, and the American Revolution was founded upon the principle that all men were created equal. Yet the framers of the Constitution feared placing too much power directly in the hands of the people. Some of those fears lay in the possibility of a newly empowered citizenry confiscating or devaluing the property of the nation's economic elite. Other concerns were not based upon class politics, however, but rather upon legitimate concerns that few people would have the knowledge to make an informed decision in a national election. Roads at that time were often little more than pitted, dirt pathways that were slow and grueling to navigate. Few people traveled more than twenty miles from their homes and were extremely unlikely to have met, seen, or heard any of the candidates for national office. Thus, the Constitution calls for the president to be chosen by a body of well-informed delegates: the Electoral College.

Even though many people are aware of the Electoral College, most are surprised to discover that the Constitution does not even grant the people the right to vote for the electors themselves. Under Article II of the Constitution, the power to appoint electors belongs to the state legislatures. This procedure was created to assure that the president would be at least somewhat independent of Congress, but also that he would be insulated from public opinion by at least two levels of intervening bodies: the Electoral College and the state legislatures that chose the members of the College.

As of 1800, only two state legislatures saw fit to select presidential electors by popular vote. In the early 1800s, however, there was a powerful movement of popular sovereignty, and by 1836 every state but South Carolina allowed its citizens to choose the state's electoral slate by popular vote. Most important, every state but Maine and Nebraska now uses a winner-take-all system, in which the winner of the popular vote receives *all* of the state's electoral votes.[10] Thus, tiny electoral margins in a large state can make all the difference in a national presidential election.

Many people are also surprised to learn that the Constitution did *not* guarantee anybody the right to vote for any office. The framers did not require landownership to vote, but they let the states determine who could vote. The Fifteenth and Nineteenth Amendments made it illegal for states to prevent anyone from voting on the basis of their race or gender. Also, the Twenty-Fourth Amendment banned poll taxes in federal elections, and the Twenty-Sixth Amendment lowered the voting age to eighteen, but otherwise the Constitution is silent on the issue of who can vote. Most states, for example, have decided not to allow convicted felons to vote, and fourteen of those states *permanently* strip persons convicted of a felony from voting.

In order to fully understand the Supreme Court's decision in *Bush v. Gore*, next we must look at how the Supreme Court has reacted to the absence of explicit protection of voting rights in the Constitution. After the Civil War, Congress proposed, and the states ratified, the vitally important Fourteenth Amendment, which guaranteed, among other things, "due process of law" and "equal protection of the law." Although the Constitution explicitly guarantees many rights, such as freedom of speech and religion, the Supreme Court has long held that the broad language of the Fourteenth Amendment implicitly protects other "fundamental rights" that are not explicitly mentioned anywhere in the text of the Constitution. These rights include the right of reproductive freedom, the right to travel from state to state, the right to marry, and, perhaps most important, the right to vote.

It has never been exactly clear what "the right to vote" means. In 1960, the Court held that the right to vote includes the right to have one's vote count as much as any other person's vote. In a landmark case, *Baker v. Carr* (1962), the Court held that, under the equal protection clause, all of the districts from which state legislators are elected must be of equal population. The Court reasoned that if each district is entitled to one legislative representative, but some districts have many more people, each individual in the larger district has less voting power than each individual in the smaller district. So for a district with, say, 10,000 voters to have the same representation as a district with twice that many voters violates the idea of "one person, one vote." (See Chapter 10 for more on *Baker v. Carr*.)

The idea that the Fourteenth Amendment protects fundamental rights that are not explicitly mentioned in the Constitution has always been controversial. As many of these rights have liberal political implications—think of the implied right to have an abortion—conservative judges in particular have argued that these rights should be defined narrowly, if, indeed, they exist at all. As we will see, one of the reasons that *Bush v. Gore* has been so thoroughly lambasted is that the conservative Supreme Court justices who wrote and joined the majority opinion had long argued for a narrow interpretation of the equal protection clause and fundamental rights, only to rely upon a novel and broad understanding of the right to vote in that case. With this constitutional background in mind, we will now look at what exactly happened in Florida and what the Court did in response.

The 2000 Presidential Election and Its Aftermath

Although Al Gore won the popular vote by more than half a million votes, the race for the electoral votes needed to become president was extremely tight. Media outlets were embarrassed by their first calling the election for Gore, then for Bush, then declaring that the race was too close to call.

As election night turned into the next morning, it became evident that the election would be decided by which candidate won Florida. Like most states, Florida awards electoral votes on a winner-take-all basis, and the popular vote in Florida was also extremely close, meaning the prize of the presidency hinged on a small number of votes. The vote was so close that, under Florida law, there was an automatic machine recount that showed that barely 300 votes separated the two men out of nearly six million votes cast.

Adding to the confusion, the Votomatic punch-card machines used to tabulate votes in a number of counties were "'alarmingly unreliable,' with a failure rate of '4 percent or more,' . . . in an election decided by a mere fraction of 1 percent of the votes cast."[11] A reason for this error is that the now-famed "chads"—the pieces of paper that are punched out of the ballots to indicate the voter's choice of candidate—could accumulate and clog the machine. The Gore camp claimed that these clogs sometimes prevented voters from cleanly breaking through the cards, resulting in mere indentations or "dimples" in the ballot or, at best, chads that were still attached to the ballots by one, two, or three corners. The Gore camp also claimed that the Votomatic machines often failed to count the ballots with these "dimpled" or "hanging" chads.

As a result, the Gore camp invoked its right to a hand recount under Florida law. This law allows a candidate to seek a recount by hand in any county in which he or she can demonstrate that a preliminary hand count of at least 1 percent of the votes indicates an error serious enough to possibly affect the outcome of the election. Naturally, the Gore campaign invoked this right in several counties that were majority Democrat, where a hand count would be more likely to find additional votes for Gore.

Under Florida law, there was a deadline for the hand counts: they all had to be completed no more than seven days after the election. After that deadline the results of the election would be certified. There was much confusion about the meaning and effect of certification. After certification, the candidates could no longer *protest* the election, but they remained free to *contest* the election. The main difference between a protest and a contest is that protests are lodged with the County Canvassing Board whereas contests are made in state courts. These technical legal distinctions, as well as the various and conflicting deadlines in different state and federal laws, proved endlessly confusing to the candidates, the courts, and perhaps most of all to the press, which appeared to have a very difficult time understanding and explaining the issues to the public.

The Bush camp was obviously concerned that a recount that was taking place only in largely Democratic counties might erase the Republicans' already razor-thin margin. They decided to seek a federal injunction—an order from a federal judge stopping the hand recounts—and based their argument on the "right to vote." As noted, the Supreme Court has held that every person is entitled to an equal vote. The Bush camp pressed a theory that the "equal vote" requirement was violated by the Florida law that, as long interpreted by the Florida courts, directed the people doing the hand count to base their count on the "intent of the voter." Bush's lawyers argued that one person might count a hanging or dimpled chad as demonstrating the intent to vote for a certain candidate, whereas another person might not. The lawyers argued that the "intent of the voter" standard was so vague that it violated the principle that every person's vote should be equal. This was a novel theory of what the equal protection clause means, and the federal judge rejected it and refused to stop the hand count.

Meanwhile, there was also a great deal of legal wrangling between the Bush and Gore teams in the Florida state courts. The Florida Supreme Court ruled that the Florida secretary of state could not certify the election until there was a reasonable opportunity to complete the hand count, which would continue under the "intent of the voter" standard that Bush had unsuccessfully challenged in Federal court.

It was at this point that the U.S. Supreme Court entered the fray. The Court refused to consider Bush's equal protection claim that the "intent of the voter standard" violated the principle that every person's vote should be equal. It agreed to consider whether the Florida Supreme Court had violated the right of the Florida legislature to determine how Florida's delegation to the Electoral College should be chosen. On December 3, the U.S. Supreme Court held that the Florida Supreme Court had violated Article II of the U.S. Constitution by extending the deadline for certification of the vote. Recall that Article II leaves it to the state legislatures to decide how each state will choose delegates to the Electoral College. The U.S. Supreme Court ruled that when the Florida Supreme Court extended the certification deadline, it usurped from the state legislature the right to decide how electors are chosen.

In the meantime, the clock was running out on the Gore campaign. Federal law provides for a "safe harbor"—if a state makes its final decision as to who its electors will be at least six days before the Electoral College actually meets to select the next president, then that decision is final and cannot be challenged. In 2000, that "safe harbor" ended on December 12, and Gore was under intense pressure to prevail or concede by that date.

At the same time, a Florida lower court judge, N. Sanders Sauls, issued an order stopping *all* of the hand counts. On December 8, just four days before the "safe harbor" deadline would pass, the Florida Supreme Court reversed Sanders Sauls's ruling and ordered the hand counts to continue. They had to tread carefully though, as the U.S. Supreme Court had just warned them against doing anything that might be construed as altering the law as passed by the Florida legislature. Therefore, in *Gore v. Harris* the Florida Supreme Court's opinion carefully tracked the language of Florida Statute 101.5614(5) and ruled as follows: "In tabulating the ballots and in making a determination of what is a 'legal' vote, the standard to be employed is that established by the Legislature in our Election Code which is that the vote shall be counted as a 'legal' vote if there is a 'clear indication of the intent of the voter.'"[12] The next day, Saturday, December 9, the U.S. Supreme Court, in a 5–4 decision, stayed all recounts, dealing Gore an extremely serious setback in his quest to have the ballots hand counted on a timely basis. Gore had argued over and over again that every vote should be counted and that, without a hand count, the votes not registered by Votomatic machines would never be counted at all. The Supreme Court's stay of all hand counts surprised many political and legal experts. Normally a court will only issue an injunction if the party seeking the injunction can demonstrate that they are about to suffer an "irreparable harm"—in other words, a harm so great that it can never be repaired or adequately compensated. For example, a court might enjoin someone from doing something that represented a serious threat to the life or health of the party seeking the injunction. By this standard, few experts could see what irreparable harm the hand counts could cause George W. Bush. Justice

Antonin Scalia wrote that the recounts might cast a "cloud" over Bush's presidency, but most experts considered that sort of vague prediction to fall far short of the kind of harm that is needed for an injunction. Furthermore, it ignored the harm caused to Gore by *not* doing the hand counts: without those hand counts, it was impossible to know if Gore actually won more votes than Bush in Florida. So the stay was extremely surprising, but what the Court did next was even more shocking and resulted in the heated controversy described in the beginning this chapter.

The Majority Decision by the U.S. Supreme Court

The Supreme Court consists of nine justices, and an opinion joined by any five of them is the Court's "majority opinion," which is the opinion that counts. All other opinions, known as concurring or dissenting opinions, are simply there to express various justices' disagreement or comments about the reasoning or holding of the majority decision. The Supreme Court issued six different opinions, including the majority opinion and various dissents and concurrences. For the sake of clarity, this chapter will discuss only the five-justice majority opinion that ended the hand counts and essentially declared George W. Bush the winner.

The opinion was handed down on the night of December 12, the end of the "safe harbor" period. It immediately provoked a storm of controversy, not only because it effectively decided the outcome of the election but also because it was so unusual in many aspects and because the five justices responsible for it are widely regarded as the most politically conservative judges on the Court. One surprising aspect of the decision was that it was not based upon the Article II grounds that the Court had relied on in its earlier injunction. In other words, the decision did not address whether the Florida Supreme Court had usurped authority from the Florida legislature. Instead, the five-justice majority based its decision on the much maligned equal protection rationale explained above.

The Court held that the recount process violated the fundamental right to vote: "having once granted the right to vote on equal terms, the state may not, by later arbitrary and disparate treatment, value one person's vote over that of another."[13] According to the majority opinion, the Florida hand counts violated the fundamental right to vote for a number of reasons. Different counties used various standards in evaluating the intent of the voter. Further, one county changed its standards during the recount. Also, different officials within the same county sometimes used different standards for determining the clear intent of the voter. The Supreme Court concluded that these inconsistencies meant different counties and different officials could end up treating identical ballots differently. The Court held that the only way the hand counts would not violate the right to vote would be if Florida adopted uniform standards as to how to judge the intent of the voter and practical procedures for implementing those standards. Finally, the Court held that any recount would have to be completed before the "safe harbor" period expired. Since the decision was handed down at 10:00 P.M. on December 12, this meant that any hand count would have to be completed within the next two hours! Obviously that was impossible; therefore the decision marked the end of the dispute and effectively decided the election in favor of George W. Bush.

Bush v. Gore and the Question of Law Versus Politics

Apart from its important result of selecting Bush as president, the *Bush v. Gore* decision has been so controversial because many view the case as violating the most basic principles of the legal system. Much was made of the fact that the majority was composed of the Court's most conservative justices, who issued a ruling that happened to put the much more conservative of the two candidates in the Oval Office. The fact that Bush would now be the one appointing the judges' future colleagues only added to speculation that the scales of justice were far from balanced in this case.

Such perceptions, if true, represent a serious threat to the rule of law in this country. "The ideal of 'the rule of law, not of men' expresses the norm that law itself should govern us, not the wishes of powerful individuals or groups."[14] A fundamental requirement of a fair and just legal system is that the outcome of a case be the product of even-handed application of preexisting, public law to the facts at hand. For the judges to favor a particular party over the other or to bend the law to achieve a certain result is a betrayal of the very foundations of our legal system. Hundreds of legal scholars have accused the *Bush v. Gore* majority of betraying these fundamental principles. More than 600 law professors signed a statement published in the *New York Times* stating: "By stopping the vote count in Florida, the U.S. Supreme Court used its power to act as political partisans, not as judges of a court of law. . . . The five Justices were acting as political proponents for candidate Bush, not as Judges."[15] Stanford law professor Margaret Jane Radin put it especially pointedly, asking "Can the Rule of Law Survive *Bush v. Gore*?"[16]

Why were so many experts convinced that the justices had defied the rule of law and placed their own political preferences above fair-minded application of the law? After all, *Bush v. Gore* was hardly the first time that the conservative five-justice majority had voted together, producing a decision with conservative political implications. Liberal judges have also voted for liberal results without generating the anger and criticism directed at the *Bush v. Gore* majority. One reason was what Posner described as the "gotcha" nature of the decision.[17] Recall that when the Supreme Court first stayed the hand count, it did so on the theory that the Florida Supreme Court violated Article II of the Constitution by usurping the authority of the Florida legislature. The Court declined to even address Bush's argument that the "intent of the voter" standard of the recount violated the equal protection clause. Indeed, by focusing on what should be the limited role of the Florida courts, the Supreme Court arguably warned the Florida courts away from any rulemaking that would have created clearer standards for the hand count but might have been viewed as usurping the lawmaking power of the Florida legislature. The action of the Supreme Court, first ruling that the role of the Florida courts should be limited and then, at the last minute, adopting a completely new legal theory that would have required the Florida courts to take an active role in directing the recount, led many to believe that the Court had created an impossible situation.

Further, the reasoning of the majority opinion rested on a novel and expansive interpretation of the right to vote that is contrary to the usual judicial philosophy of the justices who joined it. The five majority justices have all advocated, at various times, the philosophy of judicial restraint: as the Court is not democratically elected or accountable, it should not create expansive new rights that are not firmly rooted in the text of the Constitution. In the name of judicial restraint, the judges have refused to hold that school funding systems that discriminate against the poor violate the equal protection clause. Justices advocating judicial restraint have also upheld laws that discriminate against gays, lesbians, and the elderly.

Indeed, the five justices who voted in favor in *Bush* had a long history of voting for a very narrow interpretation of the equal protection clause. For example, Justice Sandra Day O'Connor, one of the five majority justices in *Bush v. Gore*, has consistently held that only *intentional* discrimination violates the equal protection clause.[18] In a case in which civil rights groups demonstrated that defendants who killed white victims were far more likely to receive the death penalty than defendants who killed African American victims, O'Connor voted to allow numerous executions to go forward anyway, because there was no proof of intentional discrimination. The contrast between her reasoning in that case and in the *Bush v. Gore* decision, which not only did not require a showing of intentional discrimination but was based on the mere *speculation* that some voters might face discrimination, is stark. Justice Anthony Kennedy has a voting record similar to O'Connor's on death penalty cases and has also emphasized that the equal protection clause protects only against intentional discrimination against an identifiable group of victims. Yet, he was also a member of the five-justice majority in *Bush v. Gore*. Chief Justice William Rehnquist has often asserted that the Court should not require that all laws have to be fair or perfect under the equal protection clause. In 1977, Rehnquist wrote: "In providing the Court with the duty of enforcing such generalities as the Equal Protection Clause, the Framers of the Civil War Amendments [including the Fourteenth Amendment] placed it in the position of Adam in the Garden of Eden . . . we are constantly subjected to the human temptation to hold that any law containing a number of imperfections denies equal protection simply because those who drafted it could have made it a fairer or better."[19] There is much to admire about the philosophy of judicial restraint, but it requires consistency to have genuine meaning. Rehnquist's words, although eloquent, hardly seemed to point to the sort of adventurous theorizing about the equal protection clause that underlies the majority decision in *Bush v. Gore*.

There was another very unusual aspect of the ruling. Although the decision broke new ground in interpreting the equal protection clause, the majority made it clear that they did not want other courts to apply the reasoning of the decision to other cases. The majority wrote: "Our consideration is limited to the present circumstances, for the problem of equal protection in election processes generally presents many complexities."[20] This statement also contradicted the fundamental premises of the rule of law. In a society governed by law, rather than by the whim or preferences of the powerful, courts must decide the cases before them according to legal principles that they are obligated to apply again and again. This vital rule of law principle makes the law more certain and predictable and also makes it fairer. This requirement that courts decide cases according to legal principles that will have to be applied in the future is a powerful tool to prevent judges from simply imposing their will upon society. For example, courts have upheld the free speech rights of members of the Nazi Party to march and wear swastikas despite the fact that the vast majority of judges presumably hold Nazis and all that they stand for in contempt. But if the courts rule that speech can be suppressed merely because it is unpopular or politically incorrect, they know that ruling can come back to haunt them when other unpopular groups, such as pro-life protesters in a liberal city or Muslim groups after the September 11 terrorist attacks, seek to exercise their free speech rights. It is a bitter pill for the courts to swallow when they have to let Nazis march (in one case the Nazis deliberately targeted a town with many Jewish Holocaust survivors), but the judges have to avoid the temptation to decide what ideas and values can be expressed because the rule of law does not allow them to pick and choose based upon their own political preferences.

Ironically, one of the most articulate advocates of this vital principle has been none other than Justice Antonin Scalia, who joined the majority opinion in *Bush v. Gore*. In 1989, Scalia wrote: "When, in writing for the majority of the Court, I adopt a general rule, and say, 'this is the basis of our decision,' I not only constrain lower courts, I constrain myself as well. If the next case should have such different facts that my political or policy preferences regarding the outcomes are quite the opposite, I will be unable to indulge those preferences; I have committed myself to the governing principle."[21] This is exactly what many people perceived the problem to be with *Bush v. Gore*. It did *not* commit itself to its own governing principle. As will be discussed below, it is not clear whether the Supreme Court even has the power to limit the reach of its own decisions in this way. But the fact that the majority has tried to do so fueled criticism of the decision.

Law in a Time of Crisis

One response to the Court's decision in *Bush v. Gore* might be a cynicism about the law and courts in general. If courts simply impose their own policy preferences on us without regard for what they have always said about the law, then are the courts not just another group of politicians and lobbyists hiding behind judges' robes? But such a response would doubtless be too cynical by far. In fact, the Supreme Court does care about legal principle and often is willing to apply those principles fairly, even when the result produces outcomes that they probably do not favor on policy grounds. The same Court that decided *Bush v. Gore* also decided cases with decidedly liberal results, based, as far as one can tell, on even-handed application of legal principles. For example, the Court struck down laws that criminalize homosexual sodomy. It also issued decisions limiting the death penalty. So the Court *is* often willing to place law over politics.

Because this is the case, a question many are asking is what happened in *Bush v. Gore*? The most likely answer is that the Court perceived the election as hopelessly deadlocked, with little likelihood of the hand counts producing a clear resolution. Faced with the prospect of continuing hand counts and yet more legal disputes as the nation had only a lame duck president and no clear successor, the Court probably felt the need to act quickly and forcefully to bring a conclusion to the disputed election. Chief Justice Rehnquist probably believed this. Defending the Supreme Court's controversial role in another disputed presidential election, between Hayes and Tilden in 1876, Rehnquist said, "There is a national crisis and only you can avert it. It may be very hard to say no."[22]

In fact, the most common defense of *Bush v. Gore* is not on its legal merits, but rather praise for the Court for making a clear decision in a time of impending national crisis. Posner argued that if the Court had not intervened, there would have been "a potential political and constitutional crisis by allowing the deadlock to continue past December 12 [the safe harbor date] and probably past December 18 [the date the Electoral College casts its votes] as well or even January 6 [the date Congress meets to count the electoral votes and formally declare the winner of the Presidential election]."[23] Justice Robert Jackson once famously wrote that "the Constitution is not a suicide pact,"[24] and if the Court truly believed that the nation was lurching toward a genuine crisis, it must have believed that there was a strong argument for putting pragmatism ahead of legal principle.

Yet, the weight of history suggests that courts should be cautious about elevating pragmatism over principle, even in times of perceived crisis. In fact, history suggests that it is during times of crisis that we most need the restraint of the rule of law. During World War I and the panic over the Russian Revolution, the Court, responding to the sense of crisis, upheld harsh prison terms for citizens who did no more than criticize the draft and the government. The Supreme Court even allowed the imprisonment of presidential candidate Eugene Debs for giving an antiwar speech. During World War II, the attack on Pearl Harbor and sense of panic over the possibility of a Japanese attack on California led the Court to uphold the shameful internment and exclusion of U.S. citizens who happened to be of Japanese descent. Although the United States indeed faced powerful and dangerous foes during World War II, much evidence has emerged over the years that the Japanese were taken from their homes largely owing to economic jealousies and racism, not legitimate national security reasons.

Further, it is far from clear that the Florida deadlock was a true impending crisis, and it certainly was not a crisis comparable to the level of World War II. Even assuming the worst-case scenario—Florida *never* agreeing on which slate of delegates to send to the Electoral College—federal law (the Electoral Count Act, now known as Title III) explicitly authorizes Congress to determine the outcome of the election. Posner argued that Congress would have been ill equipped to head off a constitutional crisis: "[H]ad the responsibility for determining who would be President fallen to Congress in January, there would have been a competition in indignation between the parties' supporters, with each side accusing the other of having stolen the election . . . that there was a real and disturbing *potential* for disorder and temporary paralysis (I do not want to exaggerate) seems undeniable."[25]

But even this is a highly speculative claim. Jeffrey Rosen, comparing the performance of Congress and the courts in handling the impeachment proceeding and lawsuits resulting from President Clinton's sexual dalliances, argued that Congress would have been a more competent institution to resolve the 2000 election deadlock if Florida had been unable to resolve it itself:

> Posner's contempt for Congress has blinded him to the fact that it is better equipped than the Court to resolve disputes that involve a mix of political and constitutional questions. In fact Congress—at least the Senate—did relatively well in adjudicating the presidential impeachment, and in balancing the complicated mix of political and constitutional questions that are inevitably implicated by a decision about whether or not to remove the president. Certainly, the Senate did far better than the Supreme Court, whose overconfident and unfounded prediction that the *Jones* case "appears to us highly unlikely to occupy any substantial amount of petitioner's time" stands as a daunting reminder of the shortcomings of ivory tower judges who fancy themselves to be armchair empiricists.[26]

The Future Implications of *Bush v. Gore*

Regardless of the merits of the Court's equal protection analysis or whether the Supreme Court, Congress, or the state of Florida was the best forum to break the election deadlock, one thing is certain: the deed is done. The question now is "what happens next?"

As one law professor has written: "But even if the *Bush v. Gore* opinion's reasoning is crucially flawed, due to intellectual dishonesty, haste or some other cause, it still represents binding case law which lower courts are bound to follow. Even the Supreme Court itself might feel pressure to follow it in some fashion, if, for no other reason than to rebut charges that it was acting in a result oriented manner."[27]

As noted, the Court itself has tried to limit the effect of its decision, saying that the decision was limited to the "present circumstances" of the 2000 presidential election. But it is far from clear that even the Supreme Court has the power to limit the reach of its own decision. Whether it likes it or not, the Court has created the principle that the right to vote, implied under the equal protection clause, is violated by irrational or arbitrary methods of vote counting. Although the Court emphasized the unique circumstances of a statewide recount, there is no apparent reason that the Court's "count all votes equally" principle should not apply to elections within a congressional district or state legislative district. *Bush v. Gore* did take place in the context of a *presidential* election, but there is nothing in the history of constitutional law that implies that the right to vote applies any less to, say, congressional elections than it does to presidential elections.

So *Bush v. Gore* has enormous potential consequences because from county to county there is wide variation in how votes are counted and what sort of technology is used to count these votes. For example, some counties utilize state-of-the-art electronic scanners while others use old-fashioned punch-card technology. Not surprisingly, the error rate is significantly greater using older technology.[28] If humans counting votes differently violates the equal protection clause, then it is difficult to see why different machines with different error rates would not also violate the Constitution. Since *Bush v. Gore*, lawsuits have been filed in federal courts in Florida, Illinois, California, and Georgia alleging that the use of error-prone technology to count votes in some districts violates the right to vote. Many of these cases allege that the disparities in voting technology have the effect of discriminating along racial and economic class lines, although that empirical claim remains to be proven, and there is some evidence to the contrary.[29] In at least one case, *Common Cause v. Jones* in California, the federal judge ordered that outdated voting technology be replaced. As of late 2003, fifty-four California counties had plans to purchase some $400 million worth of new voting equipment.[30] In Florida, the state legislature outlawed the use of punch-card ballots.

Perhaps the most notorious legal consequence of *Bush v. Gore* is that a three-judge panel of the Ninth Circuit Court of Appeals postponed the 2003 gubernatorial recall election in California. Repeatedly citing *Bush v. Gore*, the Ninth Circuit held that the recall election could not take place until six California counties had time to switch over from error-prone punch-card technology for counting ballots. An eleven-judge panel of the same court quickly overturned that decision. But the reasoning of the eleven-judge panel centered on the fact that it was too late to change the technology without seriously disrupting the election, not necessarily that the current technology was acceptable. Therefore, it appears likely that litigation, or at least the threat of litigation, will prompt many states to equalize access to the best and most accurate voting technology. If the litigants in these cases are correct that the outdated technology is more prevalent in poor and minority districts (again this claim is still in dispute nationally, but in California the counties that were affected had higher minority and poor populations), this could provide a major boost for the Democratic Party's chances of winning numerous close elections in the future, at both the state and federal level. Such a result would be an ironic but important reminder that in the field of constitutional law, not even the Supreme Court is at liberty to decide cases without giving serious thought to the legal principle they are creating, no matter how tempting the short-term results of a particular decision may be.

Notes

1. The preceding quotes came from Fried, "Unreasonable Reaction," p. 4.
2. Posner, *Breaking the Deadlock*, pp. 4–5.
3. Ibid., p. 128.
4. Epstein, "In Such Manner," p. 14.
5. Quoted in Dershowitz, *Supreme Injustice*, p. 83.
6. Yoo, "In Defense of the Court's Legitimacy," p. 775.
7. Gigot, "Liberals Discover," p. A16.
8. Krauthammer, "Defenders of the Law," p. A41.
9. Klarman, "*Bush v. Gore*," p. 1721.
10. Maine and Nebraska use a district system. If a candidate wins a plurality of the vote in a congressional district, that district's elector pledges to the candidate. The winner statewide receives the two bonus electoral votes.
11. Dershowitz, *Supreme Injustice*, p. 27.
12. *Gore v. Harris*, 772 So. 2d 1243 (2000), p. 1262.
13. *Bush v. Gore*, 531 U.S. 98 (2000), p. 104.
14. Radin, "Can the Rule of Law," p. 111.
15. *New York Times*, 13 January 2001, p. A7.
16. Radin, "Can the Rule of Law."
17. Posner, *Breaking the Deadlock*, p. 150.
18. For example, see *McCleskey v. Kemp*.
19. Quoted in Dershowitz, *Supreme Injustice*, pp. 144–145.
20. 531 U.S. 98, p. 109.

21. Scalia, "The Rule of Law," pp. 1179–1180.
22. Rosen, "Political Questions," p. 150.
23. Posner, *Breaking the Deadlock*, p. 168.
24. *Terminiello v. Chicago,* 337 U.S. 1 (1949), p. 37.
25. Posner, *Breaking the Deadlock,* p. 143.
26. Rosen, "Political Questions," p. 157.
27. Mulroy, "Lemonade from Lemons," p. 364.
28. Ibid.
29. See Knack and Kropf, "Who Uses Inferior Voting Technology?"
30. Reiterman and Nicholas, "Ex-Officials Now Behind New Voting Machines."

9

The Voting Rights Act: Addressing Age-Old Barriers in a New Milieu

Antonio Brown

Since its inception, the United States has struggled with the rights of franchise. Women, men, rich, poor, African descent, Caucasian, Latino, Asian, non-English speakers, and so many others—who among them deserves the right to vote in a nation founded on the principles of democracy? For many of us the answer appears self-evident. The legitimate existence of our free society seems dependent on a simple, straightforward principle, "one person, one vote." But, as you may have heard, appearances can be deceiving: Enter the Voting Rights Act of 1965 (VRA).

This monumental civil rights legislation was noted by President Lyndon B. Johnson as one of the greatest and most significant contributions to society completed during his tenure. Arguably, it is one of the most clearly influential and enduring developments related to the civil rights movement. Yet it has not endured without challenges and changes. Traditionally, among the most controversial interpretations regarding the VRA are those relating to redistricting and vote dilution (see Chapter 10). They are certainly not the only important aspects of the legislation, however. In this chapter, I examine the challenges that physical and technological barriers, two other issues addressed in the VRA, pose for equality of franchise historically and contemporarily. With that in mind, I will review the obstacles to suffrage posed by the events of the 2000 presidential election and the voting rights issues raised by the California recall election of 2003. But first, let's review some of the history related to the development of the VRA.

The Voting Rights Act: Balancing Race, Rights, and Regulations

Few people of African descent were enfranchised prior to the Civil War. During centuries of enslavement in America, African descent men and women were routinely denied the right to vote. There were exceptions from the time of the framing of the Constitution through the early nineteenth century. During that period there were small numbers of free black men in the North and South who were allowed to vote.[1] Yet, by the time of the Civil War, free blacks were disfranchised throughout the South and in Connecticut. In New York, black males who owned property could vote. Exemplary of the inequities of the time, however, their white male counterparts who did not own property did not face such an obstacle to suffrage.[2] Ending pernicious and pervasive disfranchisement based on racial classification as it related to African descent men (no women, regardless of color, had the right to vote during that period) in the United States became the focus for abolitionists and their supporters during the antebellum and post–Civil War eras.

The end of the Civil War saw relatively rapid movement to give blacks the vote. The Reconstruction Act of 1867 required that rebel states hold conventions, inclusive of black delegates, as a condition of readmission to the Union. This act served as an impetus for new state constitutions assuring the voting rights of black males. The Reconstruction Act of 1867 was passed despite Andrew Johnson's veto, and more than 700,000 African descent males registered to vote in the South alone.[3] Also, a combination of constitutional amendments and legislative acts—the Thirteenth Amendment (1865), which effectively forbade the practice of slavery; the Fourteenth Amendment (1868), which granted citizenship to all persons born or naturalized in the United States (thus striking down the infamous three-fifths clause[4]); the Fifteenth Amendment (1870), which made it unconstitutional to deny someone suffrage based on race, color, or previous condition of servitude; and the Enforcement Acts (1870–1871), which provided consequences for subverting the right to vote[5]—granted a basis for civil rights and voting rights for African Americans. Each of these was initially directed at establishing and sustaining the rights of franchise among the African American population in particular. With the end of slavery and ratification of these acts and amendments, it seemed that a new day was dawning for African Americans and the nation as a whole. But, as I have noted, appearances can be deceiving.

Supported and encouraged by the new acts and amendments, African Americans were registering, voting, and electing black political candidates at the local and federal levels in record numbers. The Enforcement Acts designed to put teeth into the Fifteenth Amendment were less toothsome, however, than presumed. Many white southerners sought and established means to circumvent suffrage for blacks. Additionally, although the Enforcement Acts called for the presence of federal troops to protect the rights of African Americans, their numbers were too small and the desire to disfranchise blacks by many white southerners was too strong to bring about such protection.

Finally, in the 1876 cases of the *United States v. Cruikshank*[6] and the *United States v. Reese*,[7] we observe the government's role as friend and protector of the newly freed and enfranchised black population shift to that of the benign (if not outright malicious) neglector, as it proceeded to rescind the gains acquired through the recent acts and amendments. The Supreme Court's rulings, in concert with the 1877 compromise between northern Republicans and southern Democrats to retain the Republican presidency, paved the way for the withdrawal of federal troops from the South. These actions also cleared the way for Jim Crow laws and numerous means of disfranchising African Americans and retracted the short-lived social and political gains that African Americans had made in the South (as well as the North) following the Civil War.

Tactics undertaken by opponents of suffrage for African Americans (as well as Latinos and Asian Americans) included violence and intimidation, fraud, moving polling and registration sites without proper notification, poll taxes, literacy tests, residency requirements, and the "grandfather clause,"[8] all of which often kept blacks from voting. Some African Americans were also excluded from voting due to the establishment of white primaries, which blocked blacks from participating in primary elections, usually the elections that mattered in the one-party South. These maneuvers and abuses instilled fear and installed obstacles that effectively stripped the voting rights of African Americans for nearly a century.

In 1940, approximately 3 percent of voting-age blacks throughout the South were registered to vote. By 1947, after successful litigation (see *Smith v. Allwright,* more fully discussed later in this chapter), still only 25 percent of voting-age blacks compared to 60 percent of their white counterparts were registered to vote.[9] Even as late as 1964, average black voter registration in the South approximated only 22.5 percent, and in Mississippi, as few as 6.7 percent of voting-age African Americans were registered.[10]

From the 1870s through the 1960s, many African Americans and their supporters sought means to regain the rights of franchise. Over these years, along with institutionalized devices of disfranchisement, the rise of white racist hate groups such as the Ku Klux Klan and the acquiescence of the dominant culture helped instill terror in would-be black voters. Aside from registration and voting irregularities and incongruencies, those who dared attempt to exercise franchise faced losing their jobs, intimidation, violence, and even death. All of this occurred with the tacit, if not explicit, support of the U.S. government and a large proportion of the white American public in the South and the North.[11] Faced with massive inequality and inequity, a cadre of African Americans and their supporters continued the struggle for civil rights and voting rights.

W. E. B. DuBois and the other founders of the National Association for the Advancement of Colored People (NAACP) led the charge for black suffrage in the early twentieth century. This group turned to the Supreme Court to challenge institutionalized disfranchisement. These challenges finally led to a favorable Supreme Court ruling in the 1944 case of *Smith v. Allwright*,[12] which struck down the practice of white primaries. The *Smith* ruling opened the door and increased voter registration among African Americans (although, as previously stated, voter intimidation, poll taxes, literacy tests and the like continued to diminish the numbers of black voters). Furthermore, it raised the profile of a prominent attorney in the *Smith* case, Thurgood Marshall, who became a preeminent figure in the struggle for social and political equality in the United States of America.

With the Supreme Court verdict ending white primaries, the proponents of voting rights were reinvigorated and moved forward to challenge poll taxes, literacy tests, and other obstructions to black franchise. Martin Luther King Jr. began strategizing to gain support for a voting rights bill to be presented to then president Lyndon B. Johnson. Following the horror of Bloody Sunday on March 7, 1965, which involved the violent attack on peaceful demonstrators seeking franchise in Selma, Alabama, that became a consciousness-raising media event, Johnson garnered political and national support for the Voting Rights Act of 1965. Upon its initiation, the VRA was the most decisive legislation assuring franchise for African Americans that the nation had ever seen.

Unlocking the Gates to Freedom: Key Components of the 1965 Voting Rights Act

Despite sustained resistance, primarily from white southerners, the VRA enjoyed widespread popular and congressional support. Initially, the VRA seemed to remove the voting obstacles experienced by blacks and other Americans.[13] Following is a sampling of the protections related to the VRA and its subsequent amendments.

The VRA was designed to complement and enforce the Fourteenth and Fifteenth Amendments, as is exemplified by Section 2, which denies states the ability to determine the rights of franchise and requires that the right to vote for any citizen not be abridged due to race or color.[14] This reversed the consequences of the Court's earlier finding that the states could determine voting rights (see *United States v. Reese*). Furthermore, the VRA, under varying conditions, challenged vote dilution (Section 2), banned literacy tests (Section 4),[15] provided for federal scrutiny of election and registration processes (Sections 4 and 5), and provided for the assignment of federal registrars to enroll voters (Sections 6 and 7). In 1975, Section 4 was amended to provide and protect the voting rights of non-English speakers. This amendment, intended to address the interests of Latinos,[16] created jurisdictions in which more than 5 percent of the voting-age population were members of a "single-language" minority and less than 50 percent of the voting-age population had voted in the 1972 presidential election and that election had been conducted in

English. Jurisdictions meeting those criteria are required to provide voter registration and voting information in English as well as the language of the applicable minority group(s).[17]

Additionally, the VRA defined *vote* and *voting* as all action necessary to exercise franchise, prohibited voting fraud, and provided for punishments for violators of others' suffrage (Section 14). Finally, although the VRA did not explicitly prohibit the poll tax, which had been outlawed in federal elections by the Twenty-Fourth Amendment in 1964, it did provide for a federal challenge to poll taxes (Section 10). This additional protection was added to the VRA because some in Congress feared that prohibition of the poll tax in state elections would be viewed as unconstitutional and endanger the entire Voting Rights Act. Section 10 assured that the attorney general would challenge the constitutionality of poll taxes, the remainders of which were struck down by the federal courts in 1966 in response to cases brought by the office of the attorney general against Texas, Alabama, Mississippi, and Virginia.[18]

The VRA as passed and amended undoubtedly unlocked and unblocked the passages to franchise for African Americans and others. Enhancing and enforcing the Fifteenth Amendment, the VRA secured the rights of racial minorities to vote and have those votes counted. These rights at times are challenged, however, by increasingly sophisticated means. Many argue that the 2000 presidential election and, to a lesser extent, the 2003 California recall election offer examples of obstructions to the rights of franchise and the fair and uniform counting of votes based on technological, and particularly in the case of Florida, physical obstacles.

Everything Old Is New Again

From the perspective of political scientist Hanes Walton Jr., it may not be so surprising that Florida became a lightning rod for accusations of voter intimidation, manipulation, and fraud. Walton Jr. recalled that, after the 1944 verdict in *Smith v. Allwright* outlawed white primaries, Florida began to record voter registration by race and party. Based on analysis of these records, it became clear that the numbers of African American Democrats were growing in that state.[19]

Republicans in this southern stronghold pursued means to increase support among African Americans for their party. Although some support was mustered through the efforts of Ronald Reagan, the senior George Bush, and Florida governor Jeb Bush (the brother of President George W. Bush), African American Democrats still outnumbered African American Republicans in Florida ten to one by the presidential election of 2000.[20] And, by election year 2000, that population of Democrats was energized and mobilized by Governor Jeb Bush's support for anti–affirmative action legislation. Hanes Walton

Jr. concluded that perhaps it was the perceptions that Florida could play a key role in the 2000 election and that African American voters in that state could also play a critical role in the election that inspired Republicans, and Jeb Bush in particular, to enlist Ward Connerly, a notable and influential African American conservative, to join them in Florida in order to mobilize their constituency. Walton Jr. stated that in order to promote a theory of constitutional inequality, which espoused that equal voting rights were unworthy of constitutional protections, Connerly was brought to Florida specifically "to tell White and ethnic communities that the disenfranchisement of these African American voters [those who could serve as swing votes] would help them to protect their self-interest and the Republican win."[21] And so, a familiar stage was set not only for a highly contestable election but also, arguably, for some of the most extreme challenges to the spirit and letter of the law of the Voting Rights Act since its inception in 1965.

No Accounting for the Count: New Challenges for a New Millennium

Forewarned and forearmed, Florida prepared to face what was anticipated to be a larger than typical voter turnout based on increased registration, particularly among Democrats, African Americans, and other ethnic minority groups.[22] Officials did not adequately prepare precincts in *all* communities for large numbers of voters. Although this could have been a simple error, other violations raised concerns that might be linked to a bygone era of disfranchisement based on race and color.

Evidence gathered by the U.S. Commission on Civil Rights (USCCR) pointed to at least one unauthorized law enforcement checkpoint in a predominantly African American neighborhood, where on election day a series of license checks, car checks, and the like occurred.[23] Such blockades, ostensibly planned as enforcement of vehicle registration, operation, and licensure laws, are easily construed as voter intimidation tactics. In any case, these roadblocks were perceived by many as negatively influencing the ability of African Americans and others to freely exercise their right of franchise.

Furthermore, because of Florida's policy of purging felons who are not eligible to vote from the voter registration rolls, nonfelons were also mistakenly removed. Erroneous information was utilized and violations of the full faith and credit clause, which requires Florida to recognize the rights accorded to ex-felons from other states, occurred.[24] Disregarding the full faith and credit clause in combination with erroneously tagging nonfelons as felons succeeded in disfranchising those who had the legitimate right to vote. Such errors even affected the voting privileges of a Florida supervisor of elections who was mistakenly identified as a felon. It is argued that African Americans were disproportionately affected by this series of violations.[25] These occurrences conflict with the goals of universal suffrage, which is the explicit intent of the Voting Rights Act.[26]

African Americans again were disproportionately affected by inadequate resources at polling sites that could not confirm voter-eligibility status.[27] Similarly, outdated voting machinery was found to be disproportionately located in predominantly or heavily African American precincts.[28] The USCCR found a positive correlation between race and voter disfranchisement. In particular, the commission and others found that voting machines with higher levels of ballot rejection were more likely to be in African American areas.[29] In effect, the larger number of spoiled ballots produced by error-prone punch-card machines disproportionately diminished the number of black votes that were counted. The impact as it related to the African American vote recalled the history of disfranchisement that had plagued that group and spurred the creation of the Voting Rights Act of 1965. African Americans were not the only group, however, that suffered from the no-count syndrome.

Jewish and elderly voters also received defective or incomprehensible ballots that rendered the infamous hanging chads and generated overvotes (voting for more than one presidential candidate) and undervotes (ballots where vote choice could not be discerned) among their ranks.[30] College students, many of whom were first-time voters, were disfranchised as their voter registration languished, and the laws of the National Voter Registration Act (also known as the Motor Voter bill) pertaining to timely and proper registration processing apparently were not fully or appropriately applied. Often young voters enrolled in colleges planned to vote on or near the campuses. In some instances, ballots and information regarding registrants arrived late to the campuses. Additionally, a number of young voters were among those prohibited from reaching the polls due to the roadblocks and car checks that were staged. Furthermore, in a clear reincarnation of past franchise violations in the South, polling places closed early or were simply relocated without notice. Haitian American and Puerto Rican voters were not provided language assistance when requested as required by law. And the physically disabled were not appropriately accommodated at the polls as is required by the Voter Accessibility for the Elderly and Handicapped Act of 1984.[31] For its part, Florida claimed to have followed the procedures at hand and protected the electoral process. Furthermore, although the USCCR and others posit numerous allegations, representatives of Florida respond that there is no hard evidence connecting particular Florida officials with any wrongdoing.[32] All in all, it is clear, however, that the procedures of and impediments to the Florida 2000 presidential election created challenges for the state, the nation, voting rights, and—perhaps most importantly—the very principles of contemporary U.S. democracy.

Hanes Walton Jr. compared the disfranchisement observed in Florida to that observed by Benjamin Harrison in 1888.[33] Upon his defeat of Grover

Cleveland based on a majority of electoral but not popular votes, Harrison proposed that he would have won the popular vote as well had it not been for the disfranchisement of the African American voters in the South. Harrison's statement called attention to support for democratic principles that were in place to preserve the voting rights of African Americans and all Americans. Given that Bush won Florida by less than 600 votes and that there were thousands of votes that were not cast, remained uncounted, or were inappropriately counted because of obstructions, both physical and technological, many Americans have been led to question whether the democratic principles that Harrison discussed are really cherished.

What Have We Learned from Florida? Recalling the Recall

Recalling the vagaries of election year 2000 leads one to inquire, what have we learned? And where do we go from here? A test case arose in California as the electorate prepared to recall the unpopular governor, Gray Davis, and replace him with the politically inexperienced and eminently appealing actor, Arnold Schwarzenegger. My goal here is not to review the qualities, campaigns, and various attributes of the recall candidates, nor even the political circus that defined the recall (see Chapter 1 for a brief discussion of the recall election). Rather, I will focus on the relationship of the recall procedures to the franchise of Americans, particularly ethnic-minority and impoverished Americans, in light of the issues raised by the Florida election and the legal intentions of the VRA.

Recall elections are peculiarities in the U.S. political system. They are rarely invoked devices to register a lack of confidence that a constituency has for its elected leadership. Such was the case in California, where the majority of the electorate ultimately declared that Governor Davis was no longer the desired leader and elected Arnold Schwarzenegger as the new California governor. Prior to voters registering that opinion at the polls, however, a challenge to the validity of the October 7, 2003, recall election was presented. In *Southwest Voter Registration Education Project v. Shelley*,[34] the American Civil Liberties Union (ACLU), representing several groups, argued that the election should be postponed until March 2004 when California was to have replaced all of the outmoded voting machines similar to those that cast a pox on the 2000 presidential election in Florida. A three-judge panel of the U.S. Court of Appeals for the Ninth Circuit agreed. The consideration here as it relates to the Voting Rights Act is tied to the goals of the act to assure enfranchisement of the citizenry and to ensure that those votes are equitably cast and equally counted. Finding that "punch-card voting systems are significantly more prone to errors" and agreeing that 40,000 or more voters were likely to be disfranchised due to ballot error, the judges ordered the election delayed.[35] Responses to the decision largely fell along party lines.[36]

The rationale utilized by the panel in its decision was based on the ruling in *Bush v Gore*, which is more fully discussed and analyzed by Evan Gerstmann in Chapter 8. The Ninth Circuit judges noted, "This is a classic voting rights equal protection claim. The Plaintiffs' claim presents almost precisely the same issue as the court considered in *Bush*, that is, whether unequal methods of counting votes among counties constitutes a violation of the equal protection clause."[37] Additionally, the Ninth Circuit opinion *precisely* cited *Bush v. Gore* as follows: "The press of time does not diminish the constitutional concern. A desire for speed is not a general excuse for ignoring equal protection guarantees."[38] Furthermore in the California recall case, the judges stated, "Public interest strongly favors holding the recall election during the general election in March 2004 to avoid an equal protection violation."[39] Although the finding was based on a case that played favorably for Republican interests during the election of President George W. Bush, Republicans were not pleased with the outcome. Democrats, who had been appalled by the Court's decision in *Bush v. Gore*, however, saw the possibility of a reprieve in sight. A delayed election was assumed by some as a potential increase in the possibilities of either Davis's remaining in office or another Democrat's receiving the California governorship. In any case, it becomes difficult to separate party interest from interests in maintaining the integrity of the vote as prescribed by the Constitution and the VRA.

Ultimately, however, a full eleven-judge panel of the Ninth Circuit Court reversed the earlier decision. Citing an obligation to grant deference to a lower court ruling and the goal of supporting the electoral process, the judges found that postponement of the election was unacceptable. This ruling, however, did not find that the punch-card ballot and disproportionate placement of outmoded voting machines within ethnic minority communities was not a violation of the VRA or of the Fourteenth or Fifteenth Amendments. Rather, the Ninth Circuit chose to rule narrowly on deference to a lower court and leave the touchier issues undecided.

Furthermore, indicating its respect for the electoral process, the court stated that the plaintiffs were "legitimately concerned that the use of the punch-card systems still [denies] the right to vote to some voters who must use that system."[40] The judges added, however, "A federal court cannot lightly interfere with [a state election]."[41] The court noted that absentee ballots had been cast and a great deal of resources had been expended for the October 7 recall election. Based on all of these considerations, the election went forward, regardless of the potential denial of voting rights that disproportionately burdened identifiable segments of the population. Therefore, despite potential violations to the U.S. Constitution and the Voting Rights Act of 1965 (and its amendments), California proceeded with the recall election. Regarding the full enfranchisement of the voters, both the courts and the political parties fell silent.

Silence Is Not an Answer: Whither Voting Rights in the Twenty-First Century

Regarding his observations of the voting rights violations and outcomes of the 2000 presidential election, Hanes Walton Jr. stated, "Silence permits party image to replace and substitute for the Fifteenth Amendment,"[42] and arguably the VRA. A similar silence is observed at the federal and state levels as it relates to the 2003 California recall election. Political winners appear to be without incentive to speak up for the goals of the VRA and the democratic principles of the nation. And perhaps political losers remain silent so that they do not appear to be whiners. In any case, we are left to ponder the future of VRA. Are voting rights a paramount concern of our nation and its leaders? How far are we as a country willing to go to assure "one person, one vote" in a system in which *every* vote counts?

These are clearly difficult questions. In fact, they are questions that the current Supreme Court appears either unwilling or, due to an overbooked calendar, unable to address. Since *Bush v. Gore*, it has not heard any related cases. It is fairly unlikely, had the California recall voting rights issues been presented to the Supreme Court, that it would have agreed to hear the case.

Nagging doubts fuel the voting rights issues hovering over the 2000 presidential election results. These doubts regarding possible disfranchisement have propelled to the forefront of our political consciousness issues regarding computerized touch-screen voting machines and Internet voting. Each of these approaches offers new challenges for the VRA.

The Help America Vote Act of 2002,[43] in part designed as a response to voting rights issues raised by the 2000 presidential election, has encouraged the proliferation of touch-screen terminals, known as direct recording electronic voting systems (DRE). DRE, which are being touted as the new wave in voting, are popular and have been utilized in numerous elections. This new technology raises new concerns, however. According to Dill, Schneier, and Simons, "The ideal voting technology would have five attributes: anonymity, scalability, speed, audit, and accuracy."[44] Ultimately, the goals and spirit of the VRA, and of those of us who are concerned with voting rights, seek to assure that the voter's intended selections are counted; that is, to assure that voter fraud does not occur. Unfortunately, because the current touch-screen voting process is paperless, the DRE suffer from an "audit gap," the inability to verify voter selections, which could encourage error or fraud and eliminate the possibilities of a recount in contested elections.[45]

The DRE have led to a number of notable problems. For instance, consider the following accounts discussed by Dill, Schneier, and Simons:

A March 2002 runoff election in Wellington, FL, was decided by five votes, but 78 ballots had no recorded vote. Elections Supervisor Theresa LePore claimed those 78 people chose not to vote for the only office on the ballot! In 2000, a Sequoia DRE machine was taken out of service in an election in Middlesex County, NJ, after 65 votes had been cast. When the results were checked after the election, it was discovered that none of the 65 votes were recorded for the Democrat and Republican candidates for one office, even though 27 votes each were recorded for their running mates. A representative of Sequoia insisted that no votes were lost, and that voters had simply failed to cast votes for the two top candidates. Since there was no paper trail, it was impossible to resolve either question.[46]

Clearly such outcomes, and the need to justify them in the name of technological advancement, pose important issues for voting rights in the new millennium. Although heretofore the challenge has been related to unequal access to new voting machine technologies (that is, DRE are currently disproportionately less available in ethnic-minority and low income districts), it seems that the integrity of the vote is questionable even among those with access to the latest technology as well as those who remain burdened by outdated mechanisms such as the butterfly ballot.

In order to close the audit gap, sustain voting rights, and support the goals of the VRA, possible inconsistencies related to the DRE machine must be addressed. In light of this, the Voter Confidence and Increased Accessibility Act of 2003 (H.R. 2239) introduced by Representative Rush Holt, which calls for voter-verification and audit capacity for the DRE, is gaining a great deal of support. H.R. 2239, also known as the Paper Trail Bill, has been referred to the Committee on House Administration. At the time of this writing, volunteers are phoning congressional representatives to garner increased support and co-sponsorship of the bill. Perhaps such public policies, in combination with increased and equitable access to the new voting technology, could help reconcile the new millennium election mechanism with the Voting Rights Act that seeks to ensure and enhance franchise for all Americans.

Likewise, the possibilities of Internet voting must respond to considerable obstacles related to adhering to the VRA and assuring that no voters are silenced. The advances represented by Internet technology regarding increasing voter turnout, access, and political knowledge are frequently cited among the advantages of Internet election capability (see Lee Goodman's discussion of the Internet in Chapter 7). Alternatively, concerns often involve the potential for fraud and for Internet viruses to corrupt the process.[47] A number of reviewers of the Internet election process are surprisingly silent, however, when it comes to an analysis of the impact of the digital divide on the equal and equitable access to and exercise of franchise.

It is clear that there is a widening gap between those with access who participate in our political system and those with less access who do not.[48] There is clear evidence that the digital divide discriminates against poor and ethnic minority populations. For instance, according to a Department of Commerce report involving interviews of 48,000 participants, the gap is closing, but ethnic-minority and lower–socioeconomic status families and individuals still experience less access to the Internet than the national average or than that enjoyed by their wealthier white counterparts.[49] The data show that 41.5 percent of U.S. households have Internet access. Notably, only 12.7 percent of those households earning less than $15,000 reported having access compared with 77.7 percent of households earning over $75,000. Furthermore, African American and Latino households routinely reported lower than average levels of Internet access, at 23.5 percent and 23.6 percent, respectively.[50] It seems that as we advance the potential for Internet voting, we may further silence the communities that the VRA has sought to address and redress. That is, as the goals of the VRA and the related constitutional amendments have been to generate and sustain an atmosphere of open and free elections in which each and every vote counts, it seems that technological advances may pose new (and perhaps unintended) threats to free suffrage.

As we speed through the twenty-first century, novel voting methods are being considered and may be implemented sooner than we think. As I have argued in this chapter, the Voting Rights Act was secured in order to sustain the legitimacy of our democracy by assuring the integrity, equality, and equitability of franchise. In order to meet new challenges, Americans must continue to ensure that the Voting Rights Act keeps its promise, keeps pace with technology, and assures the priority of universal suffrage and unencumbered access to voting technologies over the costs or expediency of new processes and mechanisms. The goal of the Voting Rights Act has been to lend voice to those who have been silenced at the polls. Accordingly, silence is not the answer as we assess the challenges to voting rights that continue to confront many Americans.

Notes

1. Franklin, *Reconstruction*.
2. McPherson, *The Struggle for Equality*.
3. Franklin, *Reconstruction*.
4. The three-fifths clause counted three-fifths of the slave population in apportioning representation in the House of Representatives. The framers of the Constitution believed that concessions on slavery were the price for the support of southern delegates for a strong central government. The three-fifths compromise gave the South extra representation in the House and extra votes in the Electoral College. Notably,

without the extra representation afforded by the three-fifths clause, Thomas Jefferson would have lost the election of 1800.

5. The Enforcement Acts of 1870–1871 criminalized, at the federal level, activities directed at disfranchising African Americans. These acts focused on the Ku Klux Klan and their assaults and murders of blacks who attempted to vote and otherwise participate in the political system. States were often in collusion with the Klan. Therefore, the federal involvement held some initial promise. Rather than leaving it to the states to punish offenders who sought to disfranchise and even murder blacks, federal intervention in the form of troops and martial law that brought white offenders before predominantly black juries were among the means used to help assure the enfranchisement of African Americans. Many offenders were jailed or fled, thus breaking some of the early organized resistance to black suffrage. The Reconstruction period and federal support of the Enforcement Acts soon came to an end, however. See Davidson, "The Voting Rights Act." This came as a blow to African American voters as the fate of their franchise was left to some unsympathetic state entities.

6. In *United States v. Cruikshank*, 92 U.S. 542 (1876), the Supreme Court narrowly interpreted the civil rights Enforcement Acts passed in 1870 and 1871. In this case, the Court dismissed indictments against whites for the violent attack against hundreds of blacks. The massacre of the African Americans by whites was related to disputed election results. The Court found no wrongdoing based on race.

7. In *United States v. Reese*, 92 U.S. 214 (1876), the Supreme Court found that the Fifteenth Amendment provided citizens of the United States with a new constitutional right: exemption from discrimination related to franchise based on race, color, or previous condition of servitude. In a convoluted finding, the Court held that the right to vote in the states comes from the states, but the right of exemption from discrimination comes from the United States. The right to franchise, the Court argued, had not been granted or secured by the Constitution of the United States, but freedom from discrimination in voting had been.

8. The grandfather clause was a statutory or constitutional device enacted by several southern states between 1895 and 1910 to deny suffrage to African Americans. The clause provided that those who had the right to vote prior to 1866 or 1867, and their descendants, would be exempt from educational, property, or tax requirements for voting. These clauses excluded blacks from the vote but assured the franchise to many impoverished and illiterate whites. Based on its interpretation of the Fourteenth Amendment, in *Guinn and Beal v. United States*, 238 U.S. 347 (1915), the Supreme Court declared the grandfather clause unconstitutional.

9. See Garrow, *Protest at Selma;* Price, *The Negro and the Ballot.*

10. Congressional Quarterly Service, *Congressional Quarterly Almanac*; Davidson, "The Voting Rights Act."

11. See Franklin, *Reconstruction*; McPherson, *The Struggle for Equality*; Davidson, "The Voting Rights Act"; Walton, "The Disenfranchisement of the African American Voter."

12. In *Smith v. Allwright*, 321 U.S. 649 (1944), the Supreme Court reviewed the primary practices in Texas and stated: "The right of a citizen of the United States to vote for the nomination of candidates for the United States Senate and House of Representatives in a primary which is an integral part of the elective process is a right secured by the Federal Constitution, and this right of the citizen may not be abridged by the State on account of his race or color (p. 661)." See Chapter 2 for further discussion of the *Smith* case.

13. In *Whose Votes Count?* Abigail Thernstrom argued that the goals of the VRA were altered and ameliorated by extending its reach to various other interest and eth-

nic minority groups as well as reapplying redistricting tactics in order to increase the impact of minority votes. Redistricting and its consequences are examined in Chapter 10.

14. Section 2 states, "No voting qualifications or prerequisite to voting, or standard practice, or procedure shall be imposed or applied by *any* State or political subdivision to deny or abridge the right of any citizen of the United States to vote on account of race or color" [emphasis my own].

15. Although literacy tests were initially banned in 1965, the ban was to expire in 1970. Ultimately Congress banned literacy tests in *all fifty states* beginning in 1970 through 1975 (see Davidson, "The Voting Rights Act").

16. Latinos, and to some extent Asian Americans, have been subject to voting rights infractions but to a much lesser degree than African Americans, particularly those in the South (Davidson, "The Voting Rights Act"). Of course, the Latinos, Asian Americans, and others who have endured restricted franchise have been and remain legitimately concerned about sustaining suffrage and its political impact. Or to paraphrase Martin Luther King Jr., injustice anywhere is a threat to justice everywhere.

17. See Bannon, "The Voting Rights Act."

18. Commission on Civil Rights, *Political Participation*; Davidson, "The Voting Rights Act."

19. Walton, "The Disenfranchisement of the African American Voter."

20. Ibid.

21. Ibid., p. 23.

22. Berry, "U.S. Commission on Civil Rights."

23. See ibid.; Walton, "The Disenfranchisement of the African American Voter"; United States Commission on Civil Rights, *Voting Irregularities in Florida*.

24. In *Schlenther v. Department of State, Division of Licensing,* 743 So. 2d 536 (1998), it was found that the restoration of a former felon's civil rights in one state entitled that party to such rights in another state based on the full faith and credit clause.

25. United States Commission on Civil Rights, *Voting Irregularities in Florida*; Hines, "The Silent Voices."

26. Walton, "The Disenfranchisement of the African American Voter"; Hines, "The Silent Voices."

27. Berry, "U.S. Commission on Civil Rights"; United States Commission on Civil Rights, "Voting Rights in Florida 2002"; United States Commission on Civil Rights, *Voting Irregularities in Florida*.

28. Hines, "The Silent Voices"; United States Commission on Civil Rights, "Voting Rights in Florida 2002"; United States Commission on Civil Rights, *Voting Irregularities in Florida*.

29. United States Commission on Civil Rights, *Voting Irregularities in Florida*.

30. This references the "butterfly ballot" that is a combination of a booklet on which candidates are listed and a card used by voters to make a selection by punching a stylus through the perforated point on the ballot that indicates their vote choice. The order of the candidates listed, in some instances, confused voters, who thought that they had selected the Democrat, Gore, but actually voted for the Reform Party candidate, Buchanan. Additionally, it was found that a number of the ballots were not counted because the voter's choice was unclear because portions of the perforated cardboard ballots (known as chads) were not completely detached by using the stylus to punch the cards. These were considered, in some cases, to be spoiled ballots. The combination of unclear ballots leading to voters' not selecting the candidates of their choice in combination with a large number of spoiled ballots due to attached chads is

seen by many as disfranchising eligible voters who arrived at the polls and believed that they had participated in the election process.

31. Berry, "U.S. Commission on Civil Rights"; Hines, "The Silent Voices"; United States Commission on Civil Rights, "Voting Rights in Florida 2002"; United States Commission on Civil Rights, *Voting Irregularities in Florida*.

32. United States Commission on Civil Rights, *Voting Irregularities in Florida*.

33. Walton, "The Disenfranchisement of the African American Voter"; see also Socolofsky and Spetter, *The Presidency of Benjamin Harrison*.

34. In *Southwest Voter Registration Education Project v. Shelley*, 2003 DJDAR 10500 (Ninth Circuit September 15, 2003), the American Civil Liberties Union represented several civil rights groups including the NAACP, the Southern Christian Leadership Conference of Greater Los Angeles, and the Southwest Voter Registration Education Project. The case was brought against California secretary of state Kevin Shelley. The three-judge panel included Judges Richard Paez, Harry Pregerson, and Sidney Thomas.

35. *Southwest Voter Registration Education Project v. Shelley*, 2003 DJDAR 10500 (Ninth Circuit, September 15, 2003), p. 23.

36. It is important to note that some Democrats opposed the ruling because they believed that a delayed election could cause greater harm to the state.

37. *Southwest Voter Registration Education Project v. Shelley*, 2003 DJDAR 10500 (Ninth Circuit, September 15, 2003), pp. 18–19.

38. Ibid., p. 56.

39. Ibid.

40. *Southwest Voter Registration Education Project v. Shelley,* 2003 DJDAR 10500 (Ninth Circuit September 15, 2003), p. 11.

41. Ibid., p. 8.

42. Walton, "The Disenfranchisement of the African American Voter," p. 24.

43. Public Law 107-252.

44. Dill, Schneier, and Simons, "Viewpoint," p. 29.

45. Ibid.

46. Ibid., p. 30.

47. Mohen and Glidden, "The Case for Internet Voting"; California Internet Voting Task Force, *A Report on the Feasibility of Internet Voting*.

48. Gibson, "Elections Online."

49. National Telecommunications and Information Administration, *Americans in the Information Age*.

50. Ibid.; Gibson, "Elections Online."

10

Redistricting: Racial and Partisan Considerations

Charles S. Bullock III

Few aspects of elections have been more controversial than the redistricting process that occurs for federal, state, and local offices every ten years after the census is conducted. Because of the controversy regarding the redistricting process and the laws that apply to certain states when redrawing districts, redistricting cases have been one of the most common aspects of election law heard by the courts. Drawing electoral districts has the potential for mischief, especially in political systems that use single-member districts (SMDs), since the distribution of population among districts significantly impacts the translation of votes into seats. In single-member district systems, clever mapping could enable a party conceivably to win virtually all of the seats with little more than a majority of the vote. In many cases, plans may allow a party to win a majority of the seats with less than half the votes. In contrast, political systems that use proportional representation take care of the votes-to-seats ratio by establishing that each party will receive a share of seats in the legislature roughly equal to its share of the vote.[1]

The fairness of representation of political parties is not the only concern of those who study districting patterns. Another concern is the adequacy of representation of racial and ethnic groups and urban versus rural representation. Litigation and statutes in these areas are intended to provide at least minimal protection to interests that can be outvoted in the legislature.

The topics dealt with in this chapter fit into two broad categories: sins of omission and sins of commission. The sins of omission were the first to draw judicial rebuke. Once courts admonished jurisdictions that failed to redraw their districts to reflect population shifts (sins of omission), attention shifted to the fairness accorded groups in newly drawn maps (sins of commission). Most examinations of fairness in the redistricting process have focused on implications either for racial and ethnic minorities or for political parties. These are the topics covered in this chapter.

Sins of Omission

For most of the twentieth century, inertia characterized legislative districting. At the congressional level, states that saw no change in delegation size rarely redrew district lines. Even some states that gained a representative as a result of growing more rapidly than the nation as a whole postponed redistricting. Texas (1932–1962) repeatedly held an at-large election to fill newly acquired seats. Once the electorate had made its decision in a statewide contest, the legislature drew a district around the home of the new member. Some other states, such as Connecticut (1932–1964), Oklahoma (1932–1941), and Washington (1952–1957), delayed drawing new districts for years, continuing to elect one legislator statewide. Illinois, New York, Ohio, and Pennsylvania elected multiple members at large for at least one decade of the twentieth century.

Generally states that lost districts immediately redrew, but in 1962 Alabama took no action to shrink its delegation from nine to eight. Instead, all nine incumbents ran statewide in the Democratic primary, with the eight top vote getters winning nominations and returning to Congress.

The inaction that characterized congressional districting extended down to most states, and since state legislatures infrequently changed size, district lines hardened into permanency. Geography was the primary basis for allocating representatives. Each county might be given a seat in one chamber of the state legislature. Although a state's most populous counties often got additional seats, they remained underrepresented compared with small, rural counties. At the congressional level, regions of a state, such as the upper peninsula of Michigan, argued for a representative who would specifically represent that area even though the area had a smaller population than other districts. Except in the nation's largest urban areas, counties were rarely split, even if a county's population (for example, Dallas and Harris counties in Texas) exceeded that of some congressional districts in the state.

Although a few states make use of commissions when redrawing districts, most states assign districting responsibilities to the legislature so that the legislature could, at any time, remap itself or the state's congressional districts. Since rural interests dominated most legislatures for the first half of the twentieth century, however, and these would be the losers in any effort to equalize populations among districts, no one took action. Consequently, as the nation's population became increasingly urbanized, the constituencies of rural representatives grew smaller and smaller in relation to the number of citizens represented by urban legislators.

Immediately after World War II, plaintiffs from Chicago asked a federal court to increase the number of legislators from their city. Because urban districts usually had larger populations than rural ones, the plaintiffs argued that their votes counted for less than rural voters. The Supreme Court ducked responsibility by labeling it a political issue and therefore one that must be resolved by the state legislature. In *Colegrove v. Green* (1946), Justice Felix Frankfurter warned the court not to enter "the political thicket" of redistricting.

At the end of the 1950s, the Court backed into the political thicket. Sensing the growing political activism of African Americans, white leaders of Tuskegee, Alabama, convinced the state legislature to redraw the city's boundaries to exclude virtually every prospective black voter. Tuskegee is located in Macon County, one of the most heavily black counties in the United States. Whites in Tuskegee feared that African Americans would achieve full political rights and dominate the government. Blacks who had been removed from the corporate limits filed suit, and the Supreme Court invalidated the legislature's actions on the grounds that it violated the Fifteenth Amendment of the Constitution by depriving them of their right to vote in city elections (*Gomillion v. Lightfoot*, 1960).

With the Court's having intervened in legislative mapmaking, plaintiffs in Tennessee filed suit noting that the state assembly ignored its own mandate for decennial redistricting. The Court overturned the *Colegrove* decision in *Baker v. Carr* (1962) and held that the equal protection clause of the Fourteenth Amendment guaranteed the right for citizens to have votes given approximately the same weight regardless of where they lived. By that, the Court meant that each district should have roughly the same number of people rather than some districts having only one-fifth or even one-tenth as many citizens as the most heavily populated districts. Two years later, the Supreme Court extended the logic of requiring equal populations among districts to both chambers in a state's legislature (*Reynolds v. Sims*) and to the U.S. House (*Wesberry v. Sanders*). The basis for *Wesberry* differed from that of litigation involving state legislatures, since the equal protection clause applies to states and not the federal government. The Court held that Article 1, Section 2 of the Constitution required the states to draw their congressional districts on the basis of equal population. Article I, Section 2 provides that "the House of Representatives shall be composed of members chosen every second year by the people of the several states."

The remainder of the 1960s saw dozens of challenges filed, since virtually no state's legislature had equal populations across districts. The courts became more demanding in how close jurisdictions must approach equal population. In *Brown v. Thomson* (1983), the Supreme Court upheld a plan in which the population deviation between the largest and smallest districts stood at 9.9 percent. Plus and minus 5 percent has become the standard that most state legislatures and local governments use for guidance, since courts have considered less than a 10 percent range in populations to be *de minimis*—literally so small as to not have an effect. When the range exceeds 10 percent, the burden of proof shifts to the jurisdiction being sued.[2]

Tolerances for congressional districts have been narrower,[3] although for years it appeared that if a congressional plan had a deviation no greater than plus and minus 0.5 percent it could withstand a challenge. Since *Karcher v. Daggett* (1983), however, courts have given precedence to alternative plans that minimize population deviations. In *Karcher*, the Supreme Court struck down a plan having a maximum range of 0.6984 percent in favor of one with a range between the smallest and largest districts of 0.4514 percent. Justice William Brennan's majority opinion held that for congressional districts "there are no *de minimis* population variations which could practicably be avoided, but which nonetheless meet the standard of Article I, Section 2, without justification." In 2002, a federal trial court rejected a plan with a deviation of nineteen people (*Vieth v. Pennsylvania*).

Beginning in the early 1990s, geographic information systems that merge maps with census and political data made it possible to try multiple alternatives quickly. Repeated trials could produce a plan in which the maximum population range is no more than a single person, which allowed courts to raise the standard in cases like *Vieth,* thereby eliminating a *de minimis* challenge.

Redistricting to equalize population among districts reallocated political influence from the farms to urban centers and their suburbs. These changes resulted in concerns of urban residents being given greater weight while their rural cousins had less influence.[4] In some states even following redistricting, however, rural interests retained an influence greater than their numbers as a result of filling key leadership posts in the state legislature.[5]

The redistricting revolution also brought new faces to the state legislature. In the South, Republicans were just beginning to make headway in urban areas. When urban areas were underrepresented and, especially, if a county elected all of its legislators at large, Democrats could typically continue to muster majorities. Once urban centers received numbers of legislators proportionate to their share of the state's population, however, and if legislators represented single-member districts, some districts had Republican voting majorities. Figure 10.1 shows the growth in Republican state legislators, with vertical lines at 1973 and 1993 indicating implementation of major new districting plans. Following the 2001–2002 redistricting, Republicans made further gains, but these were a continuation of the growth in the party that began in 1985. The 1993 growth is overshadowed by the advances registered in the big GOP (the Grand Old Party; the Republicans) year of 1995. Regression models show that time is strongly correlated with percent GOP. Of the redistricting years, only 1973 is a statistically significant correlate when included with time in a model.[6]

Outside the South, fairer representation of urban areas usually benefited Democrats, since Republican strength was often at its greatest on the farms. Putting additional legislators in the urban center resulted in greater numbers of districts having Democratic concentrations. Cox and Katz explained that electoral and judicial factors intersected to eliminate the Republican advan-

Figure 10.1   Percentage of Republicans in Southern Legislatures, 1971–2003

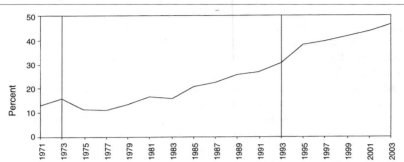

tage that had existed outside the South prior to the redistricting revolution.[7] State legislatures used the controversial tactic of gerrymandering—drawing districts to benefit a particular group—when creating new district maps. Strong Democratic tides in 1958 and 1964 left Republican state legislators unable to defend their earlier gerrymanders when federal courts, which had disproportionately large numbers of Democratic judges, went about implementing the *Wesberry* standards. States that had been strongly Republican had recently fallen into Democratic hands, and the new majority devised plans in states such as Ohio, New York, and Michigan that solidified Democratic gains in state congressional delegations and state legislatures. The onset of a larger incumbency advantage at about the same time as the one-person, one-vote revolution made these Democratic gains difficult to root out.[8]

The new district plans not only changed the partisan makeup of southern legislatures but the racial complexion as well. The redistricting revolution came along as the federal government flexed its muscles and began eradicating obstacles to black registration and voting. Although a number of rural southern counties had black majorities (therefore if African Americans had been enfranchised, blacks would have been likely elected prior to the 1960s), opportunities for blacks to participate were much greater in urban centers. As redistricting gave cities more seats, the numbers of black legislators increased. For example, after completing the post-1970 redistricting, the numbers of black state representatives increased from four to twelve in South Carolina, from fourteen to nineteen in Georgia, and from one to eight in Louisiana.

Sins of Commission

Minority political parties have been mistreated since the earliest days of the republic. The term *gerrymander* comes from a depiction of a Massachusetts district crafted by Governor Elbridge Gerry to disadvantage his foes. The distribution of African Americans and whites has been considered by legislators engaged in redistricting since Reconstruction; some redistricting plans of the 1960s and 1970s advantaged whites at the expense of blacks. In the 1990s, racial gerrymandering took on new meaning as the Department of Justice (DOJ) forced jurisdictions to draw additional majority-minority districts when possible. Initially, DOJ focused on prohibiting efforts to draw districts that disadvantaged minorities by distributing them so as to reduce their potential for electing their preferences. Then, in the wake of the 1990 census, DOJ shifted its emphasis to promoting the creation of additional majority-minority districts. These topics are covered in the next two sections.

Racial Gerrymandering: Phase I

The 1965 Voting Rights Act banned various tests and devices used in the South designed to keep African Americans from voting. The act gave special attention to seven states where less than half the voting-age population had registered or voted in 1964.[9] In these states the act prohibited literacy, understanding, good character, and other tests as prerequisites for registering.

As the path to the ballot box opened for blacks, recalcitrant southern jurisdictions turned to new techniques to thwart black political goals. Of relevance here was the use of districting plans to keep African Americans from winning office. The initial tactic used was the classic gerrymandering technique of *cracking* black population concentrations so that they did not constitute a majority in any district. As an example of cracking, consider Mississippi's Delta district, which had existed since 1882. With the densest concentration of African Americans in the country, blacks constituted a majority of the population, but disfranchising techniques allowed the white minority to control politics. Even after Mississippi lost a congressional seat following the 1960 census, it continued to have a district almost 60 percent black.[10] Despite the redrawing necessitated by the loss of a representative, Mississippi districts lacked equal populations, with one district having more than twice the population of another. In the course of addressing one-person, one-vote issues, the state eliminated the majority-black Delta district. The new plan divided the Delta among three districts running east to west across the state so that no district had a black voting-age population over 44 percent black.

Although Mississippi cracked the black population among multiple districts to prevent African Americans from winning a seat in the congressional delegation, it turned to another gerrymandering technique, *stacking,* to minimize black success in the state legislature. Stacking involves the creation of multimember districts (MMDs) so as to submerge a potential majority-minority single-member district. For example, assume the existence of a district in which two-thirds of the population is black. If that district combined with three SMDs in which the population is 75 percent white, then in the newly created four-member district, the population would be more than 60 percent white. If the electorate voted along racial lines, then all four of the representatives from the district would be white. In contrast, if the election were conducted in four SMDs and voting were along racial lines, one black and three whites would be elected. As Parker detailed, the plans for the Mississippi house and senate used MMDs in which majority-black counties were outvoted by whites in adjacent counties.[11] Because the vast bulk of the Mississippi electorate voted along racial lines, blacks had little chance of electing their preferences except in districts having sizable black majorities. A Mississippi case (*Kirksey v. Board of Supervisors of Hinds County*) spawned the "65 percent rule" based on the assumption that for African Americans to constitute a majority of the voting electorate, the district's population should be at least 65 percent black in order to offset racial differences in voting-age distribution, registration, and turnout.[12]

A third technique designed to reduce black political influence involves overpopulating a district with minorities. This technique, *packing*, usually ensures a minority representative. It is still designed to limit minority political power, however, because with an alternative configuration, the minority population could have a substantial voice in two districts instead of one.

All three techniques are considered to be dilutive since they keep a racial or partisan minority from achieving fair representation by "wasting" some votes of group members. With the first two, the minority is unable to elect any of its preferences. Packing is also dilutive since, even though a group can elect one of its preferences, this candidate wins with far more votes than needed, thereby wasting some votes. An African American candidate could carry, say, 80 percent of the vote in one district, but she only needs a plurality to win the seat. If the districts were drawn so that the black candidate won, say, 55 percent of the vote, a black candidate would still be elected (assuming racial voting), and a neighboring district would have a much stronger minority presence.

The federal government had learned from the South's obstinacy and inventiveness in developing new obstacles to school desegregation that simply eliminating old practices would not ensure equal rights. Therefore, Section 5 of the Voting Rights Act required that states targeted under the Voting Rights Act had to seek preclearance. In other words, before implementing any changes in voting laws, covered jurisdictions had to seek approval either through an administrative or judicial procedure. In the administrative process, the U.S. attorney general examines redistricting plans for fairness. The judicial approach involves a hearing before the U.S. District Court of the District of Columbia. Southern jurisdictions initially interpreted the preclearance provisions of Section 5 to mean that only legislation specifically relating to voting needed to obtain federal approval. In *Georgia v. U.S.* (1973), however, the Supreme Court held that Section 5 applied to redistricting plans, and the submitting authority had the burden of proving an absence of discrimination.[13]

Three examples demonstrate the types of discrimination that ran afoul of the Voting Rights Act prior to the 1990s. First, in the course of redrawing its congressional districts in 1971, Georgia excluded from its Fifth Congressional District (Atlanta) the homes of the two leading black candidates, former Atlanta mayor Andrew Young and future Atlanta mayor Maynard Jackson. The Justice Department invalidated this plan because it was purposely designed to hurt the electoral chances of black candidates; the legislature then recast it to include Young's home. In the next election, he joined Houston's Barbara Jordan to become the first African Americans elected to Congress from the South in the twentieth century.

Second, civil rights attorneys attacked the use of multimember districts in the Mississippi legislature, arguing that if these districts were divided into single-member districts, a number of the SMDs would have black majorities and thus allow African Americans to elect black representatives.[14] This would not be the case in the existing MMDs, in which whites comprised a majority of the population. The invalidation of MMDs (and also at-large elections in many municipalities) by courts began with *Connor v. Johnson* (1971), when the Supreme Court ruled on plans drawn by a federal district court in Mississippi. The district court had noted that the election of eleven representatives at large from Hinds County, which includes the city of Jackson, could easily cause voter confusion. In its capacity of overseeing actions by lower federal courts, the Supreme Court directed that court-drawn plans avoid MMDs and use exclusively SMDs.

Third, in a Texas case challenging the use of MMDs in Dallas and Bexar (San Antonio) counties, the Supreme Court upheld an equal protection claim brought by blacks and Hispanics. These two minority groups successfully claimed that the use of countywide at-large elections prevented the election of their candidates of choice, since the bulk of the electorate voted along racial lines and whites outnumbered minorities (*White v. Register*, 1973). According to the Court, subdividing the counties into SMDs remedied the problem.

Taken together, these decisions from the early 1970s established the principle that Section 5 preclearance applies to new districting plans and that, in drawing those plans, it is impermissible to use at-large or MMD plans if doing so dilutes the influence of minority voters. When a federal court draws the plan, that plan does not need to be precleared, but it must contain only SMDs.

Until 1990, retrogression topped the list of concerns for the Department of Justice when reviewing a redistricting plan. If a plan split existing substantial minority concentrations so as to reduce their political impact, DOJ would reject the plan, forcing the submitting authority to remedy DOJ concerns or seek approval from the District of Columbia court. It is important to note that a jurisdiction had no obligation to optimize or improve minority representation; the modest requirement was only to do no harm (*Beer v. U.S.*, 1976).

DOJ's focus changed dramatically, however, just before the round of redistricting that followed the 1990 census.

Racial Gerrymandering: Phase II

Amendments to Section 2 of the Voting Rights Act adopted in 1982 provided leverage that could be used against preexisting discrimination in the redistricting process. The original version of Section 2 was interpreted as being nothing more than a restatement of the Fifteenth Amendment. The new version of Section 2 permitted challenges to electoral practices nationwide that had the effect of diluting minority political influence even if there had been no intention to discriminate. Plaintiffs used Section 2 extensively in challenges to local at-large electoral systems. Invariably plaintiffs called for replacing MMDs or at-large elections with SMDs, in some of which minorities would be the majority of the population. In time, most MMD and at-large jurisdictions that had sizable minority populations but usually saw only whites elected had to change to SMDs. These changes made additional cities, counties, and school boards subject to periodic redistricting and therefore, in the covered jurisdictions, subject to Section 5 of the Voting Rights Act.

Section 2 also became involved in preclearance reviews of the legislative and congressional redistricting plans of covered jurisdictions. In 1990, the U.S. District Court for the Eastern District of Arkansas in *Jeffers v. Clinton* required that a large chunk of the state legislative districts in Arkansas be redrawn to create additional majority-black districts. Although the court did not find any intentional discrimination by the state, it nonetheless required a remapping that opened the way for black senators to triple to three and the number of black representatives to increase from five to nine. Even though the Supreme Court never heard *Jeffers*, DOJ incorporated the decision into the criteria used to evaluate redistricting plans. Incorporating Section 2 into Section 5 preclearance led DOJ to impose an affirmative duty on jurisdictions to expand the number of districts in which the minority population constituted a majority.

Relying on *Jeffers*, DOJ representatives warned legislators from states subject to Section 5 that they needed to draw additional majority-minority districts when possible. In an effort to increase the number of majority-black districts which would, in turn, likely produce more black elected officials, DOJ rejected North Carolina's congressional plan even though it created the state's first majority-black district in decades. In the past, a plan that enhanced black influence would have been approved. But, under Section 2, DOJ demanded that a second majority-black district be fashioned. Georgia had the same experience, and even though it added a second majority-black district, DOJ rejected its congressional plan with explicit directions to draw a third black district. In Georgia, three of eleven districts with black majorities would equal the state's overall black population percentage. In Louisiana, a districting plan for a statewide education board met a similar fate, with DOJ demanding a second majority-black district.

After the 1990 census, every southern state subject to Section 5 except Mississippi, which already had a majority-black congressional district among its five, drew at least one new majority-black district. DOJ's new expectations also prompted Florida and Texas to create additional majority-Hispanic districts. Southern states drew three new majority-Hispanic districts along with twelve new majority-black districts. Additional minority districts were also drawn in New York, Illinois, and Maryland. The new majority-minority districts often had strange shapes, since their creation required uniting minority concentrations in nonadjacent communities.

All of the new majority-black districts elected African Americans in 1992, and new Hispanic districts in Florida, Illinois, and New York, along with a new Hispanic district in the Rio Grande Valley, sent Hispanics to Congress. In the majority-Hispanic district in Houston, multiple Hispanics ran, with the strongest losing in the Democratic runoff to an Anglo.[15] At DOJ's behest, southern states also created a number of additional majority-minority state legislative districts.

Republicans used Section 2 of the Voting Rights Act to their advantage by creating coalitions with minority Democrats. In several southern legislatures, Republicans joined with minority Democrats supporting plans that crafted additional majority-minority districts,[16] and Republican political appointees at DOJ refused to preclear plans that did not maximize the numbers of black districts. Creating additional minority districts advantaged Republicans because to get a sufficient concentration of blacks for new majority-minority districts required the removal of minorities from surrounding districts. The neighboring districts now became whiter, and since blacks often give 90 percent or more of their votes to Democrats, the whiter the district, the less likely it would be to support a Democrat and the more likely that the district would elect a Republican. Many political scientists believe that these plans contributed to the GOP House majority won in 1994 and to the Republicans' ability to retain control of the House through the rest of the decade.[17] Though black representation in Congress increased, the shift in partisan control of Congress in 1994—a shift augmented by Republicans elected in bleached districts—weakened the Congressional Black Caucus's ability to influence legislation.

Petrocik and Desposato suggested that Democratic incumbents lost in 1994 because the massive redistricting split their districts, giving them many new constituents whom they had not previously represented.[18] Several other scholars contended that bleaching districts in order to create adjacent majority-minority districts made the whiter districts much more winnable by the GOP.[19] By 1995, Georgia's congressional delegation consisted of three black Democrats and eight white Republicans—a dramatic change from 1991, when the delegation had eight white Democrats, a black Democrat, and one Republican.

Some have argued that the racial gerrymandering of the early 1990s involved trade-offs between descriptive and substantive representation. The new majority-minority districts performed as anticipated and elected African Americans, thereby providing descriptive representation for that component of the population. If black policy preferences were less likely to secure enactment because Republicans now controlled the House, however, then the level of substantive representation afforded African Americans suffered.[20] Others have contended that white Democrats, who might have been elected in place of white Republicans but for the bleaching of districts to create the majority-minority districts, do not represent black interests as well as black legislators do either in terms of roll call voting[21] or in promoting black concerns.[22]

Challenges to Racial Gerrymanders
The Department of Justice's demands that states draw additional majority-minority districts, many of which were extremely contorted in shape, prompted a suit from Duke University law professor Robinson Everett. Everett found North Carolina's Twelfth Congressional District, a long, twisting strand of spaghetti that extended 160 miles from Gastonia to Durham, particularly appalling. In *Shaw v. Reno* (1993), the Supreme Court upheld Everett's efforts to have his day in court. Without ruling on the merits of the case, the Court's 5–4 opinion determined that the professor's suit was justiciable, meaning that it would be possible for a court to grant relief. Writing for the majority, Justice Sandra Day O'Connor focused on the shape of District Twelve that at times was no wider than two lanes of highway I-85. At several points, the district switched from the northbound lanes to the southbound lanes and was connected only at a touch point. O'Connor observed that in matters of legislative districts, "looks matter."

After the Supreme Court opened the way for litigating the issues involved in affirmative action gerrymandering, suits were filed in several other states. The Supreme Court next visited this issue in a Georgia case, *Miller v. Johnson* (1995). Georgia's Eleventh Congressional District stretched from the suburbs of Atlanta to Augusta on the South Carolina border and then ran along the river to Savannah. This district, spanning three metropolitan areas, was more than 60 percent black to ensure that the candidate preferred by black voters could win. In *Miller* the Court acknowledged the appropriateness of considering race when drawing districts but rejected this district because race had been the predominant factor considered by the legislature. The Court ruled that race could be a factor, but it must not trump other concerns such as compactness and respect for traditional political boundaries such as county lines.

In a Texas case regarding the drawing of congressional districts, the Supreme Court invalidated three more majority-minority districts. These districts, unlike the ones challenged in Georgia and North Carolina, each involved a single metropolitan area. Nonetheless, as in the other suits, the districts in *Bush v. Vera* (1996) were contorted as they twisted and turned, gathering together minority residents while carefully avoiding nearby concentrations of Anglos.

Because of these cases, state legislatures had to redraw their congressional district boundaries. After the invalidation of North Carolina's Twelfth Congressional District, the legislature drew a more compact version of the district and one that spanned fewer miles. Still, the new district, shaped something like a Y, stretched from Charlotte through High Point to Greensboro, with an arm that went from High Point to Winston-Salem. Everett again led a team that challenged the new district. Although he succeeded before a trial court, the Supreme Court in *Easley v. Cromartie* (2001) concluded that race had not been the dominant factor in drawing this district. The Court accepted the state's justification that it relied primarily upon partisanship in seeking to draw a safely Democratic district in order to maintain partisan balance within the state's congressional delegation.[23] The five-person majority acknowledged that, in North Carolina, African Americans provided the most loyal support for the Democratic Party and, consequently, Democratic concentrations would often also be black concentrations.

Despite warnings of dire consequences that would flow from invalidating the racial gerrymanders of the early 1990s, the actual impacts proved minimal. As states lost challenges to their districting plans and had to redraw congressional districts and disperse minority concentrations, the districts that had been drawn with majority-minority populations took on infusions of Anglos while neighboring districts added black populations.[24] Although several African-American members of Congress had to run in majority-white districts under the new plans, all who ran continued to win election until the census necessitated drawing new districts in 2002. One black member, Cleo Fields of Louisiana, left Congress and ran for governor when a new map replaced his bizarre district that had extended more than 600 miles and included parts of every urban area in the state except for New Orleans and Lake Charles.

In the course of redrawing majority-black districts, adjacent districts gained African Americans. With the infusion of black Democrats, some Republicans encountered stiff reelection challenges, but all the incumbents survived.

Disentangling Sections 2 and 5
The Department of Justice's incorporation of Section 2 considerations into Section 5 reviews had always been controversial. As stated earlier, Section 5 mandated that states and counties subject to one of the trigger mechanisms of the Voting Rights Acts of 1965, 1970, or 1975 submit redistricting plans to DOJ or to the U.S. District Court of the District of Columbia for preclearance.

Section 2 established an effects test to determine whether existing electoral rules resulted in minorities having less opportunity than whites to elect their candidates of choice. DOJ justified incorporation, noting that it would make little sense to approve a plan under Section 5 because it did not constitute retrogression while knowing that the plan could be challenged under Section 2 for diluting minority political influence. At one point, the U.S. assistant attorney general for civil rights stated his intention of dropping Section 2 considerations from preclearance reviews, but after a firestorm of criticism, he relented. Ultimately, in *Reno v. Bossier Parish School Board* (1999), the Supreme Court found incorporation of Section 2 into Section 5 reviews to be illegal. The Court ruled that had Congress wanted DOJ to assess plans for compliance with Section 2, it would have so indicated in the legislation. Since Congress did not take that step, DOJ had gone beyond its authority.

The Post-2000 Redistricting

Redistricting after the 2000 census took place in a different context than a decade earlier. Republicans controlled more governorships and legislatures than in 1991, and, in the South, Democrats were desperately trying to contain a rising tide of Republicanism. To stave off Republicans whose support from a majority of the electorate had percolated down from the presidency to statewide and congressional offices and now lapped at the edge of state legislatures required careful gerrymandering.[25] Key to the strategy of using support from a minority of the electorate to control a majority of legislative offices was the distribution of the Democratic Party's most loyal voters: African Americans. In the past, reducing black concentrations in districts in which they already constituted a majority would likely have run afoul of DOJ's nonretrogression standard.

In Georgia, Democrats brought in outside consultants to develop maps to more efficiently distribute black voters. The plan reduced the black concentration in eleven of twelve majority-black state senate districts, with the average decrease being eleven percentage points. The greatest drop, which exceeded twenty-five percentage points, reduced the district's black population from 88 percent to slightly more than 62 percent black. In five senate districts, the black share of the voting-age population (VAP) dropped below 52 percent. In four of these districts, fewer than half the registrants were black.

DOJ objected to three of the districts where it believed the reduction in black voting-age population endangered the ability of African Americans to elect their candidates of choice. In these districts, the black VAP fell to just above 50 percent, a drop of more than ten points in two districts. After the District of Columbia District Court sided with DOJ, Georgia boosted the black concentrations in those districts to approximately 55 percent of the VAP, which DOJ found acceptable.[26] Interestingly, in a fourth district where the black concentration fell from 63 to 51.5 percent of the VAP—and to which

DOJ did not object—the black incumbent, who was the president pro tem of the state senate, the senate's highest position, lost to a white Republican. In an open seat where the black VAP fell three percentage points, a Hispanic male defeated a black female in the decisive Democratic runoff. Although other factors no doubt played some role, reducing black concentrations accompanied the loss of two seats that African Americans had filled for more than a decade.

Georgia appealed the district court's decision and received a more receptive hearing before the U.S. Supreme Court. The state's expert, political scientist David Epstein, had published articles showing that even if black concentrations were lowered to less than 50 percent, blacks would still have a better than fifty–fifty chance of electing their preferences.[27] In *Georgia v. Ashcroft* (2003), the high court approved the redistribution of blacks that Democrats had carried out in a desperate effort to retain a majority of the seats with a minority of the vote. The 5–4 opinion explained that states have options under Section 5. One is to create a smaller number of districts with minority concentrations so high that the candidate preferred by the minority community will almost certainly be elected, which was DOJ's preference in the early 1990s. Alternatively, a state may draw a larger number of districts with lower minority concentrations in which the minority preference has a chance—but not a guarantee—of winning.[28] *Georgia v. Ashcroft* does not spell out how jurisdictions, DOJ, or courts should go about weighing the options. Does one district certain to elect the minority preference equal two or three minority influence districts? We must await additional suits to learn the answer.

Partisan Gerrymandering

Although partisan gerrymandering has a much longer history than racial gerrymandering, it has attracted less judicial attention. A result of the one-person, one-vote revolution launched in the mid-1960s has been to make it easier for legislative majorities to take advantage of the other party in the legislature. Once the norm of not splitting county lines fell, mapmakers dissected counties and cities to get at concentrations of partisans. Democrats could be gathered together in one district while Republicans could be corralled into another district, with the majority party maximizing its advantage by forcing the minority party to waste a number of its voters by packing or cracking them.

Prior to 1986, the Supreme Court had not acknowledged that the judiciary could grant relief to a party claiming it had been mistreated by its opponents during a redistricting. In *Davis v. Bandemer* (1986), the Supreme Court recognized a cause of action but did not find that the gerrymander under attack was so egregious as to justify judicial intervention. In *Davis*, Democrats challenged the use of MMDs because the party received a much smaller share of the seats than their share of the votes. To succeed, the Court advised, plaintiffs needed to show that discrimination was both intentional and had an actual discriminatory impact. The Court cautioned that an electoral system need not provide proportionality, meaning that a party had no right to expect that its share of votes would equal the share of seats received. Furthermore, the Court said it was insufficient to show disproportional results in a single election.

Although *Davis* opened the door for challenging partisan gerrymanders, the opportunity has remained an illusion. Thus far the Supreme Court has yet to find a partisan gerrymander so extreme that it merited intervention by the judicial branch. Since the redistricting carried out in the wake of the 2000 census has been considered to have included some of the worst examples of partisan gerrymandering,[29] further guidance from the Court would be helpful.

In 2002, a federal trial court sternly rebuffed a Democratic challenge to a Republican plan in Michigan. According to an attorney representing the Democrats, Republicans packed Democrats into five districts while making the other ten districts safe for the GOP.[30] The plan so effectively separated partisans that even if Democrats attracted ten percentage points more of the vote across the board, they would win only one more district. With 47 percent of the statewide vote, Republicans would likely win a majority of the congressional seats, a feat that would require a 58 percent share statewide for Democrats to achieve. The district court dismissed the plaintiffs' equal protection claims because they had not alleged that Democrats had been excluded *entirely* from the political process since they could still vote and work on and contribute to political campaigns (*O'Lear v. Miller,* 2002). The court also declined to intervene, citing the possibility that the current gerrymander might be undone after the next census.

The Supreme Court used a challenge to Pennsylvania's congressional districts to revisit the issue of partisan gerrymandering (*Vieth v. Jubelirer,* 2004). Democrats went to court when the state that had sent eleven Republicans and ten Democrats to the 107th Congress adopted a plan that gave Republicans majorities in fourteen of nineteen districts. In the course of eliminating the two districts lost through reapportionment, Republicans created two open seats that favored their party by combining two pairs of Democrats while a fifth Democrat shared a seat with a Republican incumbent in a district that favored the GOP.[31] As often happens with partisan gerrymanders, the perpetrators did not reap all the gains they anticipated and the delegation elected in 2002 had twelve Republicans along with seven Democrats. Despite some disappointment, by taking 63 percent of the seats, Republicans far exceeded the 46 percent of the vote that George Bush managed in his five-point loss to Al Gore in the state. As in previous court challenges to partisan gerrymander this one failed. Four of the justices wanted to go beyond rejecting the Democrats' call for redress. The four who supported the court's plurality opinion pointed out that no plaintiff has won a partisan gerrymander case, and even in *Vieth,* justices who believe the issue to be justiciable disagree on the appropriate standard of proof. This prompted four justices to call for the reversal of *Davis v. Bandemer.* Justice Kennedy, who cast the deciding vote, acknowledged that presently no standards exist that permit a plaintiff to win; nonetheless he favored keeping *Bandemer* viable since "in another case a standard might emerge that suitably demonstrates how an apportionment's *de facto* incorporation of partisan classifications burdens rights of fair and effective representation."

Although courts have shown little interest in questions of partisan gerrymandering, a sizable scholarly literature examines the topic. Political scientists acknowledge that the U.S. system of single-member districts usually awards the majority party a disproportionate share of the legislative seats. Although accepting the unlikelihood of proportional representation, two criteria permit assessment of the fairness of plans: bias and responsiveness.[32] In an unbiased plan, if two parties each get about 50 percent of the statewide vote, they will divide the legislative seats equally. Moreover, the seat bonus going to a party winning a majority of the votes is about the same for each party, which is clearly *not* the situation in the Michigan case cited previously where Republicans can win a majority of the seats with 47 percent of the vote whereas Democrats would need 58 percent of the vote to accomplish the same feat.

Responsiveness, an issue raised in *Vieth,* deals with the competitiveness of districts. The greater the number of seats offering prospects for both Democrats and Republicans, the more likely that shifts in public preferences will result in the replacement of members of one party by the opposing party. Again, the Michigan congressional plan does poorly on this dimension.

Population Deviations

Although the allowable deviation in the population across a state's congressional districts has increasingly been pushed to a single person, it was widely believed that a 5 percent deviation was a "safe harbor" for state legislative and local districts. A three-judge federal panel took a more restrictive view in a Georgia case (*Larios v. Cox,* 2004). Democrats who controlled redistricting pushed the envelope in an effort to increase their majorities in the state legislature even as their vote shares statewide declined. Rather than being normally distributed with most districts being fairly close to the ideal population (the state's population divided by the number of districts), most districts were substantially overpopulated or underpopulated. In the state senate, thirty-six of fifty-six districts had populations 4 percent off the ideal while in thirty-one districts the population deviation was 4.5 percent. Sixteen districts were 4.9 percent off the ideal and some districts were either 4.99 percent below the average or 4.99 percent above. The overpopulated districts had Republican majorities while the underpopulated ones had Democratic majorities.

The trial court held that the population deviations violated the one person, one vote standard since they could not be justified with "legitimate considerations incident to the effectuation of a rational state policy." Rationales for population variations that might have been convincing, but which the state did not raise as a defense, include a desire to avoid splitting county boundaries, to promote compactness or contiguity in districts, or to avoid pairing incumbents. The state offered two justifications. First, Democrats sought to maintain as many seats in south Georgia and inner-city Atlanta (where Republicans were weak) as possible. Second, the plans bolstered Democratic incumbents. The court rejected these since favoring south Georgia and Atlanta legislators disadvantaged other legislators and the state failed to also protect Republican incumbents.

Georgia has appealed *Larios*. If the Supreme Court allows the trial court opinion to stand, then similar suits will be filed in several other states. If *Larios* gets overturned, then a total deviation of less than 10 percent may indeed be a safe harbor.

Summary

With each passing decade, redistricting takes on greater significance. Parties begin planning and scheming years before the census is taken. Once states receive the results of the census, pitched battles are fought in legislative chambers as the majority tries to draw lines that will maximize its advantage. Geographic information systems technology facilitates the rapid production and evaluation of alternative plans so parties can maximize the number of districts in which they win.

Case law has established that when drawing congressional districts, any difference in population between the districts leaves the state vulnerable to a challenge from a plan that has a smaller population range. Increasingly, states produce congressional plans with a population deviation of one person. The constitutionality of 10 percent population deviations that have been widely used for state legislative and local districts have now been questioned in *Larios*.

Litigation pursuant to the Voting Rights Act has established that redistricting must not dilute minority influence. During the 1970s and 1980s this translated into a ban on retrogression that prevented breaking up existing minority concentrations. In the early 1990s, DOJ used amended Section 2 to require creation of additional majority-minority districts when feasible. After the Supreme Court invalidated plans drawn predominantly on the basis of race, jurisdictions ceased to have an affirmative duty to maximize minority representation, although race remains a factor when creating a map.

In the new century, some jurisdictions reduced minority concentrations—a step that in the past would have constituted retrogression—on the basis that heightened levels of minority participation and greater willingness among whites to support minority candidates lowered the threshold at which minority candidates could hope to win. In 2003, the Supreme Court indicated greater latitude for how jurisdictions dealt with minority populations. Under *Georgia v. Ashcroft,* jurisdictions could pursue the older tack of drawing districts in which the candidates preferred by minorities would win if the minority vote united. Alternatively, a jurisdiction could draw a greater number of districts in which the minority vote would be important even if not sufficient to determine the outcome. Either approach satisfies Section 5 of the Voting Rights Act.

Still to be determined is the nature of the trade-off suggested in *Georgia v. Ashcroft.* Also still up in the air is what evidence would suffice to win a claim alleging a partisan gerrymander. A third question mark hangs over whether other courts will follow *Larios* and demand narrower population tolerances for state legislative districts. Unless these questions are resolved conclusively, we can be certain that the number of redistricting plans challenged in court will not decline any time soon.

Notes

1. For a review of various systems of proportional representation, see Farrell, *Electoral Systems.*
2. The Court's rulings in *Reynolds* and *Wesberry* required population equality, but the Court did not define precisely what that meant. This is standard practice in the U.S. judiciary where courts often do not provide specific guidance, yet ban certain activities. As a series of court decisions bans more activities, it becomes clearer—and more narrowly defined—what is permitted. Thus, court-made law tends to be evolutionary. As another example, consider the evolution of what was meant by school desegregation and the amount of time permitted under "all deliberate speed."
3. The courts have been reluctant to impose more demanding standards on district plans for state legislatures because of federalism.
4. Saffell, "Reapportionment and Public Policy."
5. Sharkansky, "Reapportionment and Roll Call Voting."
6. Republicans were hurt immediately after 1973 because of Richard Nixon's resignation in 1974.
7. Cox and Katz, *Elbridge Gerry's Salamander.*
8. Mayhew, *Congress: The Electoral Connection.*
9. The states were Alabama, Georgia, Louisiana, Mississippi, South Carolina, Virginia, and about half of North Carolina.
10. Parker, *Black Votes Count,* p. 45.
11. Ibid.
12. The 65 percent rule was used at times by DOJ and judges as the threshold for black concentration needed to insure that the black population could elect its preferred candidate. By the 1990s, it was no longer needed.
13. Amendments to the Voting Rights Act in 1970 and 1975 expanded the number of states subject to preclearance. Currently all or parts of sixteen states have to obtain federal approval before putting a redistricting plan into effect.
14. Parker, *Black Votes Count.*
15. Abel and Oppenheimer, "Candidate Emergence."
16. Grofman, *Race and Redistricting in the 1990s.*

17. Lublin, *The Paradox of Representation.* A dissenter, Richard Engstrom ("Voting Rights Districts"), claimed that the racial gerrymandering of the early 1990s produced no gains for Republicans.

18. Petrocik and Desposato, "The Partisan Consequences."

19. See Lublin, *The Paradox of Representation,* for a review of these claims.

20. See Tate, *From Protest to Politics,* pp. 205–206.

21. Whitby, *The Color of Representation.*

22. Canon, *Race, Redistricting, and Representation.*

23. When this plan was drawn, the North Carolina delegation had six Democrats and six Republicans. By the time of the suit, Republicans had won a seventh seat.

24. During the mid-1990s, black districts in Florida, Georgia, Louisiana, North Carolina, Texas, and Virginia were made whiter. Hispanic districts in New York and Texas became whiter following litigation.

25. Bullock, Gaddie, and Hoffman, "Regional Variations." For an alternative perspective on the spread of Republican support and one that argued that it bubbled up from below, see Aldrich and Griffin, "Ambition in the South."

26. Georgia, which had encountered difficulties getting administrative preclearance in the past, pursued the judicial approach in 2001.

27. Cameron, Epstein, and O'Halloran, "Do Majority-Minority Districts Maximize Substantive Black Representation in Congress?"; Epstein and O'Halloran, "A Social Science Approach."

28. Reducing black concentrations had been upheld in New Jersey, a state that, unlike Georgia, is not subject to preclearance (*Page v. Bartels,* 2001). In New Jersey, reducing minority concentrations led to election of additional blacks (Hirsh, "The United States House of Unrepresentatives").

29. Hirsch, "The United States House of Unrepresentatives."

30. Ibid.

31. The best-laid redistricting plans do not always come to fruition as the Democrat beat his Republican colleague. Republicans ended up with twelve seats rather than the fourteen they had targeted.

32. Gelman and King, "A Unified Method."

11

Judicial Elections: A Different Standard for the Rulemakers?

Matthew J. Streb

There has been a plethora of studies examining presidential and congressional elections, but fewer scholars have systematically analyzed the judicial elections that thirty-nine states hold. In many election classes, professors completely ignore judicial elections, and in those that do not, students are often surprised to learn that the overwhelming majority of state judges are elected.

There are several reasons why scholars have focused more on presidential and congressional elections than judicial elections. Data collection makes it much easier to look at presidential, congressional, or even gubernatorial elections. Every two years the University of Michigan conducts the National Elections Study, a comprehensive pre/post national survey that asks respondents a variety of questions. Exit polls—polls conducted as voters leave the voting booth—are usually available to provide scholars with information on how people voted and why they voted that way. A variety of polling and news organizations conduct preelection polls that give researchers even more data to analyze. None of these sources of data usually asks questions about judicial elections.

The reason questions about judicial elections are rarely asked leads us to another explanation of why scholars have conducted little research on the subject: judicial campaigns just aren't that exciting. Citizens are engaged in presidential elections, watching television screens colored with red and blue states as if the election were some sort of athletic contest. To a lesser extent, we are engrossed in midterm elections, trying to predict which party will win control of Congress or pick up gubernatorial seats. We are more likely to understand the issues discussed in and the importance of the outcomes of these elections. They are fun to watch and interesting to study.

The excitement of judicial elections, on the other hand, has been compared to playing a game of checkers by mail.[1] Few people know who is running for judge, what the important issues are in the elections, and how the outcomes will influence the public. This is not to say, however, that judicial elections are inconsequential. Judges have a great deal of power and are deeply involved in dividing up scarce resources and deciding what kind of society we will live in. It is important, then, that we understand the rules of judicial elections and how judicial candidates' campaigns are conducted.

I begin by examining the debate between those who argue that judicial elections hold judges accountable for their rulings and those who believe that judicial elections sacrifice judicial independence. Then, I discuss how the states choose their judges and the politics of judicial elections. From there, I analyze the various rules of judicial elections in different states and how the courts have interpreted the constitutionality of those rules. Finally, I look briefly at the future of judicial elections.

Judicial Independence Versus Judicial Accountability

When writing the Constitution, the founding fathers often left many parts of the document quite vague. Of the sections relating to the three branches of government, Article III, which created a federal judicial system, was the least specific. Article III vested the judicial power of the United States "in one supreme Court, and in such inferior Courts as the Congress from time to time ordain and establish" and held that all federal judges would be appointed by the president and confirmed by the Senate.

Writing in *Federalist* No. 78, Alexander Hamilton argued that the judiciary was the least dangerous branch of the government because it had neither the power of the purse nor the sword, but "merely judgment." Hamilton was not concerned that the lifetime tenure of the justices would make them too powerful; instead, he argued that lifetime tenure was needed to secure judicial independence and "to guard the Constitution and the rights of individuals."[2]

Hamilton, like many of the founding fathers, believed that the Constitution was the "will of the people" and the job of the judiciary was to protect the Constitution from the momentary passions of a fickle public. Hamilton envisioned the judiciary as being above politics and insulated from public opinion. If judges had to be elected or reelected, their judicial independence would be compromised, and so would the Constitution. Instead of defending the Constitution, the judges would be forced to heed the momentary passions of the public and make popular rulings in order to keep their jobs. In particular, Hamilton argued that the rights of the minority would be threatened.

Because the United States' system of federalism created a dual-court system, each state would have its own judiciary, the rules for which would be spelled out in the state's constitution.[3] Immediately after the ratification of the Constitution, the thirteen states all selected their judges in a manner similar to that used by the federal government. Five of the states opted for the same system as the federal government, whereas the other eight gave the appointment power directly to the state legislatures. In no state were judges elected.

That changed with the election of Andrew Jackson, however.[4] The era of Jacksonian Democracy not only gave more power to the people; it also saw an increase in the number of states entering the Union. Many of these new states questioned the judicial appointment process used by the federal government because judicial independence kept judges from being held accountable to the people and was considered to be undemocratic. The number of states holding judicial elections increased dramatically. "Beginning with the admission of Missouri in 1832, every state which entered the Union until 1958 adopted constitutional provisions for an elected judiciary."[5] Although there have been attempts in some states to eliminate judicial elections, they have failed, largely because people are concerned with losing judicial accountability.

How States Select Their Judges

Although the federal judicial appointment system is quite simple—the president appoints, the Senate confirms—the number of variations states use is quite complex. Each state has its own rules regarding selection and length of term, but there are generally six ways in which states choose who will sit on their benches. Three of these use an appointment process:

> *Gubernatorial Appointment Without a Nominating Commission*—Two states, New Jersey and Maine, simply follow the federal model of judicial selection. The governor independently chooses a judicial nominee who is then subject to legislative confirmation. The judges in both states serve seven-year terms and are reappointed in the same manner.[6]
>
> *Legislative Appointment Without a Nominating Commission*—Virginia continues to use the plan adopted by the majority of the states after the ratification of the Constitution. Its judges are appointed (and reappointed) by the state legislature.
>
> *Merit Selection Through a Nominating Commission*—In states such as Hawaii, New Hampshire, and Rhode Island, a nominating committee—often comprising state lawyers and judges—presents a list of potential nominees to the governor from which to choose. The governor then must nominate one of those candidates. The lengths of the terms vary by state. For example, justices in Rhode Island are appointed for life. Judges in Hawaii are given ten-year terms, after which they must be reappointed by the Judicial Selection Commission. Hawaii's appointment process is especially interesting because

the governor or chief justice of the state supreme court, depending on which state court has a vacancy, chooses from a list provided by the Judicial Selection Commission. The state senate must then confirm the nominees. After the ten-year term expires, only the Judicial Selection Commission decides if the justice should be reappointed to another term.

South Carolina's judicial selection process is slightly different because the Judicial Merit Selection Commission provides a list of three candidates to the state legislature, not to the governor. Of the ten seats on the state's Judicial Merit Selection Committee, six are held by members of the General Assembly and the remaining four seats are chosen by the state legislature from the general public.

The appointment of state justices without an electoral component is not frequent, however. More than three-fourths of the states use some sort of electoral process to choose at least some of their judges. Eighty-seven percent of the general jurisdiction appellate and trial judges run in popular elections.[7] There are three types of judicial elections:

Partisan Election—States including Alabama, Illinois, Pennsylvania, and Texas elect their judges in the same manner as they vote in presidential or congressional elections. Political parties nominate candidates, who then run under the party's name. Six states hold outright partisan elections.[8]

Nonpartisan Election—Because many people believe partisan politics has no place in judicial elections, a number of states hold nonpartisan elections in which no political party is listed next to the candidates' names on the ballot. The state of North Carolina most recently voted to switch from partisan to nonpartisan elections; it will hold its first nonpartisan judicial elections in fall 2004.

Retention Elections—In several states, judges are forced to run in retention elections. Judges are appointed to the bench (usually by the governor, in some cases with a merit commission, in some cases without) for a set term. After a judge's term is completed, the public then votes whether to retain the judge. The judge does not run against an opponent; voters simply vote "Yes" to keep him or her on the bench or "No" to remove the judge. Retention elections were a creation of the Progressive Movement as an attempt to generate a compromise between judicial independence and accountability.

What makes the selection process of state justices even more confusing is that some states use different methods to choose justices for different courts. For example, in California judges for the supreme court and the courts of appeal are appointed to twelve-year terms and then must face retention elections. On the other hand, candidates for superior court must run in non-partisan elections and are elected to six-year terms.

The Politics of Judicial Elections

Judicial elections are generally low-key affairs that receive little media coverage. Because of the lack of easily accessible information in judicial elections, turnout in these elections is normally quite low. One study of voter turnout in twenty-five nonsouthern states from 1948 to 1974 found that the average turnout for judicial elections in nonpresidential years was only 24.6 percent.[9] A more recent example showed a similar finding. In 2002, fewer than 15 percent of eligible voters participated in New York City's judicial elections.[10] Also, voter rolloff (those people who cast ballots but did not vote in a judicial election) is quite high, although it varies by type of election.[11] In general, voter rolloff is less in partisan elections than in nonpartisan or retention elections, largely because an easily obtainable cue—party identification—makes it easier to vote. It is clear that many people who make the effort to turn out to vote in high-information contests (that is, president, Congress, governor) are skipping judicial elections. One study of retention elections in ten states from 1964 to 1994 found that rolloff averaged 34.5 percent.[12]

Another characteristic of judicial elections is that incumbent judges are rarely challenged and those who are challenged rarely lose (although there are signs that this trend is beginning to change in some states and counties[13]). In a study of state supreme court races from 1980 to 1995, only roughly half of the incumbents faced opposition.[14] In 2002, of the 142 superior court justices who came up for reelection in Los Angeles County, only two were opposed![15]

The few judges who are challenged normally win. One study found that 92 percent of all judges up for reelection or retention either won or were retained, and they won quite easily. It is extremely rare that a judge is removed from office in a retention election. In fact, almost 99 percent of judges are retained;[16] in some states, such as Florida, a judge has never lost a retention election.[17] On average, more than 70 percent of voters in state supreme court retention elections reaffirmed the judges; incumbents running in nonpartisan elections received an average of 75.9 percent of the vote, and those in partisan elections carried 68.3 percent of the vote.[18] Judicial scholar Lawrence Baum argued that the empirical evidence of the incumbent advantage for lower-court judges, although somewhat spotty and out of date, indicated that incumbents fared even better in those races.[19]

Many justices are given an incumbency advantage without having to actually run in an election. More than half of all elected justices are initially appointed by a governor to fill a retiring judge's term. Often judges will strategically retire if the governor is a member of the judge's party. This way the justice's replacement will be a member of the same party, and the new justice will have the incumbency advantage in his or her first election.

Even though few people participate in judicial elections, judges regularly run unopposed, and those who do not are almost always retained or reelected; the public supports judicial elections. In a survey conducted by Justice at Stake, a nonpartisan organization comprising more than thirty judicial, legal, and citizen organizations, 52 percent of respondents said they supported merit selection followed by retention election. Another 19 percent favored holding nonpartisan judicial elections, and 7 percent believed judicial elections should be partisan. Only 18 percent responded that there should be no electoral component when selecting judges.[20] Those who oppose judicial elections agree with Hamilton and the founders' contention that judicial elections lessen judicial independence because judges must worry about keeping their seat on the bench. In fact, the American Bar Association (ABA) has argued against judicial elections for more than seventy years.

Opponents of judicial elections also argue that judicial elections create an extreme conflict of interest. Judicial candidates need money to be elected (or in some cases retained) and are forced to rely heavily on groups such as trial lawyers and businesses who may very well appear before the candidate if elected. There are certainly still many instances where judges do not need money because they are unopposed. For example, 25 percent of supreme court candidates in 2000 reported raising no money.[21] But there has been a trend in recent years for some states to have extremely competitive judicial races in which campaign funding becomes incredibly important.

By far, business and lawyers were the two largest contributors to state supreme court candidates between 1989 and 2000.[22] The U.S. Chamber of Commerce spent $10 million on judicial races in 2000, mostly on judicial races in just five states. It spent $1.3 million on issue advocacy ads alone, and trial lawyers and unions combined to spend $945,000 on issue advocacy ads.[23] In 2002, the Chamber of Commerce and the Business Roundtable raised even more money, spending $25 million on that year's judicial elections.[24]

Though judicial elections often go unnoticed by the media, judicial campaigns are becoming more expensive, especially in supreme court races. "In the 2000 campaign, supreme court candidates raised $45.6 million—a 61% increase over 1998. . . . The average state Supreme Court candidate in 2000 raised $430,529—and 16 of them raised more than $1 million."[25] In 2000 in Michigan, with three justices up for reelection, a record $15 million was spent in the battle to control the state's supreme court.[26] The amount of money raised by supreme court candidates dropped slightly in 2002 to almost $33 million, still the second largest amount of money in history raised for these races.[27] The increase in campaign spending is not simply a supreme court election phenomenon. In 2002, Broward County, Florida, judicial candidates for six circuit seats spent more than $2.7 million combined.[28] Though the public supports judicial elections, 72 percent reported being concerned that the money raised by judicial candidates compromised the judges' impartiality; 26 percent of judges believed that campaign donations have at least some influence on their decisions. Forty-six percent of judges felt pressure to raise money for campaign expenses. Finally, nine in ten voters and eight in ten state judges believed that, even if judges were not being influenced, special interests were trying to use the courts to shape public policy.[29]

Because of the concern of influence that money may have on judges, many states have laws that do not allow a judicial candidate to accept money directly from a corporation, union, interest group, or individual; instead, the candidate must set up a fund-raising committee (as discussed below, however, the constitutionality of these laws has been questioned). It is unclear, although unlikely, that these laws have been effective. Even though judicial candidates may not directly accept contributions in these states, it is hard to believe that they are unaware of who is donating money.

A few states have gone further in their quest to limit the influence money has on judicial elections by publicly financing judicial campaigns in a manner similar to the one the federal government uses in presidential elections. In the late 1970s, Wisconsin took the first step at publicly financing elections for the state supreme court. In Wisconsin, a candidate who agrees to a $215,000 spending limit is eligible for state money. Candidates are not forced to accept government funds, however, and if even one candidate does not agree, none of the candidates has to follow the spending limit, which has kept the law from being effective. For example, in 1999 Chief Justice Shirley Abrahamson accepted government funds, but her opponent did not. Abrahamson ended up spending $1.36 million on her campaign.[30]

In 2002, North Carolina became the first state to adopt full public financing for all appellate-level judicial campaigns.[31] It is unclear how effective the reform will be because, as in Wisconsin, candidates are not forced to accept state funding, and much of the funding will be created from an income tax return check-off. As with the presidential election income tax return check-off, the well in states that publicly finance elections is quite dry because few people are willing to give money.[32] Also, although public financing could crack down on the direct contributions to judicial candidates that create an immense conflict of interest, it is unclear whether public financing will really affect that conflict of interest. Certainly groups can still run issue advocacy ads and support or oppose a justice without directly contributing to the campaign. In fact, noncandidate spending in the five states with the most competitive supreme court elections in 2000 totaled $16 million.[33] Although the conflict of interest in this case may not be direct, it certainly remains.

In addition, public financing of judicial elections may actually increase the incumbency advantage that judges hold. As Lawrence Baum wrote, ". . .

money is the most important key to the effectiveness of campaigns to defeat sitting judges."[34] Baum noted that "spending very large sums of money to defeat incumbents is not enough to ensure success,"[35] but campaign spending is really the only way that challengers can overcome the incumbent's possible name recognition advantage; limiting the amount of money a challenger can spend will make it difficult for the challenger to do so. Though the ABA opposes judicial elections, it has realized that they are not likely to be abolished; therefore, it supports public financing of judicial elections.

Increasingly competitive judicial elections in some states and counties have led many to argue that they have become far more negative as well. "Despite what many justices might want to believe," wrote Joseph R. Cerrell and Hal Dash, "judicial campaigns can be as rough-and-tumble politically as any other election."[36] Judicial elections are supposed to be low-key affairs that remain civil. This is certainly not always the case. A study of supreme court campaign advertisements by Justice at Stake found that most ads run by candidates were positive, but spots created by political parties or interest groups were quite negative. Although fewer than 20 percent of candidates' ads attacked their opponents, 80 percent of interest group ads were negative! A majority of ads (57 percent) run by political parties contrasted the two candidates, and 27 percent attacked the other party's candidate. Only 16.1 percent of the party ads and 9.6 percent of the interest group ads were positive.[37]

The issues salient in judicial campaigns are not usually the same issues that dominate presidential or congressional elections. Until recently judicial candidates often could not announce their positions on policy issues, and, as discussed below, questions about what a judicial candidate can and cannot say on the campaign trail remain. Instead of focusing on judicial candidates' views on issues such as abortion or the death penalty, judicial elections focus mainly on personality and qualifications.[38] Advocates of judicial elections argue that the election should be about which candidate has the most merit, not about candidates' views on a variety of issues. In addition to qualifications, candidates often highlight their religious or ethnic backgrounds.[39] On the other hand, political parties and interest groups are able to raise issues that candidates often cannot. One study of television ads during the 2000 judicial elections found that parties and interest groups highlighted three main themes: civil justice (usually tort liability and reform), crime control, and family values.[40]

It is not entirely clear that policy issues or candidate qualifications matter in judicial elections, however, or that citizens are capable of making intelligent votes. "In the great majority of contests, a large share of the voters come to their polling place without having assimilated much (or any) information about that contest," wrote Baum. "Indeed, many voters are not aware that these contests exist until they see the ballot."[41] I have already discussed that turnout is quite low, largely because the cost of obtaining information in judicial elections can be quite high. Often voters will simply rely on name recognition to cast their vote. According to one political observer, judicial candidates in Broward County, Florida, bombarded the county with billboard signs in 2002 in hope "that voters will choose the name they've seen most often and remember."[42] The odds that voters will remember judicial candidates' names are still small, however. Surveys have found that not only do voters have difficulty recalling the names of judicial candidates, but large numbers of people who vote in these contests do not even *recognize* the names of the candidates. Those who recognize the candidates' names are usually not able to rate them.[43] In one study, only 14.5 percent of voters interviewed immediately after casting their ballots could identify a single judicial candidate on the ballot.[44] Another study of judicial elections in Washington and Oregon found that a strong majority of people reported not having enough information to make an informed vote.[45] And an examination of the Ohio Supreme Court discovered that no more than 4 percent of Ohioans could name a justice on the highest court in the state.[46]

Perhaps the best indication that citizens are casting questionable votes can be found in two 1990 races for supreme court seats in Washington and Texas. In Washington, a man who did not campaign and spent only $500 beat the state's chief justice. The victor had the same name as a well-known Tacoma television anchor. In Texas, a man named Gene Kelly beat an intermediate appellate judge who was supported by both the plaintiffs' bar and the defense bar in a primary. Kelly then spent only $7,795 in the general election against an opponent who spent more than $1,000,000, mostly on ads reminding voters "He's Not That Gene Kelly." Kelly still captured 44 percent of the vote.[47]

As with other low-information contests, voters will try to find any inexpensive cue to help them cast their votes. Scholars have found that voters rely on a candidate's ethnicity[48] or gender,[49] not necessarily reliable cues. In a study of California trial court elections, Dubois concluded that occupational ballot labels influenced people's votes. Those candidates who listed some prior judicial experience in lower level courts were significantly more likely to win than those who had no previous experience.[50] Studies have discovered that voters also rely heavily on voter pamphlets distributed by the secretaries of state before the election and on newspaper and bar association endorsements when making their decisions.[51]

Perhaps the most commonly used cue in judicial contests, when available, is party identification.[52] As Baum concluded, studying Ohio's 1984 supreme court elections, "party affiliation was a strong correlate of voting decisions."[53] Squire and Smith found that when given an indirect partisan cue (in their experiment, one group was provided with the name of the governor who initially appointed the judge), people used that information when evaluating whether the justice should be retained.[54] Few states hold partisan judicial elections, however, and many people, including members of the ABA, are opposed to partisan judicial elections because they want to limit partisan involvement in these elections. In other words, the cheapest, and most likely accurate, cue is not available to most voters.

The Rules of Judicial Elections

Although judicial elections have many of the same characteristics as, say, congressional elections (for example, the role of money, the incumbency advantage, negative campaigning), many argue that judicial elections are different from elections for other offices because of the nature of the position. Judges do not have constituencies the same way that members of Congress or the state legislatures do, and they are expected to be impartial. Therefore, supporters of judicial elections seek to remove politics from the judicial selection process. They cringe at the role money has played, believe judges should not seek endorsements or run in a partisan manner, and want to limit what judicial candidates talk about on the campaign trail. All of these concerns have led judicial candidates to be subjected to much different electoral rules than candidates for other offices. Many states have enacted laws that keep judicial candidates from attending political gatherings, receiving campaign contributions directly, and seeking party endorsements.

Perhaps the biggest restriction placed on judicial candidates is the guidelines that many states have enacted, which limit the issues candidates can discuss during the campaign. There are generally four canons based on the ABA's Model Code of Judicial Conduct that states abide by in judicial elections. First, the *Announce Clause* prohibits a judicial candidate from "announcing his or her view on disputed legal or political issues."[55] Under the announce clause, a candidate could not make known his or her position on issues such as abortion, the death penalty, or gay rights. Second, the *Commit Clause* prohibits "statements that commit or appear to commit the candidate with respect to cases, controversies, or issues that are likely to come before the court."[56] Although the two are obviously quite similar, the commit clause is more specific than the announce clause. Under the commit clause, for instance, a candidate could not say she would never give the death penalty to someone convicted of murder. Third, under the *Pledges and Promises Clause*, it is illegal for judicial candidates to make "pledges or promises of conduct in office other than the faithful and impartial performance of the duties to the office."[57] Under this clause, a candidate could not, for example, state that she vows to crack down on drunk driving by giving stricter punishments. Finally, the *Misrepresent Clause* provides that a judicial candidate shall not "knowingly misrepresent the identity, qualifications, present position, or other fact concerning the candidate or an opponent."[58] Table 11.1 provides a list of states that have adopted laws similar to the clauses listed above. As the information in the table makes clear, the great majority of states that hold judicial elections limit what candidates can say when campaigning.

Table 11.1   Summary of State Provisions in the States that Hold Judicial Elections

State	Announce Clause	Commit Clause	Pledges and Promises Clause	Misrepresent Clause
Alabama			X	X
Alaska		X	X	X
Arizona	X	X	X	X
Arkansas		X	X	X
California		X		X
Colorado	X		X	X
Florida		X	X	X
Georgia		X	X	X
Idaho		X	X	X
Illinois		X		X
Indiana		X	X	X
Iowa	X	X	X	X
Kansas		X	X	X
Kentucky		X	X	X
Louisiana		X	X	X
Maryland	X		X	X
Michigan			X	X
Minnesota	X		X	X
Mississippi		X	X	X
Missouri	X		X	X
Montana			X	
Nebraska		X	X	X
Nevada		X	X	X
New Mexico	X	X	X	X
New York		X	X	X
North Carolina			X	X
North Dakota		X	X	X
Ohio		X	X	X
Oklahoma		X	X	X
Oregon			X	X
Pennsylvania	X		X	X
South Dakota		X	X	X
Tennessee		X	X	X
Texas			X	X
Utah			X	X
Washington		X	X	X
West Virginia		X	X	X
Wisconsin		X	X	
Wyoming		X	X	X

Source: Compiled by the author from information obtained from American Judicature Society, www.ajs.org.

Note: Connecticut, Delaware, Hawaii, Maine, Massachusetts, New Hampshire, New Jersey, Rhode Island, South Carolina, Vermont, and Virginia do not hold judicial elections. Maine, Rhode Island, South Carolina, and Vermont have commit clauses, pledges and promises clauses, and misrepresent clauses for their judicial nominees.

Many criticize the canons and other judicial election laws as restricting a candidate's right to free speech and keeping important information from voters. As a result, political parties and individuals have challenged these rules in court. The most documented case was filed by Minnesota judicial candidate Greg Wersal and the state's Republican Party. Wersal and the state's GOP argued that Minnesota's Code of Judicial Conduct, specifically its "announce clause" and the ban on the use of political party endorsements in judicial elections, was unconstitutional. Wersal first ran for the state's supreme court in 1996, when he criticized many of the court's previous decisions on crime, welfare, and abortion and stated that he was a strict constructionist—one who interprets the Constitution literally with the framers' intentions uppermost in mind. In one instance, Wersal's campaign distributed literature that stated that "the Minnesota Supreme Court has issued decisions which are marked by their disregard for the Legislature and a lack of common sense." Another piece criticized a Minnesota Supreme Court decision striking down a law restricting welfare benefits, stating that "it's the Legislature which should set our spending policies."[59] A complaint was made against Wersal that he had violated the state's announce clause, and Wersal decided to withdraw from the race. Two years later, Wersal once again ran for a state supreme court position and was warned that he could not make the kind of statements he had made in his previous campaign. Wersal then filed suit. Such diverse groups and individuals as the American Civil Liberties Union, the U.S. Chamber of Commerce, and Pat Robertson filed amicus briefs on behalf of the judicial candidate.

The case was first heard in the U.S. District Court for the District of Minnesota and then in the U.S. Court of Appeals for the Eighth Circuit. In both cases, the judges sided with the state of Minnesota, arguing that the canon did not violate the First Amendment because the clause reached "only to disputed issues that are likely to come before the candidate if he is elected judge."[60] The Eighth Circuit added that the announce clause did not prohibit general discussions of case law and judicial philosophy.[61] In 2002, the Supreme Court granted review of the portion of the case dealing with the announce clause (it did not hear the party endorsement challenge) and in the case of the *Republican Party of Minnesota v. White,* in a narrow 5–4 decision, overturned the Eighth Circuit's ruling.

The Court held that Minnesota's announce clause failed to meet strict scrutiny and that states did not have a compelling interest for restricting speech of judicial candidates. Writing for the majority, Justice Antonin Scalia argued that the First Amendment does not permit "leaving the principle of elections in place while preventing candidates from discussing what the elections are about."[62] He continued, "It is simply not the function of government to select which issues are worth discussing or debating in the course of a political campaign. We have never allowed the government to prohibit candidates from communicating relevant information to voters during an election."[63] In a concurring opinion, Justice Anthony Kennedy wrote, "The political speech of candidates is at the heart of the First Amendment, and direct restrictions on the content of candidate speech are simply beyond the power of government to impose."[64] He went on to say:

> Minnesota may choose to have an elected judiciary. It may strive to define those characteristics that exemplify judicial excellence. It may enshrine its definitions in a code of conduct. . . . What Minnesota may not do, however, is censor what the people hear as they undertake to decide for themselves which candidate is most likely to be an exemplary judicial officer. Deciding the relevance of candidate speech is the right of the voters, not the State. The law in question here contradicts the principle that unabridged speech is the foundation of political freedom.[65]

Not all agreed with Scalia and Kennedy's claims. Those who dissented argued that judicial elections are not the same as elections for other offices, therefore are not entitled the same First Amendment protections. According to Justice Ruth Bader Ginsburg:

> Legislative and executive officials serve in representative capacities. They are agents of the people; their primary function is to advance the interests of their constituencies. . . . Judges, however, are not political actors. They do not sit as representatives of particular persons, communities, or parties; they serve no faction or constituency. . . . Thus, the rationale underlying unconstrained speech in elections for political office—that representative government depends on the public's ability to choose agents who will act at its behest—does not carry over to campaigns for the bench.[66]

Finally, while siding with the majority, Justice Sandra Day O'Connor, the only Supreme Court justice to actually run in a judicial election, cautioned against holding judicial elections, period, because they compromise a judge's ability to remain impartial.[67] In her concurring opinion, O'Connor wrote:

> We of course want judges to be impartial, in the sense of being free from any personal stake in the outcome of the case to which they are assigned. But if judges are subject to regular elections they are likely to feel that they have at least some personal stake in the outcome of every publicized case. Elected judges cannot help being aware that if the public is not satisfied with the outcome of a particular case, it could hurt their reelection prospects.[68]

The effects of the *White* decision could be seen immediately. In Alabama, the Christian Coalition sent judicial candidates a questionnaire asking them a number of questions about personal values and positions on issues including abortion and adoption by same-sex couples. The Alabama Judicial Inquiry Commission advised judicial candidates not to answer the questionnaire, arguing that doing so would violate state restrictions on judicial campaigns. Because of the *White* ruling, the commission withdrew its advice.[69]

The Court's ruling in *White* only applied specifically to the announce clause, leaving many to speculate that more lawsuits challenging the other clauses, especially the commit clause because it is so similar, lie ahead. Indeed, fresh off his earlier victory, Wersal and the state Republican Party quickly filed another lawsuit that would strike down bans on judicial candidates' attending and speaking at political conventions, seeking party endorsements and campaign contributions directly, and identifying as members of a political party. Several of these practices are discouraged by the ABA's Code of Judicial Conduct and are restricted in many states. Wersal's goal is to have judicial elections treated like all other elections. "[Judges] do set policy," stated Wersal. "If we're going to have policymakers, then I think we want real elections where the people choose who's making policy."[70] In March 2004, the U.S. Eighth Circuit Court of Appeals upheld Minnesota's ban on judicial candidates soliciting campaign contributions directly. The court sent the remaining questions back to a federal district court for further review. Wersal's challenges have not fallen on deaf ears, however. In April, a Minnesota Supreme Court advisory board recommended that judicial candidates be allowed to identify with political parties and speak at party functions. At the time of this writing, the state supreme court was set to hear public comment on the proposed changes.

Wersal is not the only person battling judicial canons. Running in a competitive race for the Georgia Supreme Court in 1998, Atlanta lawyer George M. Weaver challenged the rules of the state's Judicial Qualifications Commission (JQC) as violating his First Amendment right to free speech. In October 2002, in the case of *Weaver v. Bonner,* the Eleventh U.S. Circuit Court of Appeals found canons that "punished candidates who made 'misleading' statements and prohibited candidates from soliciting campaign funds personally" to be unconstitutional.[71] The JQC has decided not to appeal to the Supreme Court. Because the Supreme Court did not hear the case, the Eleventh Circuit's ruling only applies to those states that fall under the Eleventh Circuit's jurisdiction. Therefore, the Minnesota ban on direct contributions to judicial candidates is not directly affected by the *Weaver* ruling.

The Future of Judicial Elections

The decisions made by the courts in *White* and *Weaver* certainly open the door for many more challenges to the rules of judicial elections. It would not be surprising in the near future to see suits filed arguing that the commit clause and the pledges and promises clause are unconstitutional. And if the rulings in *White* and *Weaver* are any indication of how the courts might rule in future cases, the landscape of judicial elections could change dramatically.

The intent to keep judicial elections distinct from elections for other elected officials is certainly threatened by the recent court rulings. Although many court scholars argue that the decision in *White* does not make it clear what a candidate can and cannot say during a campaign, certainly the implication of the decision is that candidates may campaign in a manner similar to that used by candidates for other offices. The concern expressed by many advocates of judicial elections is that the striking down of the announce clause will make judicial elections even nastier, much like elections for other offices.

The increased importance of money in many judicial elections raises many more problems. The role of money is inevitable in any election. To challenge a sitting justice, a candidate needs money. To defend a sitting justice from being challenged by a strong candidate, the incumbent needs money. Although the vast majority of incumbents run unopposed, more states are seeing competitive, expensive judicial elections. Judicial candidates raising and spending more money will likely have a negative effect on the public. It will cause the public to question even further whether judges are impartial or if they are being "bought" by special interests. Public financing of judicial elections is an interesting idea, but, as I mentioned earlier, it has major problems. It will not lessen the amount of candidate spending, will possibly lead to a greater incumbency advantage, and will be difficult for the states to finance.

Because of the concerns that judicial campaigns will focus on policy issues such as abortion and welfare instead of candidate qualifications, that campaigns for judicial seats will only become more negative, and that the role of money has made many question whether judges can remain impartial, advocates of judicial elections continually try to reform the system and keep politics out of the judicial election process. The reforms will continue to fail, however, because whenever an election occurs, politics is inevitable.

The most common reason offered by advocates in support of judicial elections is that electing justices is democracy at work. To take away a person's voice and ability to elect his or her state judges, they say, threatens democracy. This argument is misguided, however. Judicial elections might technically be democratic, but they are a type of dangerous democracy. Study after study has found, and election after election has indicated, that citizens are rarely informed about the most basic information in judicial elections, making it difficult to cast an intelligent vote. Those cues, such as party identification, that provide citizens with helpful information are often not available because of the concern that politics should play no role in judicial elections. Discussions of issues such as abortion and the death penalty that might help a person decide whom to vote for have rarely been permitted on the campaign trail. The importance of money in judicial elections will only become greater, making it increasingly difficult for a judge to appear impartial. And, interestingly, those who are so concerned about protecting democracy have shown little interest in amending the Constitution to elect federal judges. Apparently democracy only matters when choosing state justices.

If we truly want to remove politics from the judicial electoral process, we simply must eliminate judicial elections and move to a system comparable to the way federal justices are appointed. Certainly it would be naive to argue that politics is not an integral part of the federal process, but that process is less dangerous than electing judges. States including Maryland and New York have recently tried to eliminate judicial elections—but have failed to do so. Support for judicial elections remains strong. Since it is unlikely that judicial elections are going anywhere in the future, we should not be surprised then to see increasingly political judicial elections and many more cases challenging the rules guiding the ways those elections are run.

Notes

I would like to thank Lawrence Baum, Eileen Gallagher, and Malia Redick for their comments and assistance. All errors are the responsibility of the author.

1. Bayne, "Lynchard's Candidacy," p. DS1.
2. Hamilton, Madison, and Jay, *The Federalist* No. 78, pp. 396, 400.
3. In Delaware, Maryland, Massachusetts, and New Hampshire the selection process is established by executive order. See American Judicature Society, "Judicial Selection in the States."
4. Although the number of states holding judicial elections grew substantially during Jackson's presidency, in 1812 Georgia was the first state to implement judicial elections.
5. Presser et al., "The Case for Judicial Appointments." www.fed-soc.org.
6. In New Jersey, a judge over the age of seventy cannot be reappointed.
7. Kozlowski, "Robed and Running," p. 35.
8. In judicial elections in Ohio for all courts and in Michigan for the Supreme Court, candidates' partisan affiliations are not listed on the ballot, but they are nominated in partisan primary elections. Illinois and Pennsylvania use partisan elections for the initial selection of a justice, who then must face retention elections after ten-year terms.
9. Dubois, "Voter Turnout in State Judicial Elections," p. 870.
10. Jockers, "Recent Events Fuel Debate," p. 12.
11. Dubois, "Voter Turnout in State Judicial Elections"; Dubois, *From Ballot to Bench*. Dubois found, however, that voter turnout in judicial elections was no less than in other "down-ballot" contests.
12. Aspin et al., "Thirty Years of Judicial Retention Elections," p. 12.
13. Hanes, "Balto. County Judges."
14. Hall, "State Supreme Courts in American Democracy." Judges running in partisan elections were more likely to be challenged than judges running in nonpartisan ones.
15. Guccione, "Elected Judges Are a Rare Breed."
16. Aspin et al., "Thirty Years of Judicial Retention Elections"; Presser et al., "The Case for Judicial Appointments." About half of those not retained came from Illinois, which requires that judges receive a 60 percent affirmative vote.
17. Schotland, "Financing Judicial Elections," p. 225.

18. Hall, "State Supreme Courts in American Democracy," p. 318.

19. Baum, "Judicial Elections and Judicial Independence."

20. Justice at Stake, "Poll of American Voters."

21. Goldberg, Holmes, and Sanchez, *The New Politics of Judicial Elections*, p. 11.

22. Ibid., p. 9.

23. Carter, "Boosting the Bench," p. 29.

24. Stone, "The Blitz to Elect Business-Friendly Judges."

25. Goldberg, Holmes, and Sanchez, *The New Politics of Judicial Elections*, p. 4.

26. Wohl, "Judge on the Stump," p. 15.

27. Institute on Money in State Politics, "National Overview."

28. Florida Department of State Division of Elections.

29. Justice at Stake, "Poll of American Voters"; Justice at Stake, "Poll of State Judges."

30. Kay, "A Taxing Thought," p. A1.

31. The new North Carolina law does not go into effect until November 2004. Also, no state publicly funds trial-level campaigns, although Florida attempted to do so in 2002. The measure failed.

32. Kay, "A Taxing Thought," p. A1.

33. Schotland, "Financing Judicial Elections," p. 213.

34. Baum, "Judicial Elections and Judicial Independence," p. 32.

35. Ibid., p. 38.

36. Cerrell and Dash, "Issues in Judicial Election Campaigns," p. 39.

37. Goldberg, Holmes, and Sanchez, *The New Politics of Judicial Elections*, p. 17.

38. Certainly congressional candidates often highlight their backgrounds and qualifications, but policy issues also are important aspects of the campaigns.

39. Kay, "Judicial Spending Spree."

40. Goldberg, Holmes, and Sanchez, *The New Politics of Judicial Elections*, p. 13.

41. Baum, "Judicial Elections and Judicial Independence," p. 19.

42. Kay, "Judicial Spending Spree," p. A1.

43. Johnson, Schaefer, and McKnight, "The Salience of Judicial Candidates and Elections"; Baum, "Voters' Information in Judicial Elections."

44. Johnson, Schaefer, and McKnight, "The Salience of Judicial Candidates and Elections," p. 371.

45. Lovrich and Sheldon, "Voters in Contested, Nonpartisan Judicial Elections."

46. "Cash v. Quality," *Cleveland Plain Dealer,* p. B8.

47. Schotland, "Financing Judicial Elections," p. 216.

48. Squire and Smith, "The Effect of Partisan Information." Interestingly, Dubois did not find that ethnic voting was a significant variable in his study of trial court elections (see "Voting Cues in Nonpartisan Trial Court Elections").

49. Dubois, "Voting Cues in Nonpartisan Trial Court Elections."

50. Ibid.

51. Lovrich and Sheldon, "Voters in Contested, Nonpartisan Judicial Elections"; Dubois, "Voting Cues in Nonpartisan Trial Court Elections."

52. Baum, "Explaining the Vote in Judicial Elections"; Klein and Baum, "Ballot Information and Voting Decisions in Judicial Elections."

53. Baum, "Explaining the Vote in Judicial Elections," p. 364. Ohio conducts nonpartisan supreme court elections, but partisan primaries.

54. Squire and Smith, "The Effect of Partisan Information."

55. Coyle, "It Won't Be Long," p. A8.

56. American Bar Association, *Model Code of Judicial Conduct*, p. 27.

57. Ibid.

58. Ibid.

59. *Republican Party of Minnesota v. White* (Scalia, opinion), p. 2533.

60. Ibid., p. 772.

61. Ibid., p. 703.

62. Ibid., p. 713.

63. Ibid., p. 782.

64. *Republican Party of Minnesota v. White* (Kennedy, concurring), p. 793.

65. Ibid., p. 717.

66. *Republican Party of Minnesota v. White* (Ginsburg, dissenting), p. 806.

67. In her concurring opinion, O'Connor only briefly discussed the constitutional issues related to the announce clause in the last paragraph. The vast majority of the concurring opinion was devoted to arguing against judicial elections.

68. *Republican Party of Minnesota v. White* (O'Connor, concurring), p. 789.

69. Cohen, "ABA Considers Judicial Campaign-Related Issues."

70. Whereatt, "Judicial Hopefuls Haven't Tried New Freedoms," p. 1B.

71. Ringel, "Court Kills GA's Judicial Campaign Curbs," p. 4.

Acronyms

AARP	American Association of Retired Persons
ABA	American Bar Association
ABC	American Broadcasting Companies
ACLU	American Civil Liberties Union
ACT	America Coming Together
AFL-CIO	American Federation of Labor–Congress of Industrial Organizations
BCRA	Bipartisan Campaign Reform Act
CBM	Citizens for Better Medicare
CBS	Columbia Broadcasting System
DOJ	Department of Justice
DRE	direct recording electronic [voting systems]
FCC	Federal Communications Commission
FEC	Federal Election Commission
FECA	Federal Election Campaign Act
GOP	Grand Old Party
GOTV	get-out-the-vote
HIAA	Health Insurance Association of America
IRS	Internal Revenue Service
JQC	Judicial Qualifications Commission
MMD	multimember district
NAACP	National Association for the Advancement of Colored People
NBC	National Broadcasting Company
NCPAC	National Conservative Political Action Committee
NRA	National Rifle Association
PAC	political action committee
PEJ	Project for Excellence in Journalism

PhRMA	Pharmaceutical Research and Manufacturing Association of America
PIN	personal identification number
PR	proportional representation
RCA	Radio Corporation of America
SMD	single-member district
USCCR	U.S. Commission on Civil Rights
VAP	voting-age population
VRA	Voting Rights Act

References

Abel, Douglas D., and Bruce Oppenheimer. "Candidate Emergence in a Majority Hispanic District: The 29th District in Texas." In *Who Runs for Congress?* ed.
Thomas A. Kazee. Washington, DC: CQ Press, 1994.

Abramson, Paul R., John H. Aldrich, and David W. Rohde. *Change and Continuity in
the 2000 and 2002 Elections*. Washington, DC: CQ Press, 2003.

Adelstein, Jonathan S. "Press Statement." 2 June 2003. www.fcc.gov/Daily_Releases/
Daily_Business/2003/db0602/DOC-235047A8.doc.

Ahrens, Frank. "FCC Eases Media Ownership Rules." *Washington Post*, 3 June 2003,
A1.

Aldrich, John H., and John D. Griffin. "Ambition in the South: The Emergence of
Republican Electoral Support, 1940–1998." Paper presented at the Citadel Sym-
posium on Southern Politics, Charleston, SC, 2–3 March 2000.

Alexander, Herbert E. "The Political Process After the Bipartisan Reform Act of
2002." *Election Law Journal* 2 (2003): 47–54.

Alvarez, R. Michael, and Jonathan Nagler. "The Likely Consequences of Internet Voting for Political Representation." *Loyola of Los Angeles Law Review* 34 (2001):
1135–1137.

American Bar Association. *Model Code of Judicial Conduct*. 2000 ed. Chicago, IL:
1999.

American Judicature Society. "Judicial Selection in the States: Appellate and General
Jurisdiction Courts." Des Moines, IA: 2002.

Annenburg Public Policy Center Ads Collection, University of Pennsylvania. 21
March 2001. www.appcpenn.org/issueads/NAR.htm.
———. 3 June 2001. www.appcpenn.org/issueads/estimate.htm.

Ansolabehere, Stephen, and Alan Gerber. "The Effects of Filing Fees and Petition
Requirements on U.S. House Elections." *Legislative Studies Quarterly* 21 (1996):
249–264.

Aspin, Larry, William K. Hall, Jean Bax, and Celeste Montoya. "Thirty Years of Judicial Retention Elections: An Update." *Social Science Journal* 37 (2000): 1–17.

Aufderheide, Patricia. *Communications Policy and the Public Interest: The Telecommunications Act of 1996*. New York: Guilford Publications, 1999.

Bagdikian, Ben H. *The Media Monopoly*. 5th ed. Boston: Beacon Press, 1987.

Balkin, Jack M. "Supreme Court Compromises Its Legitimacy." *Boston Globe*, 12 December 2000, A23.

Bannon, Nancy K. "The Voting Rights Act: Over the Hill at Age 30?" *Human Rights* 22 (1995): 10–15.

Bartels, Larry M. "Partisanship and Voting Behavior, 1952–1996." *American Journal of Political Science* 44 (2000): 35–50.

Baum, Lawrence. "Explaining the Vote in Judicial Elections: The 1984 Ohio Supreme Court Elections." *Western Political Quarterly* 40 (1987): 361–371.

———. "Judicial Elections and Judicial Independence: The Voter's Perspective." *Ohio State Law Journal* 64 (2003): 13–41.

———. "Voters' Information in Judicial Elections: The 1986 Contests for the Ohio Supreme Court." *Kentucky Law Journal* 77 (1989): 645–665.

Bayne, William C. "Lynchard's Candidacy, Ads Putting Spice into Justice Race." *Commercial Appeal*, 29 October 2000, DS1.

Bennett, Daniel, and Pam Fielding. *The Net Effect: How Cyberadvocacy Is Changing the Political Landscape*. Lorton, VA: Capitol Advantage Publishing, 1999.

Berg, John C. "Spoiler or Builder? The Effect of Ralph Nader's 2000 Campaign on the U.S. Greens." In *The State of Parties*, 4th ed., ed. John C. Green and Rick Farmer. Lanham, MD: Rowman and Littlefield, 2003.

Berry, Mary Frances. "U.S. Commission on Civil Rights: Status Report on Probe of Election Practices in Florida During the 2000 Presidential Election." *The Black Scholar* 31 (2001): 2–5.

Bibby, John F. "In Defense of the Two-Party System." In *Multiparty Politics in America*, ed. Paul S. Herrnson and John C. Green. Lanham, MD: Rowman and Littlefield, 1997.

Bibby, John F., and Thomas M. Holbrook. "Parties and Elections." In *Politics in the American States*, 8th ed., ed. Virginia Gray and Russell L. Hanson. Washington, DC: CQ Press, 2003.

Bibby, John F., and L. Sandy Maisel. *Two Parties—Or More?* 2nd ed. Boulder, CO: Westview Press, 2003.

Blaine, Ryan L. "Election Law and the Internet: How Should the FEC Manage New Technology?" *North Carolina Law Review* 81 (2003): 722–725.

Blumenfeld, Laura. "Soros' Deep Pockets vs. Bush." *Washington Post*, 11 November 2003, A3.

Born, Richard. "The Influence of House Primary Election Divisiveness on General Election Margins, 1962–76." *The Journal of Politics* 43 (1981): 640–661.

"Briefly in Kansas." *Topeka Capital-Journal*, 9 October 2003. www.cjonline.com/stories/041603/kan_ksbrfs.shtml.

Bullock, Charles S., III, Ronald Keith Gaddie, and Donna R. Hoffman. "Regional Variations in the Realignment of American States, 1944–2000." Paper presented at the annual meeting of the Southwestern Political Science Association, New Orleans, LA, 27–30 March 2002.

Burden, Barry C. "Minor Parties in the 2000 Presidential Election." In *Models of Voting in Presidential Elections: The 2000 U.S. Election*, ed. Herbert F. Weisberg and Clyde Wilcox. Stanford, CA: Stanford Law and Politics, 2004.

California Internet Voting Task Force. *A Report on the Feasibility of Internet Voting*. Sacramento, CA: 2000.

Cameron, Charles, David Epstein, and Sharyn O'Halloran. "Do Majority-Minority Districts Maximize Substantive Black Representation in Congress?" *American Political Science Review* 90 (1996): 794–812.

Canon, David T. *Race, Redistricting, and Representation: The Unintended Conse-quences of Black Majority Districts*. Chicago: University of Chicago Press, 1999.

Cantor, Joseph E., and L. Paige Whitaker. "Bipartisan Campaign Reform Act of 2002: Summary and Comparison with Existing Law." *Congressional Research Service Report RL31402*, 2 May 2002. www.house.gov/shays/hot/CFR/RL31402.pdf.

Carter, Terry. "Boosting the Bench: The U.S. Chamber of Commerce Is Spending Big Bucks to Influence Judicial Elections." *ABA Journal* (October 2002): 28–33.

"Cash v. Quality." *Cleveland Plain Dealer*, 5 March 2003, B8.

Cerrell, Joseph R., and Hal Dash. "Issues in Judicial Election Campaigns." In *State Judiciaries and Impartiality: Judging the Judges*, ed. Roger Clegg and James D. Miller. Washington, DC: The National Legal Center for Public Interest, 1996.

Cigler, Allan J. "Enron, a Perceived Crisis in Public Confidence, and the Bipartisan Campaign Reform Act of 2002." *Review of Policy Research* 2 (2004): 231–250.

———. "Interest Groups and Financing the 2000 Elections." In *Financing the 2000 Elections*, ed. David B. Magleby. Washington, DC: The Brookings Institution Press, 2002.

———. "The 1998 Kansas Third Congressional District Race." In *Outside Money: Soft Money and Issue Advocacy in the 1998 Congressional Elections*, ed. David B. Magleby. Lanham, MD: Rowman and Littlefield, 2000.

Cigler, Allan J., and Burdett A. Loomis. "The Changing Nature of Interest Group Politics." In *Interest Group Politics*, 6th ed., ed. Allan J. Cigler and Burdett A. Loomis. Washington, DC: CQ Press, 1999.

Clarke, Peter, and Susan Evans. *Covering Campaigns: Journalism in Congressional Elections*. Stanford, CA: Stanford University Press, 1983.

CNN News. "MoveOn.org Becomes Anti-Bush Powerhouse." www.cnn.com/2004/TECH/internet/01/12/moveon.org.ap/index.html.

Cohen, Mark. "ABA Considers Judicial Campaign-Related Issues." *The Minnesota Lawyer*, 19 August 2002, 1.

Collet, Christian, and Martin P. Wattenberg. "Strategically Unambitious: Minor Party and Independent Candidates in the 1996 Congressional Elections." In *The State of the Parties*, 3rd ed., ed. John C. Green and Daniel M. Shea. Lanham, MD: Rowman and Littlefield, 1999.

Comment. "Election Law and the Internet: How Should the FEC Manage New Technology?" *North Carolina Law Review* 81 (2003): 697–723.

Commission on Civil Rights. *Political Participation: A Study of Participation by Negroes in the Electoral and Political Processes in 10 Southern States Since the Passage of the Voting Rights Act of 1965*. Washington, DC: 1968.

Congressional Quarterly Service. *Congressional Quarterly Almanac*. Washington, DC: 1968.

Congressional Record. 105th Cong., 2nd sess. 25 February 1998, S.997.

Converse, Phillip. "The Nature of Belief Systems in Mass Publics." In *Ideology and Discontent*, ed. David Apter. Glencoe, IL: Free Press, 1964.

Convio, Inc. "Howard Dean Uses Convio to Raise $7.4 Million Online in Third Quarter, $11 Million via Internet Since April 2003." www.convio.com.

Corrado, Anthony. "Financing the 1996 Election." In *The Election of 1996*, ed. Gerald Pomper. Chatham, NJ: Chatham House Publishers, 1997.

———. "The Legislative Odyssey of BCRA." In *Life After Reform: When Bipartisan Campaign Reform Act Meets Politics*, ed. Michael J. Malbin. Lanham, MD: Rowman and Littlefield, 2003.

Cox, Gary W., and Jonathan N. Katz. *Elbridge Gerry's Salamander: The Electoral Consequences of the Reapportionment Revolution*. New York: Cambridge University Press, 2002.

Coyle, Marcia. "It Won't Be Long: Supreme Court Took a Narrow View in Ruling on Judicial Candidates Talking on Issues, so Lawsuits Are Expected Soon." *Broward Daily Business Review*, 17 July 2002, A8.

Cummings, Jeanne. "The E-Team—Behind the Dean Surge: A Gang of Bloggers and Webmasters." *Wall Street Journal*, 14 October 2003, A1.

CyberAtlas. *Population Explosion!* www.cyberatlas.com.

Davidson, Chandler. "The Voting Rights Acts: A Brief History." In *Controversies in Minority Voting*, ed. Bernard Grofman and Chandler Davidson. Washington, DC: The Brookings Institution, 1992.

Demers, David. "Corporate Newspaper Bashing: Is it Justified?" *Newspaper Research Journal* 20 (1999): 83–97.

Dershowitz, Alan. *Supreme Injustice: How the High Court Highjacked Election 2000*. New York: Oxford University Press, 2001.

Dill, David L., Bruce Schneier, and Barbara Simons. "Viewpoint: Voting and Technology: Who Gets to Count Your Vote?" *Communications of the ACM* 46 (2003): 29–31.

Dionne, E. J., Jr. "Supremely Partisan, Will the High Court Besmirch Itself?" *Pittsburgh-Post Gazette*, 12 December 2000, A19.

Disch, Lisa J. *The Tyranny of the Two-Party System*. New York: Columbia University Press, 2003.

Dubois, Philip. *From Ballot to Bench: Judicial Elections and the Quest for Accountability*. Austin: University of Texas Press, 1980.

———. "Voter Turnout in State Judicial Elections: An Analysis of the Tail on the Electoral Kite." *The Journal of Politics* 41 (1979): 865–887.

———. "Voting Cues in Nonpartisan Trial Court Elections: A Multivariate Assessment." *Law and Society Review* 18 (1984): 395–436.

Duverger, Maurice. *Political Parties*. New York: Wiley, 1954.

Dwyre, Diana, and Victoria A. Farrar-Myers. *Legislative Labyrinth: Congress and Campaign Finance Reform*. Washington, DC: CQ Press, 2001.

Dwyre, Diana, and Robin Kolodny. "Throwing Out the Rule Book: Party Financing of the 2000 Election." In *Financing the Election*, ed. David B. Magleby. Washington, DC: The Brookings Institution Press, 2002.

Eisenberg, Arthur N. "Buckley, Rupert Murdoch, and the Pursuit of Equality in the Conduct of Elections." *Annual Survey of American Law* 451 (1996): 459–460.

Engstrom, Richard. "Voting Rights Districts: Debunking the Myths." *Campaigns and Elections*. 16 (April 1995): 24, 46.

Epstein, David, and Sharyn O'Halloran. "A Social Science Approach to Race, Redistricting and Responsiveness." *American Political Science Review* 93 (1999): 187–191.

Epstein, Leon D. *Political Parties in the American Mold*. Madison: University of Wisconsin Press, 1986.

Epstein, Richard A. "In Such Manner as the Legislature Thereof May Direct: The Outcome in *Bush v. Gore* Defended." In *The Vote: Bush, Gore, and the Supreme Court*, ed. Cass R. Sunstein and Richard A. Epstein. Chicago: University of Chicago Press, 2001.

Falk, Erika. "Issue Advocacy Advertising Through the Presidential Primary 1999–2000 Election Cycle." Press Release, 20 September 2000. www.appcpenn.org/issuea/foris/2000issuead.htm (accessed May 2001).

Farrell, David M. *Electoral Systems*. New York: Palgrave, 2001.

Federal Communications Commission. "FCC Sets Limits on Media Concentration." Press Release, 2 June 2003.

Florida Department of State Division of Elections. 6 August 2003. www.election.dos.state.fl.us.

Foerstel, Karen. "As Groups File Lawsuits, Bush Spurns Signing Ceremony for 'Flawed' Fundraising Law." *Congressional Quarterly Weekly* 60 (2002): 868.

Ford, Frederick W. "The Meaning of the Public Interest, Convenience and Necessity." *Journal of Broadcasting* 5 (1961): 205–218.

Franklin, John Hope. *Reconstruction: After the Civil War*. Chicago: University of Chicago Press, 1961.

Fried, Charles. "Unreasonable Reaction to a Reasonable Decision." In *Bush v. Gore: The Question of Legitimacy*, ed. Bruce Ackerman. New Haven: Yale University Press, 2002.

Garrett, Elizabeth. "Political Intermediaries and the Internet 'Revolution.'" *Loyola of Los Angeles Law Review* 34 (2001): 1055.

Garrow, David J. *Protest at Selma: Martin Luther King, Jr., and the Voting Rights Act of 1965*. New Haven: Yale University Press, 1978.

Geer, John G., and Mark E. Shere. "Party Competition and the Prisoner's Dilemma: An Argument for the Direct Primary." *Journal of Politics* 54 (1992): 741–761.

Gelman, Andrew, and Gary King. "A Unified Method of Evaluating Electoral Systems and Redistricting Plans." *American Journal of Political Science* 38 (1994): 514–554.

Gerber, Elisabeth R., Kristin Kanthak, and Rebecca B. Morton. "Selection Bias in a Model of Candidate Entry Decisions." Working Paper, University of Michigan, 1999.

Gerber, Elisabeth R., and Rebecca B. Morton. "Electoral Institutions and Party Competition: The Effects of Nomination Procedures on Electoral Coalition Formation." Working Paper, University of Michigan, 1998.

———. "Primary Election Systems and Representation." *Journal of Law, Economics, and Organization* 14 (1998): 304–324.

Gibson, Rachel. "Elections Online: Assessing Internet Voting in Light of the Arizona Democratic Primary." *Political Science Quarterly* 116 (2001/2002): 561–584.

Gigot, Paul A. "Liberals Discover the Tyranny of the Courts." *Wall Street Journal*, 15 December 2000: A16.

Gillespie, J. David. *Politics at the Periphery*. Columbia: University of South Carolina Press, 1993.

Goldberg, Deborah, Craig Holman, and Samantha Sanchez. *The New Politics of Judicial Elections*. Washington, DC: Justice at Stake Campaign, 2002.

Greenhouse, Linda. "The Supreme Court: The Ruling; Justices, in 5-to-4 Decision, Back Campaign Finance Law that Curbs Contributors." *New York Times,* 11 December 2003, A24.

Grofman, Bernard. *Race and Redistricting in the 1990s*. New York: Agathon Press, 1998.

Guccione, Jean. "Elected Judges Are a Rare Breed." *Los Angeles Times*, 22 February 2002, B2.

Guth, James L., Lyman A. Kellstedt, John C. Green, and Corwin E. Smidt. "A Distant Thunder? Religious Mobilization in the 2000 Elections." In *Interest Group Politics,* 5th ed., ed. Allan J. Cigler and Burdett A. Loomis. Washington, DC: CQ Press, 1998.

Hall, Melinda Gann. "State Supreme Courts in American Democracy: Probing the Myths of Judicial Reform." *American Political Science Review* 95 (2001): 315–330.

Hamilton, Alexander, James Madison, and John Jay. *The Federalist*. New York: The Macmillan Company, [1787–1788] 1948.

Hanes, Stephanie. "Balto. County Judges Get Aggressive in Election." *Baltimore Sun*, 13 April 2003, 1B.

Herrnson, Paul. *Congressional Elections: Campaigning at Home and in Washington*. Washington, DC: CQ Press, 1997.

———. "Parties and Interest Groups in Post-Reform Congressional Elections." In *Interest Group Politics*, 5th ed., ed. Allan J. Cigler and Burdett A. Loomis. Washington, DC: CQ Press, 1998.

Herrnson, Paul S., and James G. Gimpel. "District Conditions and Primary Divisiveness in Congressional Elections." *Political Research Quarterly* 48 (1995): 117–134.

Hershey, Marjorie Randon. *Party Politics in America*. 11th ed. New York: Longman, forthcoming.

Heyser, Holly A. "Minnesota Governor: The End of the Ventura Interlude." In *Midterm Madness*, ed. Larry J. Sabato. Lanham, MD: Rowman and Littlefield, 2003.

"High Court's Integrity at Risk." *New York Daily News*, 12 December 2000, 50.

Hines, Revathi I. "The Silent Voices: 2000 Presidential Election and the Minority Vote in Florida." *The Western Journal of Black Studies* 26 (2002): 71–74.

Hirsch, Sam. "The United States House of Unrepresentatives: What Went Wrong in the Latest Round of Congressional Redistricting." *Election Law Journal* 2 (2003): 179–216.

———. "Unpacking *Page v. Bartels*: A Fresh Redistricting Paradigm Emerges in New Jersey." *Election Law Journal* 1 (2002): 7–23.

Hofstadter, Richard. *The Age of Reform*. New York: Vintage, 1955.

Holman, Craig B., and Luke P. McLoughlin. *Buying Time 2000: Television Advertising in the 2000 Federal Elections*. New York: Brennan Center for Justice at New York University School of Law, 2001.

"Independent Voter Sues for Right to Vote in Primary." *Pennsylvania Law Weekly,* 14 December 1998, 2.

Institute for Politics, Democracy and the Internet. *The Virtual Trail: Political Journalism on the Internet*. Washington, DC: George Washington University, 2002.

Institute on Money in State Politics. "National Overview." 6 August 2003. new.followthemoney.org.

Jewell, Malcolm E., and Sarah M. Morehouse. "What Are Party Endorsements Worth? A Study of Preprimary Gubernatorial Endorsements." *American Politics Quarterly* 24 (1996): 338–362.

Jockers, Ken. "Recent Events Fuel Debate About How We Choose State Judges." *New York Law Journal*, 2 June 2003, 12.

Johnson, Charles A., Roger C. Schaefer, and R. Neal McKnight. "The Salience of Judicial Candidates and Elections." *Social Science Quarterly* 49 (1978): 371–378.

Jolly, W. P. *Marconi*. New York: Stein and Day, 1972.

Justice at Stake. "Poll of American Voters." Conducted by Greenberg, Quinlan, Rosner Research Inc. 30 October–7 November 2001. www.justiceatstake.org.

———. "Poll of State Judges." Conducted by Greenberg, Quinlan, Rosner Research Inc. 5 November 2001–2 January 2002. www.justiceatstake.org.

Kanthak, Kristin, and Rebecca B. Morton. "The Effects of Electoral Rules on Congressional Primaries." In *Congressional Primaries and the Politics of Represen-*

tation, ed. Peter F. Galderisi, Marni Ezra, and Michael Lyons. Lanham, MD: Rowman and Littlefield, 2001.

———. "Turnout and Primaries." Paper presented at the annual meeting of the American Political Science Association, Philadelphia, PA, 28–31 August, 2003.

Kay, Julie. "Judicial Spending Spree." *Miami Daily Business Review*, 30 August 2002, A1.

———. "A Taxing Thought: Move Afoot in South Florida to Have Public Money Fund Judicial Elections Throughout the State." *Palm Beach Daily Business Review*, 17 July 2002, A1.

Keith, Bruce E., David B. Magleby, Candice J. Nelson, Elizabeth Orr, Mark Westlye, and Raymond E. Wolfinger. *The Myth of the Independent Voter*. Berkeley: University of California Press, 1992.

Kenny, Patrick J. "Explaining Primary Turnout: The Senatorial Case." *Legislative Studies Quarterly* 11 (1986): 65–73.

———. "Sorting Out the Effects of Primary Divisiveness in Congressional and Senatorial Elections." *The Western Political Quarterly* 41 (1988): 765–777.

Kenny, Patrick J., and Tom W. Rice. "The Effect of Primary Divisiveness in Gubernatorial and Senatorial Elections." *The Journal of Politics* 46 (1984): 904–915.

———. "The Relationship Between Divisive Primaries and General Election Outcomes." *American Journal of Political Science* 31 (1987): 31–44.

Key, V. O. *American State Politics: An Introduction*. New York: Knopf, 1956.

———. *Southern Politics in State and Nation*. New York: Vintage Books, 1949.

King, David C. "Congress, Polarization, and Fidelity to the Median Voter." Working paper, Harvard University, 2003.

Klain, Maurice. "A New Look at the Constituencies: The Need for a Recount and a Reappraisal." *American Political Science Review* 49 (1955): 1105–1119.

Klarman, Michael J. "*Bush v. Gore* Through the Lens of Constitutional History." *California Law Review* 89 (December 2001): 1721.

Klein, Alec, and David A. Vise. "Media Giants Hint That They Might Be Expanding." *Washington Post,* 3 June 2003, A6.

Klein, David, and Lawrence Baum. "Ballot Information and Voting Decisions in Judicial Elections." *Political Research Quarterly* 54 (2001): 709–728.

Knack, Stephen, and Martha Kropf. "Who Uses Inferior Voting Technology?" *PS*, September 2002, 541–548.

Kozlowski, Mark. "Robed and Running: Striking Prohibitions on Elected Judges' Political Speech Threatens Further Erosion of Public Faith in Their Capacity to Act Impartially." *Legal Times,* 8 July 2002: 35.

Krauthammer, Charles. "Defenders of the Law." *Washington Post*, 15 December 2000, A16.

Kuhnhenn, James. "Election Financing Turns Creative." *Kansas City Star,* 14 December 2003, A16.

Kurtz, Howard. "Local News Heroes." *Washington Post Magazine*, 24 October 1993, W16.

Labaton, Stephen. "Deregulating the Media: The Overview; Regulators Ease Rules Governing Media Ownership." *New York Times*, 3 June 2003, A1.

Lawson, Kay. "The Case for a Multiparty System." In *Multiparty Politics in America,* ed. Paul S. Herrnson and John C. Green. Lanham, MD: Rowman and Littlefield, 1997.

Lee, Jennifer. "On Minot, N.D., Radio, A Single Corporate Voice." *New York Times*, 29 March 2003, C7.

Lijphart, Arend. *Electoral Systems and Party Systems*. New York: Oxford University Press, 1994.

"Local TV News Coverage of the 2002 General Election." Report from the Lear Center Local News Archive, 2003. www.localnewsarchive.org.

Lovrich, Nicholas P., Jr., and Charles H. Sheldon. "Voters in Contested, Nonpartisan Judicial Elections: A Responsible Electorate or a Problematic Public." *Western Political Quarterly* 36 (1983): 241–256.

Lublin, David. *The Paradox of Representation*. Princeton: Princeton University Press, 1997.

Magleby, David B. *Dictum Without Data: The Myth of Issue Advocacy and Party Building*. Provo, UT: Brigham Young University, Center for the Study of Elections and Democracy, 2000.

———. "Executive Summary." In *Election Advocacy: Soft Money and Issue Advocacy in the 2000 Elections*, ed. David B. Magleby. Provo, UT: Brigham Young University, Center for the Study of Elections and Democracy, 2000.

Malbin, Michael J. "Thinking About Reform." In *Life After Reform: When the Bipartisan Campaign Reform Act Meets Politics*, ed. Michael J. Malbin. Lanham, MD: Rowman and Littlefield, 2003.

Mann, Thomas E. "Linking Knowledge and Action: Political Science and Campaign Finance Reform." *Perspectives on Politics* 1 (2003): 74.

Mayhew, David R. *Congress: The Electoral Connection*. New Haven: Yale University Press, 1974.

McNitt, Andrew D. "The Effect of Preprimary Endorsement Competition for Nominations: An Examination of Different Nominating Systems." *The Journal of Politics* 42 (1980): 257–266.

McPherson, James M. *The Struggle for Equality: Abolitionists and the Negro in the Civil War and Reconstruction*. Princeton: Princeton University Press, 1964.

Meyerson, Michael I. "Ideas of the Marketplace: A Guide to the 1996 Telecommunications Act." *Federal Communications Law Journal* 49 (1997): 252–287.

Milbank, Dana. "Virtual Politics." *The New Republic*, 5 July 1999, 22–27.

Mintz, John, and Susan Schmidt. "Stealth PACs Report Campaign Financing: First Data Available Under New Reform Law." *Washington Post*, 1 November 2000, A17.

Mohen, Joe, and Julia Glidden. "The Case for Internet Voting." *Communications of the ACM* 44 (2001): 72–85.

Morehouse, Sarah M. "Money Versus Party Effort: Nominating for Governor." *American Journal of Political Science* 34 (1990): 706–724.

Morris, Dick. "Direct Democracy and the Internet." *Loyola of Los Angeles Law Review* 34 (2001): 1033.

Mulroy, Steven J. "Lemonade from Lemons: Can Advocates Convert *Bush v. Gore* into a Vehicle for Reform?" *Georgetown Journal of Law and Policy* 9 (2002): 357.

National Elections Study Data. www.umich.edu/~new/nesguide/toptable/tab2a_1.htm.

National Telecommunications and Information Administration. *Americans in the Information Age: Falling Through the Net Toward Digital Inclusion*. Washington, DC: U.S. Department of Commerce, 2000.

Norrander, Barbara. "Explaining Cross-State Variation in Independent Identification." *American Journal of Political Science* 33 (1989): 516–536.

Ortiz, Daniel. "Constitutional Restrictions of Campaign Finance Regulations: Introduction." In *Campaign Finance Reform: A Sourcebook*, ed. Anthony Corrado, Thomas E. Mann, Daniel Ortiz, Trevor Potter, and Frank J. Sorauf. Washington, DC: The Brookings Institution, 1997.

Parker, Frank R. *Black Votes Count*. Chapel Hill: University of North Carolina Press, 1990.

Patterson, Thomas E., and Robert D. McClure. *The Unseeing Eye: The Myth of Television Power in National Politics*. New York: Putnam, 1976.

Persily, Nathaniel. "Toward a Functional Defense of Political Party Autonomy." *New York University Law Review* 76 (2001): 750.

Petrocik, John R., and Scott W. Desposato. "The Partisan Consequences of Majority-Minority Redistricting in the South, 1991 and 1994." *Journal of Politics* 60 (1998): 613–633.

Pew Internet and American Life Project. *The Ever-Shifting Internet Population*. Washington, DC, 2003.

Pew Research Center for the People and the Press. "Public's News Habits Little Changed by September 11." 9 June 2002. http://people-press.org.

———. "Strong Opposition to Media Cross-Ownership Emerges." 13 July 2003. http://people-press.org.

Pomper, Gerald M. "The Presidential Election." In *The Election of 2000*, ed. Gerald M. Pomper. New York: Chatham House, 2001.

Posner, Richard A. *Breaking the Deadlock: The 2000 Election, the Constitution and the Courts*. Princeton: Princeton University Press, 2001.

Potter, Trevor. "Issue Advocacy and Express Advocacy: Introduction." In *Campaign Finance Reform: A Sourcebook*, ed. Anthony Corrado, Thomas E. Mann, Daniel Ortiz, Trevor Potter, and Frank J. Sorauf. Washington, DC: The Brookings Institution, 1997.

Powell, Michael V. "Press Statement." 2 June 2003. www.fcc.gov/Daily_Releases/Daily_Business/2003/db0602/DOC-235047A3.doc.

Presser, Stephen B., John L. Dodd, Christopher Murray, Mark Pulliam, Alfred W. Putnam, and Paula M. Stannard. "The Case for Judicial Appointments." Washington, DC: Federalist Society for Law and Public Policy Studies, 2003.

Price, Margaret Walzem. *The Negro and the Ballot in the South*. Atlanta, GA: Southern Regional Council, 1959.

Radin, Margaret Jane. "Can the Rule of Law Survive *Bush v. Gore*?" In *Bush v. Gore: The Question of Legitimacy*, ed. Bruce Ackerman. New Haven: Yale University Press, 2002.

Rapoport, Ronald B., and Walter J. Stone. "Ross Perot Is Alive and Well and Living in the Republican Party." In *The State of the Parties*, 4th ed., ed. John C. Green and Rick Farmer. Lanham, MD: Rowman and Littlefield, 2003.

"Record Number of Libertarians Seeking Votes." *Hoosier Times*, 3 November 2002, B4.

Reichley, A. James. *The Life of the Parties*. Lanham, MD: Rowman and Littlefield, 1992.

———. "The Future of the American Two-Party System." In *The State of the Parties*, 4th ed., ed. John C. Green and Rick Farmer. Lanham, MD: Rowman and Littlefield, 2003.

Reiterman, Tim, and Peter Nicholas. "Ex-Officials Now Behind New Voting Machines." *Los Angeles Times*, 10 November 2003, A1.

Rice, Tom W. "Gubernatorial and Senatorial Primary Elections: Determinants of Competition." *American Politics Quarterly* 13 (1985): 427–446.

Ringel, Jonathan. "Court Kills GA's Judicial Campaign Curbs." *The Legal Intelligencer*, 23 October 2002, 4.

Rosen, Jeffery. "Political Questions and the Hazards of Pragmatism." In *Bush v. Gore: The Question of Legitimacy*, ed. Bruce Ackerman. New Haven: Yale University Press, 2002.

Rosenstiel, Tom, and Amy Mitchell. "Does Ownership Matter in Local Television News: A Five-Year Study of Ownership and Quality." Report from the Project for Excellence in Journalism, Washington, DC: 29 April 2003.

Rosenstone, Steven J., Roy L. Behr, and Edward H. Lazarus. *Third Parties in America*. 2nd ed. Princeton: Princeton University Press, 1996.

Rozell, Mark, and Clyde Wilcox. *Interest Groups in American Campaigns*. Washington, DC: CQ Press, 1999.

Ryden, David K. "'The Good, the Bad, and the Ugly': The Judicial Shaping of Party Activities." In *The State of the Parties*, 3rd ed., ed. John C. Green and Daniel M. Shea. Lanham, MD: Rowman and Littlefield, 1999.

Sabato, Larry. *PAC Power*. New York: Norton, 1985.

Saffell, David. "Reapportionment and Public Policy: State Legislators' Perspective." *Policy Studies Journal* 9 (1980–1981): 916–936.

Sandalow, Marc. "Turbulent Election Taints Top Court's Reputation for Neutrality." *San Francisco Chronicle*, 12 December 2000, A1.

Scalia, Antonin. "The Rule of Law as a Law of Rules." *University of Chicago Law Review* 56 (1989): 1175.

Scarrow, Howard A. *Parties, Elections, and Representation in the State of New York*. New York: New York University Press, 1983.

Schaffner, Brian F., and Patrick J. Sellers. "Structural Determinants of Local Congressional News Coverage." *Political Communication* 20 (2003): 41–57.

Schantz, Harvey L. "Contested and Uncontested Primaries for the U.S. House." *Legislative Studies Quarterly* 5 (1980): 545–562.

Schotland, Roy A. "Financing Judicial Elections." In *Financing the 2000 Election*, ed. David B. Magleby. Washington, DC: Brookings Institution Press, 2002.

Schram, Martin. *Running for President 1976: The Carter Campaign*. New York: Stein and Day, 1977.

Schumaker, Paul, and Burdett A. Loomis. *How Should We Elect Our President? The Electoral College and Beyond*. New York: Chatham House, 2001.

Sharkansky, Ira. "Reapportionment and Roll Call Voting." *Social Science Quarterly* 51 (1970): 129–137.

Shays, Rep. Christopher. "Statement on Today's Campaign Finance Reforms Supreme Court Oral Arguments." Press Release. 8 September 2003. www.house.gov/shays.

"Short Summary of Shays-Meehan." From the Offices of Congressmen Christopher Shays and Marty Meehan. 14 February 2002. www.house.gov/shays/hot/CFR/ssum22356.htm.

Sniderman, Paul M. "Taking Sides: A Fixed Choice Theory of Political Reasoning." In *Elements of Reason*, ed. Arthur Lupia, Mathew D. McCubbins, and Samuel L. Popkin. New York: Cambridge University Press, 2000.

"Soapbox Monopoly." *St. Louis Post-Dispatch*, 19 May 2002, D6.

Socolofsky, Homer E., and Allan B. Spetter. *The Presidency of Benjamin Harrison*. Lawrence: University Press of Kansas, 1987.

Squire, Peverill, and Eric R.A.N. Smith. "The Effect of Partisan Information on Voters in Nonpartisan Elections." *Journal of Politics* 50 (1988): 169–179.

Stone, Peter H. "The Blitz to Elect Business-Friendly Judges." *National Journal*, 16 February 2002, 480.

Swoboda, Frank. "AFL-CIO Plots Push for Democratic House." *Washington Post*, 18 February 1999, A1.

Tate, Katherine. *From Protest to Politics: The New Black Voters in American Elections*. Cambridge: Harvard University Press, 1993.

Taylor, Chris, and Karen Tumulty. "Internet Politics: MoveOn's Big Moment." *Time* 162 (2003): 32.

Teeter, Dwight L., Jr., and Don R. Le Duc. *Law of Mass Communications*. New York: Westbury Press, 1992.

Thernstrom, Abigail M. *Whose Votes Count?: Affirmative Action and Minority Voting Rights*. Cambridge: Harvard University Press, 1987.

Tillinghast, Charles H. *American Broadcast Regulation and The First Amendment*. Ames: Iowa State University Press, 2000.

Trister, Michael. "The Rise and Reform of Stealth PACs." *The American Prospect* 11 (2000): 32–39.

True, Christy. "Presidential Candidates Cast for Votes in Cyberspace." *Seattle Times*, 27 February 2000, C1.

"2000 Presidential Race First in History Where Political Parties Spent More on TV Ads Than Candidates." 23 March 2001. www.brennencenter.org/presscenter/pressrelease_2000_1211cmag.html.

United States Commission on Civil Rights. *Voting Irregularities in Florida During the 2000 Presidential Election*. Washington, DC: Government Printing Office, 2001.

———. *Voting Rights in Florida 2002: Briefing Summary*. Washington, DC: Government Printing Office, 2002.

United States Department of Commerce. *A Nation Online: How Americans Are Expanding Their Use of the Internet*. Washington, DC: Government Printing Office, 2002.

Van Drehle, David. "McCain-Feingold Ruling Angers Activists on Both Left and Right." *Washington Post*, 11 December 2003, A1.

Walsh, Edward. "Ruling Marked by the Words of a Dissenter." *Washington Post*, 17 December 2000, A32.

Walton, Hanes, Jr. "The Disenfranchisement of the African American Voter in the 2000 Presidential Election: The Silence of the Winner and the Loser." *The Black Scholar* 31 (2001): 21–24.

Ward, Kenneth. "Looking for Law in All the Wrong Places: A Critique of the Academic Response to the Florida Election." *University of Miami Law Review* 57 (2002): 55–99.

Weinstein, Henry. "Courts See Delay as Too Disruptive." *Los Angeles Times*, 24 September 2003, A22.

Weiss, Todd R. "Democrat Howard Dean Strikes an Online Chord with Campaign." *ComputerWorld*, 3 July 2003, email newsletter. www.computerworld.com.

Weissberg, Robert. "Collective vs. Dyadic Representation in Congress." *American Political Science Review* 72 (1978): 535–547.

Wekkin, Gary D. "Why Crossover Voters Are Not Mischievous Voters: The Segmented Partisanship Hypothesis." *American Politics Quarterly* 19 (1991): 229–247.

West, Darrell M. "How Issue Ads Have Reshaped American Politics." In *Crowded Airwaves*, ed. James A. Thurber, Candice Nelson, and David Dulio. Washington, DC: Brookings Institution Press, 2000.

West, Darrell M., and Burdett A. Loomis. *The Sound of Money*. New York: W. W. Norton Press, 1998.

Whereatt, Robert. "Judicial Hopefuls Haven't Tried New Freedoms: They're Now Allowed to Share Their Political Views with Voters, But Few Have." (Minneapolis) *Star Tribune*, 19 October 2002, 1B.

Whitby, Kenny J. *The Color of Representation: Congressional Behavior and Black Interests*. Ann Arbor: University of Michigan Press, 1997.

White, John Kenneth, and Daniel M. Shea. *New Party Politics*. 2nd ed. Belmont, CA: Wadsworth, 2004.

"Who Can Own Media?" *Washington Post*, 1 June 2003, B6.

Wilson, Craig. "The 2000 Montana Senate Race." In *Election Advocacy*, ed. David B. Magleby. Provo, UT: Brigham Young University, Center for the Study of Elections and Democracy, 2000.

Winger, Richard. "11th Circuit Upholds Georgia Law." *Ballot Access News* 18 (2002): 1.

————. "Injunction Issued Against West Virginia Restriction." *Ballot Access News* 19 (2004) 1.

————. "Institutional Obstacles to a Multiparty System." In *Multiparty Politics in America*, ed. Paul S. Herrnson and John C. Green. Lanham, MD: Rowman and Littlefield, 1997.

————. "Minor Party and Independent Vote for Top Offices Is Best Mid-Term Result Since 1934." *Ballot Access News* 18 (2002): 1.

Wohl, Alexander. "Judge on the Stump: What Can—and Can't—Judicial Candidates Say?" *The American Prospect*, 12 August 2002, 15.

Yoo, John. "In Defense of the Court's Legitimacy." *University of Chicago Law Review* (2001): 775–789.

Court Cases

Anderson v. Celebrezze, 460 U.S. 780 (1983).

Austin v. Michigan Chamber of Commerce, 494 U.S. 652 (1990).

Baker v. Carr, 369 U.S. 186 (1962).

Beer v. U.S., 425 U.S. 130 (1976).

Brown v. Thomson, 426 U.S. 835 (1983).

Buckley v. Valeo, 424 U.S. 1 (1976).

Burdick v. Takushi, 504 U.S. 428 (1992).

Bush v. Gore, 531 U.S. 98 (2000).

Bush v. Vera, 517 U.S. 952 (1996).

California Democratic Party v. Jones, 530 U.S. 567 (2000).

Cartwright v. Barnes, 304 F.3d 1138 (2002).

Colegrove v. Green, 328 U.S. 549 (1946).

Colorado Republican Federal Campaign Committee v. Federal Election Commission, 518 U.S. 604 (1996).

Common Cause v. Jones, 235 F. Supp. 2d 1076 (2002).

Connor v. Johnson, 402 U.S. 690 (1971).

Cruikshank, U.S. v., 92 U.S. 542 (1876).

Davis v. Bandemer, 478 U.S. 109 (1986).

Democratic Party of the United States v. Wisconsin ex. Rel. La Follette, 489 U.S. 214 (1981).

Democratic Party v. Reed, 343 F.3d 1198 (2003).

Easley v. Cromartie, 532 U.S. 234 (2001).

Eu v. San Francisco County Democratic Central Committee, 489 U.S. 214 (1989).

Faucher v. Federal Election Commission, 928 F.2d 468 (1991).

Federal Election Commission v. Christian Action Network, 110 F.3d 1049 (1997).
Federal Election Commission v. Colorado Republican Federal Campaign Committee, 533 U.S. 431 (2000).
Federal Election Commission v. Furgatch, 869 F.2d 1256 (1987).
Federal Election Commission v. Massachusetts Citizens for Life, Inc., 479 U.S. 238 (1986).
Federal Election Commission v. National Conservative PAC, 470 U.S. 480 (1985).
Federal Election Commission v. Phillips Publishing, 517 F.Supp.1308 (1981).
First National Bank of Boston v. Bellotti, 435 U.S. 765 (1977).
Foster v. Love, 522 U.S. 67 (1997).
Fox Television Stations, Inc. v. Federal Communications Commission, 280 F.3d (2003).
Georgia v. Ashcroft, 156 L. Ed. 2d. 428 (2003).
Georgia v. U.S., 411 U.S. 526 (1973).
Gitlow v. New York, 268 U.S. 652 (1925).
Gomillion v. Lightfoot, 364 U.S. 339 (1960).
Gore v. Harris, 772 So. 2d 1243 (2000).
Gray v. Sanders, 372 U.S. 368 (1963).
Guinn and Beal v. United States, 238 U.S. 347 (1915).
In Re Barkman, Commonwealth Court of Pennsylvania, 726 A.2d 440 (1998).
Jeffers v. Clinton, 740 F. Supp. 585 (E.D. Ark. 1990).
Karcher v. Daggett, 426 U.S. 725 (1983).
Kirksey v. Board of Supervisors of Hinds County, 544 F. 2d 139 (5th Cir. 1977).
Larios v. Perdue, Civil Action No. 1:03-CV-693-CAP (N.D. Ga., 2003).
Maine Right to Life Committee v. Federal Election Commission, 914 F. Supp. 8 (1996).
McCleskey v. Kemp, 481 U.S. 279 (1987).
McConnell v. Federal Election Commission, 124 S.Ct. 619 (2003).
McIntyre v. Ohio Elections Commission, 514 U.S. 334 (1995).
Miller v. Johnson, 515 U.S. 900 (1995).
NAACP v. Alabama, 357 U.S. 449 (1958).
Nader v. Schaffer, 429 U.S. 989 (1976).
National Broadcasting Company v. U.S., 319 U.S. 190 (1943).
Nixon v. Condon, 286 U.S. 73 (1932).
Nixon v. Herndon, 273 U.S. 536 (1927).
Nixon v. Shrink Missouri Government PAC, 528 U.S. 377 (2000).
O'Lear v. Miller, 222 F. Supp. 2d 850 (E.D. Mich., 2002).
Osburn v. Cox, 1:02-CV-2721 (2003).
Page v. Bartels, 144 F. Supp. 2d 346 (D.N.J. 2001).
Readers Digest Association v. Federal Election Commission, 509 F.Supp. 1210 (1981).
Red Lion Broadcasting v. Federal Communications Commission, 319 U.S. 367 (1969).
Reese, U.S. v., 92 U.S. 214 (1875).
Reno v. Bossier Parish School Board, 528 U.S. 320 (1999).
Republican Party of Minnesota v. White, 536 U.S. 765 (2002).
Reynolds v. Sims, 377 U.S. 533 (1964).
Schlenther v. Department of State, Division of Licensing, 743 So. 2d 536 (1998).
Shaw v. Reno, 509 U.S. 630 (1993).
Smith v. Allwright, 321 U.S. 649 (1944).
Southwest Voter Registration Education Project v. Shelley, 344 F.3d 882 (2003).
Tashjian v. Republican Party of Connecticut, 479 U.S. 1024 (1986).
Terminiello v. Chicago, 337 U.S. 1 (1949).
Terry v. Adams, 345 U.S. 461 (1953).

Timmons v. Twin Cities Area New Party, 520 U.S. 351 (1997).
Van Allen v. Democratic State Committee of New York, N.Y. Misc. Lexis 1209 (2003).
Vieth v. Jubelirer, 241 F. Supp. 2d 478 (M.D. Pa. 2003).
Vieth v. Pennsylvania, 195 F. Supp. 2d 672 (M.D. Pa., 2002).
Weaver v. Bonner, 309 F.3d 1312 (2002).
Wesberry v. Sanders, 376 U.S. 1 (1964).
White v. Register, 412 U.S. 755 (1973).
Williams v. Rhodes, 393 U.S. 23 (1968).

The Contributors

Matthew J. Streb is assistant professor of political science at Loyola Marymount University and writes on political behavior, public opinion, elections, and race. He is the author or coeditor of three books, including *The New Electoral Politics of Race* and *Polls and Politics: The Dilemmas of Democracy,* and has published more than a half-dozen articles in journals, including *Political Research Quarterly, Public Opinion Quarterly, Social Science Quarterly*, and *Election Law Journal.*

Antonio Brown is assistant professor of political science at his alma mater, Loyola Marymount University. His teaching and research focus on quantitative and qualitative studies of political culture and national identity in the United States and Western Europe. He is currently editing a book titled *Getting Men to Get It: Perspectives on Men and Women and Politics.*

Charles S. Bullock III holds the Richard B. Russell Chair in Political Science at the University of Georgia. He is the author, coauthor, or coeditor of seventeen books and more than 150 articles and book chapters dealing with topics relating to southern politics and legislative politics.

Allan J. Cigler is Chancellors Club Teaching Professor of Political Science at the University of Kansas. His research and teaching interests include group politics, participation, political parties, and campaigns. He is the coeditor of *Interest Group Politics,* sixth edition, and *U.S. Agriculture Groups* and has recently published *Perspectives on Terrorism.*

Victoria A. Farrar-Myers is associate professor of political science at the University of Texas at Arlington and specializes in presidential-congressional relations and the policymaking process. She is the coauthor of *Legislative Labyrinth: Congress and Campaign Finance Reform* and has published articles in *Congress and the Presidency, White House Studies*, and *American*

Review of Politics. During 1997 and 1998, she served as an American Political Science Association Congressional Fellow.

Evan Gerstmann is associate professor of political science at Loyola Marymount University. His research interests are in the area of constitutional law, specifically the equal protection clause. He is the author of *The Constitutional Underclass: Gays, Lesbians and the Failure of Class-Based Equal Protection* and *Same-Sex Marriage and the Constitution*.

Lee E. Goodman is an election law attorney in private practice in Washington, D.C., where he advises clients on compliance with federal and state campaign finance laws, ethics and lobbying rules, and First Amendment rights of political participation. He also advises several major Internet-based clients on a wide range of New Economy legal and policy matters. He previously served as legal counsel and policy adviser to the governor of Virginia and is a veteran of several national and statewide political campaigns.

Marjorie Randon Hershey is professor of political science at Indiana University, specializing in political parties and election campaigns. She is the author of three books (most recently, *Party Politics in America*, tenth edition) and a number of articles in professional journals.

Kristin Kanthak is assistant professor of political science at the University of Arizona. Her research focuses on legislative behavior, particularly in the U.S. Congress. Her work has appeared in *Journal of Theoretical Politics*, *Public Choice*, and edited volumes. Her current projects include research on leadership political action committees in the House of Representatives and the evolutionary effect of members' decisions to retire from the House on the remaining House parties.

Brian F. Schaffner is assistant professor of political science at American University. He has published articles in the *American Political Science Review*, *Political Research Quarterly*, *Public Opinion Quarterly*, *Legislative Studies Quarterly*, and *Political Communication*. Currently, he is studying how the local media coverage of politics and campaign advertising influence congressional elections.

Jeffrey Williams is a Ph.D. student in the Political Science Department at the University of Arizona. His research interests include elections, the courts, and Congress.

Index

Act, 44, 61, 102; and the Internet, 114; and Latino representatives, 160; and literacy tests, 148n.15; and media consolidation, 77–78; and Medicare, 60; and Radio Act (1912), 80; and Radio Act (1927), 81; and seat allocation, 12; and Telecommunications Act (1996), 85; and Voter Confidence and Increased Accessibility Act, 145; and Voting Rights Act, 139, 163. *See also* Congressional Black Caucus; House of Representatives; Senate
Congressional Black Caucus, 160
Connecticut, 13, 18, 136, 152
Connecticut Party, A, 41n.6
Connerly, Ward, 140
Connor v. Johnson, 158
Conservative Party, 35, 44
Constitution, 127, 136, 143, 186; and campaign finance, 45; interpretation of, 182; and the judiciary, 172–173; ratification of, 56; and right to vote, 121–122, 131. *See also* Article I, Section 2; Article I, Section 4; Article II; Article III; Electoral College; Equal protection; Fifteenth Amendment; First Amendment; Fourteenth Amendment; Freedom of speech; Nineteenth Amendment; Thirteenth Amendment; Three-fifths clause; Twenty-Fourth Amendment; Twenty-Sixth Amendment
Contributions. *See* Campaign contributions
Converse, Phillip, 94n.4
Convio, Inc., 115n.9–11
Corporations: and Bipartisan Campaign Reform Act, 52, 70, 71; and Federal Election Campaign Act, 44, 62–63; and Federal Election Commission, 105–106; and judicial elections, 176, 177; and media exemption provision, 108; and soft money, 50; and Supreme Court rulings, 104–105; and Tillman Act, 102. *See also* Business Roundtable; U.S. Chamber of Commerce
Corrado, Anthony, 74n.19, 75n.28, 75n.35
Cox, Gary W., 154, 168n.7
Coyle, Marcia, 188n.55
Cummings, Jeanne, 115n.8
CyberAtlas, 115n.6

Dallas County, TX, 152, 158
Dash, Hal, 178, 187n.36
Davidson, Chandler, 147n.5, 147n.10, 148n.15–16, 148n.18

Davis, Gray, 2, 5n.6, 34, 142–143
Davis v. Bandemer, 164–166
Dean, Howard, 99–101, 109
Death penalty, 127, 129, 178, 180, 185
Debs, Eugene, 130
Delegate representation, 48–50
Demers, David, 95n.35
Democratic Party, 39; and advertising, 74n.17; and African American support, 162, 163; in Arizona, 113–114, 117n.70; and ballot access laws, 31; in California, 58n.22; and California recall, 2, 143; and Citizens for Better Medicare, 67; and 1877 compromise, 137; and express advocacy, 65; and FCC, 87; in Georgia, 7, 20; and Medicare, 60, 67; and 1994 elections, 160; party identification, 38; and Populists, 25; and public funding of presidential candidates, 36; and public support of, 37; and punch-card ballots, 132; and redistricting, 155, 163–167; and soft money, 51, 56, 66, 74n.24; and the South, 30, 154; two party dominance, 30, 40; 2004 presidential nomination, 101. *See also California Democratic Party v. Jones; Democratic Party of the United States v. Wisconsin ex. Rel. La Follette; Democratic Party v. Reed; Eu v. San Francisco County Democratic Central Committee*
Democratic Party of the United States v. Wisconsin ex. rel. La Follette, 17–18
Democratic Party v. Reed, 20
Denver, 79, 87
Department of Defense. *See* U.S. Department of Defense
Department of Justice (DOJ), 156, 158–164, 167, 168n.12
Dershowitz, Alan, 119, 132n.5, 132n.11, 132n.19
Descriptive representation, 161
Desposato, Scott W., 160, 169n.18
Dill, David L., 144, 145
Dionne, E. J., 1, 5n.4
Direct mail, 112
Direct recording electronic voting systems (DRE), 131, 144–145
Disabled, 141
Disch, Lisa J., 42n.46
Dixiecrats, 41n.16
Dnet.org, 113
DOJ. *See* Department of Justice
Dooley, Cal, 64

Vermont, 27, 36, 99
Viacom, 87, 90
Video Monitoring Service, 78, 87
Vieth v. Jubelirer, 165–166
Vieth v. Pennsylvania, 154
Virginia, 110, 139, 168n.9, 169n.24, 173
Vote-Smart.org, 113
Voter Accessibility for the Elderly and
   Handicapped Act (1984), 141
Voter Confidence and Increased
   Accessibility Act (2003), 145
Voter rolloff, 175
Voting: disfranchisement of voters,
   135–138, 140–142; physical barriers to,
   135, 139, 142; technological barriers to,
   135, 139, 142; and 2000 presidential
   election, 123–127
Voting, as a right, 120–122, 131, 135; for
   college students, 141; for the disabled,
   141; for the elderly, 141; for Jews, 141;
   for non-English speakers, 138. *See also*
   African Americans; Equal protection;
   Voting Rights Act (1965)
Voting Rights Act (VRA) (1965), 109,
   140–145, 148n.13; and redistricting,
   135, 157–159; and Section 2, 138,
   148n.14, 159–160, 162–163, 167; and
   Section 4, 138; and Section 5, 138,
   157–158, 159–160, 162–163, 164, 168;
   and Section 6, 138; and Section 7, 138;
   and Section 10, 139; and Section 14;
   139; and vote dilution, 135, 138,
   157–159, 163, 167. *See also* African
   Americans; Equal protection; Voting
Voting Rights Act (1970, 1975), 162,
   168n.13
Voting Rights Act (1982), 159
Votomatic punch-card machines, 122–123,
   124. *See also* Punch-card machines
VPAP.org, 113
VRA. *See* Voting Rights Act

Wallace, Geroge, 29
Walsh, Edward, 5n.5
Walton, Hanes, Jr., 139–140, 141–142,
   144, 147n.11, 148n.19–21, 148n.23,
   148n.26, 149n.33, 149n.42

Warren, Brad, 23, 40
Washington, 8, 18, 19–20, 35, 42n.37, 152,
   179
Washington, D.C., 111
Washington Post, 90, 95n.31, 97
Watergate, 44, 102
Wattenberg, Martin P., 42n.30, 42n.41
Weaver, George M., 184
Weaver v. Bonner, 184
Weicker, Lowell, 41n.6
Weinstein, Henry, 6n.8
Weiss, Todd R., 115n.12
Weissberg, Robert, 57n.12
Wekkin, Gary D., 21n.20
Welfare, 182, 185
Wellington, FL, 145
Wersal, Greg, 182, 184
Wesberry v. Sanders, 153, 155,
   168n.2
West, Darrell M., 73n.2, 73n.3–4
Whereatt, Robert, 188n.70
Whigs, 25
Whitby, Kenny J., 169n.21
White, Byron, 48, 57n.9, 82–83
White, John Kenneth, 42n.29
White primary, 137, 138, 139. *See also*
   Smith v. Allwright; White Primary
   Cases
White Primary Cases, 13, 14–15, 21n.15.
   See also Smith v. Allwright; White
   primary
White v. Register, 158
Whitiker, L. Paige, 58n.18
Wicker, Tom 98
Williams v. Rhodes, 42n.38
Wilson, Craig, 74n.26
Winger, Richard, 41n.5, 41n.20–21, 42.n
   23–27, 42n.32
Winston-Salem, 162
Wisconsin, 17, 24, 177
Wohl, Alexander, 187n.26
WorldTraveler magazine, 107
World War I, 130
World War II, 130, 152

Yoo, John, 120, 132n.6
Young, Andrew, 158

About the Book

How much money can a candidate for political office legally collect, and from what sources? What can and can't be said in campaign ads? Who determines the process of redistricting, and what is the overall effect on U.S. democracy? *Law and Election Politics* analyzes the rules of the electoral game, helping readers to understand how politics influences and is influenced by electoral laws and court rulings.

The authors address the most important—and sometimes controversial—decisions that the courts have made on campaign finance, political parties, issue advocacy, voting, campaigning, redistricting, and judicial elections. The result is an engaging and accessible study of how election laws and politics intertwine.

Matthew J. Streb is assistant professor of political science at Loyola Marymount University. He is author of *The New Electoral Politics of Race*.